Questions on an Ethics of Divine Commands

Notre Dame Texts in Medieval Culture
Vol. 3

The Medieval Institute
University of Notre Dame

John Van Engen and Edward D. English, Editors

EDITED, TRANSLATED, AND WITH AN INTRODUCTION BY
Janine Marie Idziak

Questions on an Ethics of Divine Commands

Andrew of Neufchateau, O.F.M.

University of Notre Dame Press
Notre Dame, Indiana

Library of Congress Cataloging-in-Publication Data

André, de Neufchateau, 14th cent.
[Primum scriptum sententiarum. Distinction 48, question 1–2.
English & Latin]
Questions on an ethics of divine commands / Andrew of Neufchateau;
edited, translated, and with an introduction by Janine Marie Idziak.
    p.   cm.   —(Notre Dame texts in medieval culture)
Includes bibiographical references.
ISBN 0-268-03977-1 (alk. paper)
1. Divine commands (Ethics)   I. Idziak, Janine Marie.   II. Title
III. Series.
BJ47.A5313 1996   96-26435
    171'.1—dc20   CIP

∞ The paper used in this publication meets the minimum
requirements of the American National Standard for Information
Sciences—Permanence of Paper for Printed Library Materials, ANSI Z39.48-1984.

To

My Parents
John and Jeannette Idziak

Contents

PREFACE

Contemporary philosophers and theologians have shown considerable interest in an ethics of divine commands. In fact, the theory has a long history. Initial work on historical discussions of an ethics of divine commands, recorded in the anthology *Divine Command Morality: Historical and Contemporary Readings* [1], suggested a richness of literature that had not been entirely explored. This work led us to believe that, especially in the medieval period, the main dispute on an ethics of divine commands had not yet been uncovered. The present edition and translation of the work of Andrew of Neufchateau is the result of these scholarly intuitions.

The section of Andrew's commentary on the *Sentences* containing his discussion of an ethics of divine commands is preserved only in a 1514 printed edition *Primum Scriptum Sententarium*, of which five copies are known to be extant [2]. This printed edition still bears a strong resemblance to a manuscript in terms of type of script, layout, use of abbreviations, and the absence of a modern system of punctuation and of sentence and paragraph structure. Consequently, not only are there few copies of Andrew's discussion of divine command ethics still in existence, but the text is preserved in a format which many find forbidding and inaccessible. In order to make Andrew's discussion available to the community of philosophers and theologians interested in the divine command theory, both a modernized Latin text and an English translation of distinction forty-eight, questions one and two have been produced. Into this redaction of Andrew's discussion are incorporated as many features of a standard modern edition as the extant text permits.

Spelling has been standardized according to Lewis and Short's *A Latin Dictionary* [3] and according to R.E. Latham's *Revised Medieval Latin Word-List* [4] with the exception that, in accordance with current editing practices, no uses of the letter *i* have been changed to the letter *j*. Angle brackets < > in the text indicate *addenda* of the editor. Small case letters represent *textual notes*, which include corrections of the Latin printed text, notation of textual lacunae and other printing errors, and explanations of the translation. Numerals represent *reference notes*. In these notes the actual texts of citations are given on a selective basis, where such enhance the understanding of Andrew of Neufchateau's discussion. Authors and texts from whom Andrew may have borrowed are also indicated in these notes.

A microfilm copy of Andrew's *Primum Scriptum Sententiarum* was obtained from the British Library. This edition and translation are part of a larger project on the history of divine command ethics conducted at the Medieval Institute of the University of Notre Dame with grants from the National Endowment for the Humanities and the American Council of Learned Societies. We are very much indebted to these institutions for the assistance provided for this project.

As well as being intended for medieval scholars, this book is meant for philosophers and theologians who are interested in the topic of an ethics of divine commands. It will open up new areas of discourse on this ethical theory.

Janine Marie Idziak

NOTES

1. Toronto & New York: Edwin Mellen Press, 1980.
2. See Appendix B.
3. Oxford: Clarendon Press, 1975.
4. London: Oxford University Press, 1973.

INTRODUCTION

I

During the last several decades there has been renewed interest on the part of philosophers and theologians in an *ethics of divine commands*. Most basically, a divine command moralist holds that the standard of right and wrong is constituted by the commands and prohibitions of God. According to the divine command theory, "an action or kind of action is right or wrong if and only if and *because* it is commanded or forbidden by God" [1]. In other words, the theory stipulates that "what ultimately *makes* an action right or wrong is its being commanded or forbidden by God and nothing else" [2]. According to a divine command moralist, it is *not* the case that God commands a particular action because it is right, or prohibits it because it is wrong; rather, an action is right (or wrong) because God commands (or prohibits) it. An ethics of divine commands is often expressed in terms of right and wrong being determined by the *will of God*.

The divine command ethical theory has a long history. It was the subject of vigorous debate in the literature of the British modern period. William Paley clearly espouses an ethics of divine commands [3], and John Locke shows proclivities towards this position [4]. In discussing the prominent moral standards of his day, John Gay delineates a scheme in which these standards are all ultimately founded on the criterion of the will of God [5]. On the other hand, an ethics of divine commands was rejected by Ralph Cudworth [6], Samuel Clarke [7], Thomas Chubb [8], Richard Price [9], George Rust [10], Anthony Early of Shaftesbury [11], Francis Hutcheson [12], and Jeremy Bentham [13].

Even earlier divine command ethics had played a part in Reformation theology. Remarks characteristic of the divine command position are found in the writings of both Martin Luther [14] and John Calvin [15]. Within the Calvinist tradition, an ethics of divine commands is articulated by James Usher [16]; among English Puritans this position is held by William Perkins [17] and John Preston [18]. The divine command theory even made its way to colonial New England. Samuel Willard, who served as pastor of the South Church in Boston and as Vice-President of Harvard College, makes note of the existence of a dispute over the divine command theory in a sermon of November 5, 1689 [19].

Intellectual historians trace the roots of the divine command position found in the literature of the Reformation and modern periods to the philosophical theology of the late Middle Ages [20]. Divine command ethics in the medieval period has been associated to some extent with Duns Scotus [21], but primarily with William Ockham [22] who is renowned for the claim that the acts of theft, adultery, and hating God could be performed meritoriously if they should come under a divine precept [23]. Yet Scotus and Ockham represent but the beginning of the medieval dispute over this ethical position, and by no means exhaust the list of philosophers and theologians involved in the development and critique of the divine command theory.

Two seventeenth century writers have provided a list of medieval proponents of divine command ethics. One is the Cambridge Platonist Ralph Cudworth in his *Treatise Concerning Eternal and Immutable Morality*:

...divers modern theologers do not only seriously, but zealously contend in like

manner, that there is nothing absolutely, intrinsically, and naturally good and evil, just and unjust, antecedently to any positive command or prohibition of God; but that the arbitrary will and pleasure of God...by its commands and prohibitions, is the first and only rule and measure thereof. ...For though the ancient fathers of the christian church were very abhorrent from this doctrine...yet it crept up afterward in the scholastic age, Ockham being among the first that maintained: Nullum actum malum esse nisi quatenus a Deo prohibitum, et qui non possit fieri bonus si a Deo praecipiatur; et e converso. That there is no act evil but as it is prohibited by God, and which cannot be made good if it be commanded by God. And so on the other hand as to good.--- And herein Petrus Alliacus and Andreas de Novo Castro, with others, quickly followed him. [24]

A second and earlier source is the Jesuit scholastic Francisco Suarez in his treatise *De Legibus ac Deo Legislatore*. While confirming Cudworth's list of William Ockham, Peter of Ailly, and Andreas de Novo Castro, Suarez adds the name of Jean Gerson:

> The second opinion...is that the natural law consists entirely in a divine command or prohibition proceeding from the will of God as the Author and Ruler of nature...
>
> This is the view one ascribes to William of Ockham...Gerson also inclines to this opinion...Peter of Ailly...too, defends this view at length, saying that the divine will is the primary law... The same opinion is supported at length by Andreas a Novocastro.
>
> ...Their opinion would assuredly seem to be founded upon the fact that actions are not good or evil, save as they are ordered or prohibited by God.... . [25]

Without doubt, the most interesting and provocative discussion of divine command ethics yet to be found in the medieval literature is given by the individual on these lists who is least known to contemporary philosophers and theologians: Andreas de Novo Castro [26]. He discusses the divine command theory in his commentary on the first book of the *Sentences*, distinction forty-eight, questions one and two.

The identification and biography of Andreas de Novo Castro have been matters of dispute among medieval scholars. The best evidence is that he is *Andrew of Neufchateau*, a French Franciscan whose academic career is to be located at the University of Paris during the second half of the fourteenth century. In particular, Andrew may have engaged in the exercise of commenting on the *Sentences* as early as the academic year 1358-59. His honorific title is *doctor ingeniosissimus*, most ingenious doctor. [27]

No manuscript copies appear to be extant of that part of Andrew's commentary of the first book of the *Sentences* which contains his treatment of the divine command theory. Thus reliance must be placed on a single printed edition entitled *Primum Scriptum Sententiarum*, printed at Paris in 1514. At present, only five copies of the printed text are known to be extant. [28]

In covering twelve folio pages in print [29], Andrew's consideration of the divine command position represents the most extended treatment of the theory among known medieval sources. He explicitly and unabashedly espouses a thoroughgoing ethics of divine commands, and is one of the

clearest examples of a divine command moralist to be found in the historical literature in general [30]. The text of Andrew contains the most extensive record of argumentation about the divine command theory of any known medieval text on the subject, and represents the most elaborate attempt to defend this position in the medieval period.   In passing mention of the work of Andrew, a contemporary medievalist has commented that it is "not among the great contributions to the history of medieval thought" [31].   Such an assessment can only be made in ignorance of Andrew's contribution to the field of ethics [32].

II

An ethics of divine commands forms the subject of the first and second questions of distinction forty-eight of Andrew of Neufchateau's commentary on the first book of the *Sentences*:

Is all good other than God contingently good from the free decree of the divine will? [33]
Is everything which is an evil of fault for a rational creature evil because it is freely and contingently prohibited by God? [34]

In extended responses to these questions Andrew unqualifiedly commits himself to the divine command position.

Andrew begins his consideration of an ethics of divine commands by distinguishing and defining various kinds of good and evil [35].   His most basic distinction is between what is *good in itself and absolutely* and what is *good for the sake of another* [36].   The former category concerns good as it is related to being [37].   The second category is subdivided into *natural, useful, pleasant,* and *noble and just good* [38].   According to the definitions given by Andrew, good in itself and absolutely, natural good, useful good, and pleasant good are all instances of what would be classified today as goodness in a *non-moral* sense [39].   It is noble and just good which we would recognize as being goodness of the *moral* variety [40], speaking of good as studied either in philosophical ethics or moral theology.   Noble and just good, the type of concern to the present study, is subdivided by Andrew into three classes: *generic goodness, moral goodness,* and *supernatural or theological and charitable goodness* [41].   Andrew's scheme also includes delineation of an evil opposite to each type of good for another [42].   Textually, emphasis is placed on the *evil of fault,* the type of evil opposed to supernatural goodness [43].   This form of evil is also distinguished categorically from the *evil of penalty for the senses* [44].

Andrew's thoroughgoing commitment to the divine command position is indicated by the fact that he puts forward three separate *conclusions* relating the divine will to be aforementioned types of good and evil.   Thus he asserts that

All created good, whether good in itself and absolutely or good for the sake of some other, is this kind of good because the divine will freely wills and decrees it to be such good [45].

In support of this thesis Andrew offers proofs specifically for good in itself and absolutely, good for the sake of some other in general, useful good, pleasant good, generic good, and moral good [46]. Further, Andrew claims that

> Everything which is a simply just and meritorious good for a viator is this kind of good for him because the divine will freely wills and decrees it to be good in this way... [47].

The good here described as "simply just and meritorious" is a characterization of supernatural goodness [48]. Finally, Andrew asserts the divine command thesis explicitly of the evil of fault which opposes supernatural goodness:

> Whatever is an evil of fault for a rational creature is this kind of evil because it deviates from a divine law or decree and because it is antecedently prohibited or discouraged or in some way reprobated by the divine will [49].

As a consequence of his divine command position on the foundation of morals, Andrew defends the additional theses that any morally good act or supernaturally good act can fail to have this status [50]; with some expressed reservation, he also argues the thesis that any evil of fault can fail to be evil [51]. These theses effectually deny the existence of intrinsically good or intrinsically evil acts in the moral realm.

The basic contention of the divine command moralist, viz., that what is morally right and wrong is fundamentally dependent on decisions made by God, can be formalized, elaborated, and refined in a variety of ways. In the contemporary literature the most familiar division among divine command ethical systems is that between *metaethical* and *normative* theories [52]. Given that Andrew begins his discussion of the divine command theory by distinguishing and defining the various kinds of good, and concomitantly, the various kinds of evil, one can meaningfully ask the question whether he articulated a metaethical divine command theory.

In the category of noble and just good, good and evil of the generic and moral varieties are explicated by Andrew without reference to divine commands [53]; indeed, right reason is central to the three definitions of moral goodness reported by him [54]. It is only when Andrew reaches the level of supernatural goodness that he brings in divine law and the divine will. Initially, Andrew defines supernatural goodness as "the conformity of the will to right reason prescribing completely about the circumstances required according to the Catholic faith and the law of God delivered to us" [55]. While reference is made to divine law in this definition, conformity of the will to right reason remains central. It is in a second definition that Andrew indicates that supernatural goodness may be defined in terms of God's will in its legislative capacity: "..or we say that it is the conformity of the created will in acting or living to the divine will as preceptive or persuasive and approving" [56]. This latter orientation is carried over into the definition of the opposing evil of fault and injustice as "the lack of a circumstance which is due or the addition of an undue circumstance contrary to the preceptive or consultative law of God" [57].

Is it thus fair to attribute to Andrew of Neufchateau a *metaethical* version of divine command ethical theory? It seems that one can categorize Andrew as a metaethical divine command moralist

only in a restricted, rarified sense. First, Andrew defines in terms of God 's will only one variety of (ethical) goodness recognized by him, namely, supernatural goodness. Second, Andrew juxtaposes, without apparent preference, two definitions of supernatural goodness, only one of which bespeaks a divine command metaethics. This juxtaposition makes questionable the extent to which Andrew was conscious of and committed to divine command ethics as a specifically metaethical theory.

Of far greater interest for Andrew's work is another contemporary formulation of the divine command theory which has been developed by Philip Quinn. Initially Quinn worked with theories based on *logical* relations such as strict equivalence:

> It is necesssary that, for all *p*, it is required that *p* if and only if God commands that *p*.
> It is necessary that, for all *p*, it is permitted that *p* if and only if it is not the case that God commands that *not-p*.
> It is necessary that, for all *p*, it is forbidden that *p* if and only if God commands that *not-p*. [58]

But in a subsequent paper Quinn set out "to explore a somewhat different terrain" [59], formulating a *causal* normative theory:

> For every proposition which is such that it is logically possible that God commands that *p* and it is logically contingent that *p*, a sufficient causal condition that it is obligatory that *p* is that God commands that *p*, and a necessary causal condition that it is obligatory that *p* is that God commands that *p*.
> For every proposition which is such that it is logically possible that God commands that *p* and it is logically contingent that *p*, a sufficient causal condition that it is forbidden that *p* is that God commands that *not-p*, and a necessary causal condition that it is forbidden that *p* is that God commands that *not-p*.
> For every proposition which is such that it is logically possible tht God commands that *p* and it is logically contingent that *p*, a sufficient causal condition that it is permitted that *p* is that it is not the case that God commands that *not-p*, and a necessary causal condition that it is permitted that *p* is that it is not the case that God commands that *not-p*. [60]

According to Quinn, the attempt to construe the relation between divine commands and moral duty in causal terms is meant to incorporate a view held by at least some divine command moralists which the logical formulations of the theory fail to embody. Specifically, it is meant to capture an intuitive picture of God as an agent *bringing about* or *creating* moral obligations and prohibitions by means of his legislative activity [61].

Thus it is noteworthy that Andrew uses causal terminology in the course of his discussion of an ethics of divine commands. Such terminology occurs too often to be purely accidental. Andrew speaks of "the first cause and rule of goodness" [62], of the "first cause and reason for good" [63], and of the "first cause and rule and measure of rectitude" [64]. On several occasions the causal force in morals is identified with God explicitly. Thus Andrew states that "the rectitude of human action

and reason and of the dictate and law of nature are reduced to the rectitude of the divine will and proceed from it causally..." [65]. Again he describes God as "the effective and the final and as it were the formal and the exemplary and the regulative and the measuring cause of this (viz., moral) goodness" [66].

It would be easy to pass over these descriptions in reading Andrew's lengthy text. Quinn's construction of a causal version of divine command theory in explicit contrast to other possible formulations serves to focus attention on the terminology used by Andrew. His stated rationale for the articulation of a causal theory suggests that Andrew's choice of terminology is by no means insignificant.

To say that right and wrong are determined by divine *commands* is a thesis in need of further clarification, for we have not yet been told *what* in the divine nature is responsble for issuing the commands and prohibitions which make moral laws. A common interpretation is to see divine command ethics as a *voluntaristic* thesis [67]. In other words, the term *command* is taken as referring to an act of the will, and an ethics of divine commands is interpreted as a system making morality dependent on God's will specifically.

This perception of the divine command theory is shared by medievalists who have claimed that adherence to this ethical position was a function of attaching importance to the faculty of will [68]. This interpretation also leads to what has been considered a major defect in an ethics of divine commands. For if morality is not grounded in the properties of actions, persons, and things, and if it does not fall within the sphere of rational determination, but if it is based solely on the choices of the divine will, then morality seems to take on an *arbitrary* and *capricious* character unbefitting to the seriousness of the moral enterprise [69].

In view of this line of criticism, one can only describe Andrew of Neufchateau as a divine command moralist who bites the bullet. First, Andrew makes a statement of a purely voluntaristic version of divine command ethics into an explicit thesis:

> THIRD CONCLUSION: For no activity of a rational creature which is simply good and just is it the case that the divine will wills and decrees it to be good and just because it is good and just in itself by its nature. In other words, because first it is antecedently dictated and judged to be good and just by the divine intellect, so that it is not the divine will as will but the dictate of the divine intellect which is the first reason and rule or measure of his activity which is simply good and just. [70]

Thus Andrew affirms that the divine will *per se* is the first rule of goodness and justice, and that the moral commands of the divine will are not based upon and directed by prior judgments of the divine intellect. Further, Andrew brings forward various considerations intended to show that the notion of God making moral pronouncements by sheer will is not the odious view one might think [71]. In defending his ethical voluntarism, Andrew makes claims about the nature of divine action in general as well as considering the ethical realm specifically.

For one thing, Andrew calls attention to biblical texts which present God's activity in a voluntaristic light. For example, in the gospel parable about the owner of a vineyard who paid as much in wages to those who had worked only one hour as to those who had worked the whole day, the only explanation given is indicative of behavior of a purely discretionary character: "I want to give

to this last just as I give to you. Am I not allowed to do what I want?" [72]. The same holds true of the explanation recorded in *Matthew* for the concealment of the mysteries of the kingdom from the wise and the revelation of them to children: "Yes, Father, because so it was pleasing before you" [73]. These two scriptural texts may well have been taken by Andrew from Thomas Bradwardine's listing of arguments against the view that reason directs the divine will [74].

Again repeating a line of argument from the discussion of Bradwardine, Andrew further defends his voluntaristic position by describing cases in which human beings perform just actions stemming not from a decision of reason, but from a sheer choice of will. For suppose that someone has been given the power to pardon one, and only one, of two persons placed under a death sentence, and that he can find no relevant differences between them. In such a case, there is no better reason for pardoning the one than for pardoning the other. However, he justly frees the one whom he chooses to pardon, although reason did not move his will to make this choice. And from the very fact that he wills to free this particular one, the act of freeing him is just. The same sort of situation occurs when one is in a position to bestow some gift or benefit on only one of two or more persons who are equally worthy of receiving it. The point of these cases is that, since we allow that justness can stem from the human will unguided by reason, there is surely nothing inappropriate or reprehensible about the same thing occurring in the case of the divine will [75].

The espousal of an ethics of divine commands has been perceived by medievalists as connected with the valuing and preservation of God's *liberty*. This claim has been made about the position of Duns Scotus by Bernard Landry [76], about the position of William Ockham by Francis Oakley [77], about the position of Gabriel Biel by C. Ruch [78] as well as about the position of Jean Gerson by Frederick Copleston [79]. God's liberty was clearly on the mind of Andrew of Neufchateau in his articulation of the divine command position. In his very statement of the questions which raise the issue of an ethics of divine commands and in statements of the divine command thesis itself, Andrew includes mention of the activity of the divine will as *free*:

> Is all good other than God contingently good from the free decree of the divine will? [80]
>
> Is everything which is an evil of fault for a rational creature evil because it is freely and contingently prohibited by God? [81]
>
> All created good, whether good in itself and absolutely or good for the sake of some other, is this kind of good because the divine will freely wills and decrees it to be such good. [82]
>
> Everything which is a simply just and meritorious good for a viator is this kind of good for him because the divine will freely wills and decrees it to be good in this way.... [83]

Indeed, the description of the divine will and its decrees, determinations, commands, approbations, and prohibitions as *free* occurs much too frequently in the course of Andrew's discussion of divine command ethics to be purely accidental [84]. Thus it is not surprising that Andrew employs the notion of the divine liberty in his argumentation in favor of a voluntaristic version of divine command ethics.

In considering the whole realm of divine action *ad extra*, Andrew postulates a fundamental

voluntarism in God's external activity, claiming that "for no outward activity of God is it the case that the divine will wills and decrees it because first it is antecedently dictated and judged by the divine intellect as it were from reason antecedently moving and stating why it must be done so, and not supposing a free decree of the will" [85]. Andrew goes on to argue for his ethical voluntarism by claiming that the nature of divine action *ad extra* is indicative of the character of God's activity in issuing moral commands governing the action of a rational creature. He supports this analogical inference by an appeal to the notion of divine liberty, pointing out tht both cases of divine activity are free with complete liberty of contradiction [86].

In addition, several of the arguments which Andrew brings forward in support of his claim about the nature of divine action *ad extra* have the form of showing that the opposing view infringes on God's liberty. For one thing, Andrew contends that the opposing position entails that the divine will is *necessitated* to act *ad extra*. For let us suppose that reason does move the divine will in God's activity *ad extra*, and that the divine intellect sees a reason, *r*, for doing *x*. Since there cannot be a divergence between will and reason in God, the will of God necessarily agrees with this reason. And therefore, God *necessarily* does *x* [87]. Furthermore, the supposition that reason moves the divine will in God's activity *ad extra* entails the false view that God could not work otherwise than he does nor make better things than he does make. For if reason dictates doing *x*, then the divine will does *x*; and if reason does not dictate doing *x*, then the divine will cannot do *x*. And Andrew is careful to point out that "the dictating...will not be free since it is understood prior to every dictate of the free divine will" [88].

Another line of argument of this type put forward by Andrew has the form of demonstrating that the rationalist position opposed to his own ethical voluntarism either is reducible to voluntarism or leads to a denial of God's liberty. For let us suppose that the divine will wills and decrees that *Socrates doing b is good* because the divine intellect first dictates and antecedently judges this to be good. That *Socrates doing b is good* is either a necessary or a contingent truth, and concomitantly, the divine will either necessarily or contingently judges that this is the case. If the option of contingency obtains, then the truth of the proposition *Socrates doing b is good* is ultimately reduced and resolved into the free decree of the divine will, since the divine will is the basis of all contingency. On the other hand, if we suppose that *Socrates doing b is good* is a necessary truth, then the divine will is necessitated so to decree, or else it would not be conformed to the judgment of the divine intellect and would not be right. But to say that God is *necessitated* to command Socrates to do *b* is simply false [89].

Andrew develops this line of argument even further. If, as the rationalist position maintains, *Socrates doing b is good* because the divine intellect so judges from a rational cause not reducible into a decree of the divine will, then the reason on account of which the divine intellect pronounces that *doing b is good* will be reducible to the nature of the created thing. But if rightness is based on the nature of things and hence on something external to God, then God will be subject to laws which are not enacted by his will and which are not within his power [90]. And to think of God as subject to laws not within his control is to place restrictions on the divine liberty and omnipotence.

In the seventeenth century the British philosopher George Rust wrote a treatise *A Discourse of Truth* in which, among other things, he attacks an ethics of divine commands. At one point, he considers the contention of divine command moralists that grounding morality in the nature and mutual respects of things is effectually "to bind and tye up God, who is an absolute and independent

Being, to the petty formalities of Good and Evil, and to fetter and imprison freedom, and liberty it self, in the fatal and immutable chains, and respects of things" [91]. Rust offers this reply:

> To the second part of the *Objection*, the strength whereof is, that to tye up God in his actions to the reason of things, destroys His Liberty, Absoluteness, and Independency. I answer, it is no imperfection for God to be determined to Good; It is no bondage, slavery, or contraction, to be bound up to the eternal Laws of Right and Justice...*Stat pro ratione voluntas*, unless it be as a redargution and check to impudent and daring Inquirers, is an account no where justifiable. The more any Being partakes of reason and understanding, the worse is the imputation of acting arbitrariously, *et pro imperio*...for a man of reason and understanding, that hath the Laws of goodness and rectitude...engraven upon his mind, for him to cast off these golden reins, and to set up arbitrarious Will for his Rule and Guide, is a piece of intolerable rashness and presumption. This is an infallible rule, that liberty in the power or principle is no where a perfection, where there is not an indifferency in the things or actions about which it is conversant... These things need no proof, indeed cannot well be proved, otherwise than they prove themselves: for they are of immediate truth, and prove themselves they will, to a pure unprejudiced mind. [92]

Rust nowhere mentions Andrew of Neufchateau by name. In fact, he does not identify any particular source for the argument to which he is replying. Nevertheless, Rust's comments unquestionably represent a response to the kind of position which Andrew so clearly articulated.

III

Natural law theory is associated with the Thomistic philosophical tradition, which stands in opposition to an ethics of divine commands. It may thus seem surprising that Andrew makes use of the concept of natural law [93]. And he does more than merely make mention of natural law in the course of his discussions. As a subsidiary point in one line of objection, Andrew mentions the view that "natural law would be destroyed if nothing were just by its nature but from a free and voluntary extrinsic decree" [94]. In replying Andrew asserts that "God established natural law and certain laws according to which many acts regularly are simply good and certain ones are generically good" [95]. What is important to notice in this statement is the point that it is God who institutes the natural law. And this statement is not an aberration. Andrew elsewhere speaks of "the order of natural law established by God" [96], and directly claims that

> the rectitude of human action and reason and of the dictate and law of nature are reduced to the rectitude of the divine will and proceed from it causally, for the former rule is subordinated to the latter one [97].

Andrew thus incorporates the concept of natural law into an ethics of divine commands by making

natural law dependent on God [98]. Further, Andrew assigns an epistemological function to natural law. In responding to a hypothetical situation in which it seems that a creature is obligated to perform an act *a* although God has in no way made this obligation known [99], Andrew comments that "the inconsistency is that God should will and shall have decreed simply and finally that Socrates ought to do *a* and that God shall not have given notification of this in any way, neither by a natural law written radically and seminally in the rational mind, nor by another special law, nor by revelation, nor by inspiration" [100]. This statement indicates that Andrew regards natural law as one of the ways in which we come to know God's commands [101]. In fact, he suggests that natural law can serve as our *immediate* rule of action: "For reason and the dictate of natural law in our intellect can be a rule directing our intellect without actually looking to the decree of the divine will, although it is in accordance with the will of God" [102].

Andrew also finds a place in his ethical system for the traditional concept of *right reason*, mentioning it throughout his discussion of the divine command theory [103]. Most notably, Andrew uses right reason in one of the arguments he develops in explicit support of an ethics of divine commands:

> The same (viz., the divine command theory) is likewise proved of moral good. For it is this kind of good because it is conformed to prudence and to moral right reason according to natural law; but such reason is right because the divine intellect and will so dictates and decrees and approves. [104]

In sum, Andrew makes right reason into a *second-order* moral principle dependent for its validity on divine commands. The subordination of right reason to divine commands also represents a strain in the thought of William Ockham [105].

IV

From the point of view of intellectual history, Andrew of Neufchateau's two questions on an ethics of divine commands are especially useful in providing an extensive catalogue of arguments for and against this ethical theory and its related theses. However, Andrew is silent on the source of the arguments he brings forward. He does not indicate whether they are of his own invention, or whether he is repeating points which had already been raised in the philosophical and theological disputations of the period. Elsewhere in *Primum Scriptum Sententiarum* Andrew makes reference to Thomas Bradwardine's *De Causa Dei* [106] and to the views of Gregory of Rimini [107]. As a matter of fact, there are clear parallels between some points raised by Andrew in his consideration of the divine command theory and what is found in earlier discussions of Bradwardine, Gregory of Rimini, and even Thomas Buckingham [108]. That Andrew's argumentation is to some extent borrowed from other sources cannot be precluded. Indeed, it would be surprising if he did not make mention of the contemporary disputation on an ethics of divine commands. At the same time, Andrew's own contributions to the debate cannot be given short shrift.

The citation of authorities is a familiar element of the medieval style of argumentation, and

Andrew of Neufchateau is no exception. Some of the authoritative statements cited by Andrew take the form of connecting justness with God, more specifically, with God's will. Of this nature is a statement made of the divine will by Anselm in the *Proslogium*: "For only what You will is just, and only what You do not will is not just" [109]. Or again, the divine will is described as "the sole and true justice" in the Pseudo-Cyprian's *De Singularitate Clericorum*, and a corresponding claim is made that if something which seems unjust in the eyes of human beings should be commanded by God, it may be believed to be just and may be done [110].

Another type of authoritative statement brought forward by Andrew concerns the explanatory sufficiency of the divine will. Thus is cited a statement made by Anselm in *Cur Deus Homo* that the will of God, never being irrational, ought to suffice us as a reason when he does anything [111]. Such a statement may be interpreted as indicative of the ultimacy of the divine will in ethical matters.

Yet other authoritative statements have to do with the concept of sin. In his treatise *De Peccatorum Meritis et Remissione et De Baptismo Parvulorum* Augustine remarks that "sin will not exist...if it is not divinely commanded that it not be" [112]. In *Contra Faustum* Augustine goes so far as to define sin as "any deed or word or desire contrary to the eternal law," which law is "the divine reason or the will of God commanding that the natural order be maintained and forbidding that it be disturbed" [113]. Ambrose similarly explicates sin in *De Paradiso*, defining it as "transgression of the divine law and disobedience to the divine precepts" [114]. Andrew likewise calls attention to the scriptural glosses of Augustine in *Enarrationes in Psalmos*, citing Augustine's identification of the "upright in heart" of Psalm 35:11 as those who follow the will of God [115].

An authoritative text given by Andrew which is especially worthy of note comes from Hugh of St. Victor's *De Sacramentis* [116]. We quote in its entirety the stretch of text from which Andrew's citation is taken:

> The first cause of all things is the will of the Creator which no antecedent cause moved because it is eternal, nor any subsequent cause confirms because it is of itself just. For He did not will justly, because what He willed was to be just, but what He willed was just, because He Himself willed it. For it is peculiar to Himself and to His will that that which is His is just; from Him comes the justice that is in His will by the very fact that justice comes from His will. That which is just is just according to His will and certainly would not be just, if it were not according to His will. When, therefore, it is asked how that is just which is just, the most fitting answer will be: because it is according to the will of God, which is just. When, however, it is asked how the will of God itself is also just, this quite reasonable answer will be given: because there is no cause of the first cause, whose prerogative it is to be what it is of itself. But this alone is the cause whence whatever is has originated, and it itself did not originate, but is eternal. [117]

This text suggests a connection between the dependency of what is just on the divine will and God's recognized status as *first and uncaused cause*. Although the text is somewhat obscure, it bears the following interpretation. When trying to determine what is just, we look to what accords with the will of God, for the divine will is considered to be paradigmatically just. Now in seeking the foundation of justice, it does not make sense to seek something else beyond the divine will. For the

divine will is the first cause of all things and, as such, it is uncaused and has no cause prior to it. Thus, there is no cause of the justness of the divine will; rather, the divine will itself generates justness.

This text from *De Sacramentis* is significant from the point of view of the history of the development of the divine command ethical theory. For the connection suggested by Hugh of St. Victor between an ethics of divine commands and God's status as *first cause* and *uncaused cause* is a connection which recurs in the historical literature, in somewhat varying forms. The connection is found in several of the arguments mentioned by Thomas Aquinas in a discussion of the divine command position in his treatise *De Veritate* [118]. The connection is also found in Reformation and early Protestant theology: in Martin Luther's *The Bondage of the Will* [119], in John Calvin's *Institutes of the Christian Religion* [120], in *The Doctrine of Absolute Predestination* of Jerome Zanchius [121], in John Preston's *Life Eternall* [122], and in *An Exposition of the Symbole or Creed of the Apostles* of William Perkins [123].

The contemporary theologians Carl Henry and Emil Brunner have claimed that an ethics of divine commands represents the *biblical* system of ethics [124]. Thus it is noteworthy that Andrew of Neufchateau makes use of biblical cases in the course of his discussion of an ethics of divine commands. In particular, Andrew uses biblical cases as one argument in support of his subsidiary thesis that there is no intrinsic evil of fault, citing the cases of Abraham preparing to kill Isaac, of the Israelites despoiling (i.e., stealing from) the Egyptians on their way out of Egypt, of Hosea taking a wife of fornication, of Samson killing himself, of Jacob lying to deceive his father, of the Israelites divorcing foreign wives, and of the patriarchs engaging in polygamy [125]. Moreover, when presenting an objection having to do with the issue of dispensation from precepts, Andrew quotes Bernard of Clairvaux's interpretation of the cases of Hosea, the Israelites plundering the Egyptians, and Samson's suicide [126]. Such appeals to the Bible were continued in discussions of divine command ethics in Reformation and Puritan theology, with focus on the case of Abraham and Isaac [127].

The defense of any ethical theory operates on two levels: the presentation of positive reasons in support of the position, and the refutation of objections which may be brought against it. In order to make Andrew's text more accessible, we have attempted to organize and systematize the various objections mentioned by him against an ethics of divine commands and its subsidiary theses, and offer the following catalogue.

(1) *An ethics of divine commands has counterintuitive consequences.*

Andrew of Neufchateau records a number of counterintuitive consequences which supposedly follow either from the basic divine command position or the subsidiary thesis denying the existence of intrinsically evil actions. For example, it might be claimed that an ethics of divine commands allows there to be "just good in inanimate beings and in animals because they live and operate and behave conformably to the decree and prescription of the divine will and as God wills" [128]. The achievement of impeccability also becomes trivialized through the possibility of God simply releasing an individual from every precept and obligation [129]. Or again, it seems that an individual being reprobated turns out to be good and just, and that the misery of hell becomes the highest good for someone who is damned, because these states are willed and decreed by God [130]. Indeed, God

could have made it the case that what the damned Lucifer now suffers is a good for him rather than an evil [131]. Furthermore, if whatever is evil is such because prohibited by the divine will, then some would contend that we are in the uncomfortable position of saying that evil comes from God, and concomitantly, that God is responsible for making a human being and an act to be evil [132]. On the other hand, it might be argued that the divine command thesis precludes the actual occurrence of evil. For if a particular act, a, is performed and willed by God, then it is good; but if God is unwilling that a be done, then a can occur only on the supposition that God is powerless [133].

As a further counterintuitive consequence of the divine command moralist's denial of the existence of intrinsically good acts, Andrew considers the point that the act of loving God above all could turn out to be evil [134]. Concomitantly, Andrew considers the objection that the divine command moralist's denial of intrinsically evil acts entails that "God could command a human being that beatitude be unwilled and that he lie and sin and fly and do contradictory things at the same time" [135].

(2) *An ethics of divine commands cannot account for degrees of good and evil.*

Andrew deals with a series of objections all having to do with the notion of *degrees* of good and evil. For one thing, the point may be raised that certain types of actions are acknowledged to be better or worse than others. It is thought, for example, that grace and supernatural gifts enable one to perform better acts than one is able to perform by purely natural capability. Or again, it is thought that the evil of fault, the evil opposed to supernatural goodness, is a greater evil than the evil of penalty for the senses. But it is alleged that, on the divine command theory, these priorities do not necessarily hold true [136]. Indeed, the point is repeatedly raised that the divine command theory obliterates any distinction of degrees of good and evil in that all things which are good or evil turn out to be *equally* good or evil [137]. Furthermore, if the existence of degrees of evil cannot be explained through the divine command theory's notion of prohibition, then it seems that the alternative view must be adopted that being a greater (or lesser) evil is intrinsic to actions themselves. And thus one seems entitled to draw the further conclusion that the very fact of something being evil at all is not due to a prohibition, as the divine command moralist claims [138]. Concomitantly, if it is admitted that one action is better than another from the nature of the thing and not because of a divine decree, it seems it must also be acknowledged that the fact of being good at all is not due to a divine command [139].

(3) *A divine precept is neither a necessary nor a sufficient condition for the existence of evil and sin.*

For the first part of this line of objection, Andrew mentions the contention that, apart from any precept of law, such actions as blaspheming God and doing harm to an innocent person are evil according to the dictate of right reason and are to be avoided by the definitions of their terms [140]. Andrew also records an objection which takes issue with the sufficiency of the divine will for establishing morals: an action can deviate from the divine will and be reprobated and hated by God yet not be vicious and culpable, should God fail to make his determination known to his creatures [141].

(4) *An ethics of divine commands fails, from a practical point of view, in leading to skepticism about morals.*

In the contemporary literature this type of objection has been considered at length by Philip Quinn [142]. The version mentioned by Andrew is that the divine command moralist's denial of intrinsically evil acts entails that "judgment is lost as well as the exercise of justice and the condemnation of evildoers" because "it will be uncertain and unknown whether the acts have been done rightly or not wrongly, not will it be possible to establish the opposite with certainty" [143].

(5) *Divine commands cannot be the ultimate foundation of morality since God's power to create moral obligations presupposes an obligation to obey God which rests on grounds other than divine commands.*

As a subsidiary point in a discussion on the virtue of obedience, Andrew records the following argument:

> ...What is just and presupposed by every divine precept or counsel as naturally prior is not contingently just because freely commanded or decreed by God. But that one ought to obey God and to obey God is of this type.
>   I prove this as follows. God would unsuitably give higher precepts unless first it were true and right that one ought to obey his will, for giving a precept presupposes a just subjection and lordship. Therefore, it is presupposed as being just that one ought to obey. And therefore, a precept is fittingly given to a rational creature because God ought to be obeyed. [144]

Historically, this proved to be an important line of objection. Among British moralists of the modern period it is found in the writings of Ralph Cudworth [145], Thomas Chubb [146], and Richard Price [147].

(6) *Contrary to the contention of the divine command moralist, there are acts which are intrinsically good and intrinsically evil.*

Andrew assesses various candidates for something having the status of being intrinsically good: the habit of infused justice or of charity and grace existing in a created will [148], the virtue of obedience [149], the vision and enjoyment of the blessed [150], fulfilling the commandments and counsels of God [151], a created will willing conformably to the divine decree [152]. Concomitantly, Andrew discusses the contention that an act of express disobedience to the divine will, as an act necessarily deviating from right reason, is an act which is intrinsically evil [153].

One line of argument falling into this category is based on an analogy between the realm of epistemology and the realm of ethics. Goodness is likened to truth, with the point being made, for transference to the case of goodness, that "something is true according to itself by its nature in such a way that it cannot fail to be true" [154]. Similarly, the relation of evilness to the first good is compared to the relation of falsity to the first and highest truth, with the claim that "something is false

of itself in such a way that, through the first truth, it cannot fail to be false" [155].

One particular candidate for an intrinsically evil act deserves special attention.

V

William Ockham claimed that the hatred of God, theft, and adultery would become right and meritorious acts if they should be commanded by God [156]. In the initial argumentation in response to the question whether evils of fault owe their status to divine prohibitions [157], the argument that Andrew of Neufchateau chooses to mention for a negative answer to this question, and concomitantly, against an ethics of divine commands, involves the hatred of God:

> *The answer seems to be no*, for <otherwise> the hatred of God could fail to be prohibited, and consequently, be licit and permitted [158].

In his consideration of the issue of intrinsically evil actions, Andrew singles out the act of hating God for special and prolonged attention not accorded to the other actions which allegedly cannot fail to be evil [159]. The same attention to this issue was subsequently displayed by the divine command moralist Jean Gerson. Gerson's discussion of divine command ethics is intermittent and not particularly extensive, and dates from the time immediately following the most active period of dispute [160]. But the temporal position of his discussion coupled with its very brevity directs our attention all the more to the fact that the one objection to the theory mentioned by him is that "a certain act is evil in such a way that it can never be good, and conversely" and that the one example of an intrinsically evil action given and considered by him is the hatred of God [161].

The importance of the issue of hating God in the critique of the divine command position is indicated by its recurrence in discussions of the theory in Renaissance scholasticism and in early modern philosophy. Against the divine command moralist, Francisco Suarez claims that the "divine volition...is not the whole reason for the good or evil involved in the observance or transgression of the natural law," but that "it necessarily presupposes the existence of a certain righteousness or turpitude in these actions" [162]. In support of this contention Suarez mentions the legitimation of the hatred of God as a counterintuitive consequence of the divine command theory:

> ...if the hatred of God, for example, involved no essential and intrinsic evil existing prior to its prohibition, then it would be possible for this hatred to be unprohibited. For why shall it not be allowed, if it is not in itself evil? Hence, it could be permitted, and it could be righteous. But this conclusion is clearly repugnant [to reason]. [163]

When considering the disclaimer of intrinsically evil actions made by divine command moralists, Jacques Almain also cites as a consequence of this position the concession that "the hatred of God can be exhibited by a human being and will not be evil" [164]. In fact, Almain distinguishes two issues of debate: first, whether the hatred of God can fail to be evil and can be licit, and second, whether the hatred of God can be good and meritorious of eternal life [165].

In the seventeenth century Nathaniel Culverwell repeated Suarez's line of argument in *An Elegant and Learned Discourse of the Light of Nature* [166]. Against the divine command moralist,

Culverwell describes the hatred of God as an evil which "is so full of evil, as that it cannot but be forbidden" and which "therefore is an evil in order of Nature before the prohibition of it" [167]. In a *Treatise Concerning Eternal and Immutable Morality*, another seventeenth century British philosopher, Ralph Cudworth, also mentions as an objectionable consequence of the divine command theory that to "command the hatred of God, is not inconsistent with the nature of God, but only with his free will" [168].

During the late Middle Ages the issue of the hatred of God was by no means limited to the internal disputations of proponents and opponents of the divine command ethical theory. It was a widely debated issue in the fourteenth century. Its prominence is indicated most forcefully by the fact that four major condemnations of the fourteenth century include articles having to do with hating God: the articles against William Ockham at Avignon in 1326 [169], those against Nicholas of Autrecourt in 1346 [170] and John of Mirecourt in 1347 [171], and the list of articles prohibited to the theological faculty of the University of Bologna issued by Hugolino or Orvieto in 1364 [172].

In considering the dispute on the hatred of God as related to the divine command ethical theory, Andrew of Neufchateau presents a line of objection having two parts. Specifically, it is objected that a divine command system entails the following apparently unacceptable positions: (1) that the act of hating God can fail to be evil, or, in other words, that it is not intrinsically evil; and the yet stronger position (2) that the act of hating God can be good and meritorious. We will examine both the case made by Andrew in favor of the acceptability of the first consequence, and his rather different response to the second point.

Andrew reports three arguments in support of the contention that the act of hating God is not intrinsically evil, arguments which can be formulated in the following way:

(I)   (1) If act *a* is evil in itself, then there is no case in which an agent performs *a* and *a* fails to be evil.
       (2) The act of hating God is not sinful when performed by a dreamer or a madman.
       (3) Therefore, the act of hating God is not evil in itself.
       (4) And therefore, the act of hating God could be performed by anyone, including those who are sane, and fail to be evil, at least with respect to the absolute power of God. [173]

(II)   (1) The act of loving God above all things fails to be good when it is performed by a dreamer, madman, or infidel or when it is performed contrary to conscience.
       (2) Therefore, the act of loving God above all things is good only contingently, not in itself.
       (3) The act of loving God above all things and the act of hating God have an analogous moral status.
       (4) Therefore, the act of hating God is not evil in itself. [174]

(III) (1) The act of hating God can be caused in the will by God alone.
       (2) It is a necessary condition of act *a* being a sin that the will do *a* actively and freely.
       (3) In the case described in (1), the will is functioning in a purely passive fashion.
       (4) Therefore, in this case, the will does not sin in hating God. [175]

The cases cited in (I-2) and (II-1) are instances of a strategy used by Andrew in arguing

against intrinsically good and intrinsically evil acts. Andrew gives the performance of an act *a* by a dreamer or a madman as reason for claiming that any morally good act *a* can fail to be morally good [176], that any supernaturally good act *a* can fail to have such goodness [177], and that any act *a* which is an evil of fault can fail to be such [178]. The possibility of performing an act contrary to conscience is used in the argumentation against intrinsically good acts of both the moral and supernatural varieties [179]. Similarly, argument (III) represents a broader strategy of argumentation. The possibility of an act being caused in the will by God alone is given as a reason why nothing has intrinsic moral goodness [180] or intrinsic supernatural goodness [181], and why nothing is intrinsically an evil of fault [182].

Andrew prefaces his statement of argument (I) with the phrase "certain persons say" [183]. Andrew indeed did not originate the appeal to the deeds of a dreamer or a madman in argumentation against intrinsically evil acts. Such a strategy of argumentation goes back at least to Thomas Bradwardine's *De Causa Dei contra Pelagium*:

> But further, if something were evil through itself, this would be apparent most of all in the case of a morally evil act...
>
> Again, homicide and adultery are not evil through themselves, nor are any exterior acts, because they are not evil in children, fools, sleepers, or even in madmen since these lack the free choice of the causal will...
>
> But further, it seems that no interior act is evil through itself, because neither is blasphemy nor the hatred of God, which can be demonstrated just as this has been shown of exterior acts in the case of fools and even madmen. [184]

This line of argument was subsequently repeated, though not endorsed, by Gregory of Rimini [185].

As the text quoted indicates, Bradwardine attributes the absence of evil in the acts of a sleeper or a madman to an absence of free will in the performance of these acts [186]. A similar explanation is given by Andrew of Neufchateau for the case of a madman who hates God: "he does not act freely, but more is impelled as is an animal" [187]. Yet other texts indicate that Andrew considered free will and the use of reason as prerequisites for goodness and virtuousness, both of which are absent in a madman or dreamer [188].

In two discussions of the divine command ethical theory from the period of Renaissance scholasticism, it is interesting to note the explicit inclusion of stipulations about *voluntariness of action* in descriptions of intrinsically evil acts:

> The other, more probable opinion is that there are some acts which are intrinsically evil, so that it is not within the power of God to bring it about that such acts be freely performed by a human being but not be evil... [189].

> ...although the natural law, as properly a divine law, includes the commands and prohibitions of God, it nevertheless assumes that there dwells in its subject-matter an intrinsic righteousness or wickedness, wholly inseparable from that matter. ...And though we may suppose, indeed, that an additional prohibition imposed through the will of God may be withdrawn, nevertheless, it is wholly repugnant to that which is

essentially and intrinsically evil that it should cease from being evil... Consequently, no act of the sort in question can be freely performed, without being evil and discordant with rational nature... This fact, indeed, would appear to be self-evident. For how could it ever happen that a voluntary act of hatred of God, or of lying, should not be wrong? [190]

The first comment comes from Jacques Almain, and the second, from Francisco Suarez. One can speculate that arguments of the form advanced by Thomas Bradwardine and Andrew of Neufchateau may have brought about this refinement in the critique of the divine command position [191].

In discussing argument (III) Andrew focuses on premise (1), which claims that the act of hating God can be caused in the will by God alone. Historically, there was debate over this claim both before and after the time of Andrew. When considering the cause of the obstinacy of the evil angels, William Ockham gives as an explanation that God causes totally whatever is absolute in the act of rejecting and hating God [192]. Ockham supports the contention that God can cause such an act in the created will with a whole series of arguments, based on the separability of acts from their moral qualities, on God's causal powers, and on the notion of the hatred of God qualifying as formally a sin [193]. Ockham's arguments, or variants of them, were repeated by John of Mirecourt [194]. The possibility of God producing in a creature the hatred of himself continued to be an issue in the late fourteenth century and in the fifteenth century among such philosophical theologians as John Brammart [195] and Gabriel Biel [196]. In fact, this line of argument may be responsible for a qualification in the description of intrinsically evil acts found in the Renaissance scholastic Jacques Almain. After claiming that there are some acts which are intrinsically evil and which cannot be freely performed by a human being without being evil, Almain explicitly adds the following condition: "It is said specifically *by a human being* for if they are produced by God alone, they cannot at this time be evil" [197]. Thus, within an historical context it can be seen that Andrew's discussion of proposition (1) of argument (III) is by no means a trivial exercise.

In defending premise (1) of argument (III), Andrew appeals first to the Articles of Paris of 1277. These articles included condemnation of the view that God cannot produce the effect of a secondary cause without the secondary cause itself [198]. Andrew translated this condemned view into a positive principle which he uses in support of premise (1): The act of hating God can be caused in the will by God alone for the reason that every effect which God can cause through a secondary cause, he can cause by himself immediately [199]. This argument seems to presuppose a theory of human action according to which the following is the case: Whenever an agent x hates God (or, more generally, whenever an agent x performs an act a), God participates causally in the effecting of the action. It is not unreasonable to think that such a rule of action theory is an implicit assumption of Andrew's supporting argument, for one of Ockham's arguments that God can be the total cause with respect to the act of hating God uses both a version of the general causal principle invoked by Andrew and the premise that "God is a partial cause with respect to anything positive, especially anything absolute, which is produced by a creature" [200]. When arguing against the existence of intrinsic evils of fault in general, Andrew brings in a universalized version of premise (1) of argument (III), viz., that an evil of fault can be totally caused in the rational soul by God alone [201]. In this case, Andrew defends his point not only by appealing to the aforementioned causal principle derived from the Articles of Paris of 1277, but also by deducing this claim directly from the omnipotence of

God [202]. Further, in giving his defense of premise (1) of argument (III) Andrew briefly alludes to yet another line of argument involving the principle that whatever God can annihilate, God can produce again [203]. With respect to the first condition, Andrew presumably has in mind the power of God's grace in bringing about repentance for action, including the act of hating God [204].

Among the objections against premise (1) considered by Andrew is the condemnation of a position held by John of Mirecourt: "That holding, as is commonly held, that understanding, volition, and sensation are qualities existing subjectively in the soul which God can by himself cause and put where he will, they have to assert or to say that God can bring it about by himself that a soul should hate his neighbor and God, and not demeritoriously" [205]. Andrew's reply embodies two different approaches to the condemned article. On the one hand, Andrew acknowledges a realm in which the condemnation holds true. This concession is based on linguistic analysis. Considering the phrase *hatred of God*, Andrew distinguishes broad and strict interpretations of its meaning:

> If *hatred* is taken in a broad sense and generally for the act which is naturally contrary to love, that act would be called *hatred of God*. But in taking *hatred of God* properly and strictly according to the meaning in which it is accustomed to be taken, then, whether from imposition or from use, it implies a disordered circumstance and a divergence from right reason and the due order towards its end and a certain perversion of the suitable order towards its end. For although the term *hatred*, taken absolutely and in itself, does not signify this since it is suitable to hate sin in a way that is not disordered, nevertheless, as *hatred* is determined by a term signifying the highest good and as it is specified to be brought to bear upon the final end, it implies a circumstance of disorder... [206].

And most importantly, Andrew denies that, in the strict, proper, and customary sense of its meaning, the hatred of God can be caused in the will by God alone [207].

In making this statement Andrew appears to recant premise (1) of argument (III). However, he goes on to indicate possible interpretations of the condemnation which are compatible with his line of argument. Invoking the distinction between the *absolute* and *ordained* powers of God [208], Andrew suggests that the condemnation might be taken as claiming only that, according to the ordained power of God and the laws which in fact have been established, it is not possible for God alone to cause the hatred of himself in the will of a creature; his own argument, however, may be seen as working within the framework of what is possible according to God's absolute power [209]. This move is consistent with Andrew's general qualifications that his discussion (and denial) of intrinsically good and intrinsically evil actions, within which is found the treatment of the issue of hating God, operates with reference to the absolute power of God [210]. Second, Andrew considers not the position *per se* that God alone could cause the hatred of himself, but the *inference* of this position from the view that understanding, volition, and sensation are merely qualities of the soul. He suggests that the condemnation may constitute a censure of the opinion that the qualities theory *necessitates* one to hold that God alone could cause the hatred of himself in the will. It remains possible, Andrew believes, to maintain the former position without adhering to the latter [211]. On this second interpretation of the article, the condemnation is not really addressed to premise (1) of argument (III) as such.

Andrew prefaces his presentation and discussion of arguments (I), (II), and (III) with a qualifying statement: "I will proceed not in the manner of making an assertion but in the manner of discussion and disputation" [212]. Given the condemnations which were issued during the fourteenth century, Andrew's disclaimer might simply be a protection against charges of heresy for views he himself felt inclined to espouse. On the other hand, Andrew's disclaimer might be genuine, cautioning the reader against taking as his own popular lines of argument of the period which he is simply reporting and exploring [213]. In any case, the reader is left wondering what position was in fact taken by this paradigmatic divine command moralist of the Middle Ages. The question is complicated by the fact that Andrew's statement of the generalized thesis denying the existence of intrinsic evils of fault also contains the explicit qualification that he is speaking "without assertion and disputatively after the manner of a laudable discussion" [214].

It seems there is reason to think that Andrew himself believed that the act of hating God can fail to be evil and hence is not intrinsically evil. First of all, arguments (I), (II), and (III), used to support this contention, represent *types* of argument which Andrew repeats at various places in the text [215], sometimes in a context which does not have the puzzling prefatory qualification [216]. Second, when considering an article against John of Mirecourt as a possible objection to premise (1) of argument (III), Andrew takes pains to show that there are ways of interpreting the article which are compatible with accepting that line of argument. Thus he clears the way for maintaining that argument and its conclusion without being accused of heresy. Finally, when Andrew considers the stronger claim that the act of hating God can be good and meritorious, he explicitly rejects it [217]. No such explicit rejection of the possibility of the hatred of God failing to be evil is to be found in his writings.

Andrew's discussion of the act of hating God has two parts. First, as just seen, he examines at length the issue of the intrinsic evilness of the act, that is, whether such an act can fail to be evil. Second, he takes up consideration of the even stronger claim, supposed to follow from an affirmataive answer to the first question, that the act of hating God can be *good, virtuous, and meritorious* [218]. This second issue was not gratuitously invented by Andrew, but reflects a wider discussion and debate. In his most celebrated statement of a divine command position, William Ockham asserts that the hatred of God could be meritoriously performed by an earthly pilgrim if it should come under a divine precept [219]. The thesis that a creature could hate God virtuously and meritoriously is sustained in the *Tractatus de Principiis Theologiae* [220], a compilation of Ockhamist thought [221]. The arguments of the *Tractatus* were subsequently reported by both Gregory of Rimini [222] and Peter of Ailly [223]. And Nicholas of Autrecourt was censured for maintaining that "God can command a rational creature to hold him in hatred, and that that creature in obeying would gain more merit than if he would love God according to a precept..." [224].

When Andrew came to deal with the issue whether his ethical system entails the counterintuitive consequence that the hatred of God could be good and meritorious, he records the following line of argument for an affirmative answer to this question. The aforementioned arguments (I), (II), and (III) conclude that the hatred of God can fail to be evil; but if any act (including the act of hating God) can fail to be evil, then it seems that it can be good, virtuous, and meritorious. For an act which is neither good nor evil in itself can not only be permitted and allowed as licit, but can even be commanded to be done. And since an act performed in obedience to a command or precept gains merit, it follows that an act of hating God so performed would be good and meritorious [225].

The Renaissance scholastics Jacques Almain [226] and Francisco Suarez [227] make note of similar lines of argument.

The ethical system of Andrew of Neufchateau is undoubtedly one of the purest examples of an ethics of divine commands to be found in the historical or contemporary literature. Thus it is noteworty that he explicitly shies away from allowing that the act of hating God could be good and meritorious [228]. He indicates that he does not regard argument (I), involving the act of hating God as performed by a dreamer or a madman, as committing him to the more extreme position presently at issue. He claims that "certain things suffice for that act not to be vicious, which do not suffice for it to be virtuous." Specifically, "such an act is not virtuous unless it is elicited freely by the one performing it and conformably to reason existing in him and prescribing to him and that he does it for the sake of God as the final end supremely loved in an orderly manner..." [229]. And these conditions simply are not satisfied in the case of a dreamer or a madman [230].

While Andrew makes mention of the article against Nicholas of Autrecourt on the subject of the meritoriousness of hating God [231], he does not offer any comments upon it. A later divine command moralist, Peter of Ailly, raised questions about the legitimacy and scope of the article. In particular, Ailly asserts that "he who wished to say that God can obligate to the hatred of himself could nevertheless uphold the article of Paris." This could be done, Ailly suggests, by denying the legitimacy of the inference from *He has a precept concerning the hatred of God and fulfills the precept* to *Therefore, he merits*, a denial allowed by the fact that God could fail to accept that act for merit [232]. Moreover, Ailly goes on to invoke the distinction between the absolute and ordained powers of God [233], further suggesting that if someone "wished to maintain the consequent with the first opinion, he could restrict that article to the ordained law by saying that that article was made more for restraining the arrogant lest they should offend pious ears than on account of the falsity of it" [234]. Ailly concludes his remarks on the article with the disclaimer, "Nevertheless I here affirm nothing" [235]. Particularly in view of his second point of reply to the article, the reader is left to wonder if the disclaimer is not merely a conventional shield against charges of heresy for a position which Peter of Ailly himself maintained.

In the contemporary literature on the divine command ethical theory the objection has been raised that God could command actions to be performed with seem to us to be abhorrent and obviously immoral in character, such as acts of gratuitous cruelty. According to the divine command system, such acts would have to be regarded as right. But to consider right such acts as the gratuitous torture of young children goes against all our moral intuitions. Therefore, since an ethics of divine commands has these counterintuitive consequences, the objection concludes that the theory must be rejected [236].

The medieval objection against the divine command theory which we have been considering is of the same ilk as this contemporary line of criticism. Surely, hating God was a paradigm case of an action intuitively repugnant to the medieval mentality, and medieval philosophers and theologians considered the implications of an ethics of divine commands for sanctioning such behavior.

In the contemporary literature replying to this line of objection, Robert Merrihew Adams has suggested that an ethics of divine commands is developed within the context of certain beliefs about God's nature, specifically, that God *loves* his human creatures. This presupposition of a divine command ethics effectually rules out the practical possibility of God commanding such abhorrent acts as gratuitous cruelty [237].

The response of medieval divine command moralists to the objection, on the other hand, can be described as one of biting the bullet. Unlike Adams, Andrew of Neufchateau did not take the position that God would not in fact command an abhorrent action, such as the hatred of himself. Indeed, Andrew brings foward the case of God himself causing such hatred in the created will. Rather, Andrew attacks the objection by asking us to reconsider our moral intuitions. He proposes and reviews cases in which we are supposed to agree that hating God is not evil, and thus accept the consequence to which an ethics of divine commands apparently leads. William Ockham, and probably Peter of Ailly, were even willing to go beyond Andrew's position by committing themselves to the yet stronger claim that the seemingly immoral act of hating God could conceivably be meritorious.

NOTES

1. William K. Frankena, *Ethics*, 2nd ed. (Englewood Cliffs, NJ: Prentice-Hall, 1973), p. 28

2. *Ibid.*

3. William Paley, *The Principles of Moral and Political Philosophy*, 2nd ed., I, 7; II, 3, 4, 9, 10; III, I, 4; VI, 3 (London: R. Faulder, 1786).

4. John Locke, *Essays on the Law of Nature* I, VI edited by W. von Leyden (Oxford: Clarendon, 1965); *An Essay Concerning Human Understanding* I, II, 6; II, XXVIII edited by Alexander Campbell Fraser (New York: Dover Publications, 1959). The ambiguities of Locke's position have been discussed in the introduction to *Essays on the Law of Nature*, pp. 40-59 and by Francis Oakley and Elliot W. Urdang in "Locke, Natural Law, and God," *Natural Law Forum* 11 (1966): 92-109.

5. John Gay, *Preliminary Dissertation Concerning the Fundamental Principle of Virtue or Morality*, Introduction, Sect. II in William King, *An Essay on the Origin of Evil*, 4th ed., translated by Edmund Law (Cambridge: W. Thurlbourn & J. Woodyer, 1758).

6. Ralph Cudworth, *Treatise Concerning Eternal and Immutable Morality* I, I-III in *The True Intellectual System of the Universe*, vol. 2 (New York: Gould & Newman, 1838).

7. Samuel Clarke, *A Demonstration of the Being and Attributes of God* in *the Works of Samuel Clarke* (reprint New York: Garland Publishing, 1978), pp. 575-6.

8. Thomas Chubb, *The Comparative Excellence and Obligation of Moral and Positive Duties* (London: J. Roberts, 1730; reprint New York: Garland Publishing, 1978), pp. 17-20.

9. Richard Price, *A Review of the Principal Questions in Morals* I, 1, 3; V (reprint New York: Burt Franklin, 1974).

10. George Rust, *A Discourse of Truth* I-XVI in Joseph Glanvill, *Two Choice and Useful Treatises* (London: James Collins & Sam. Lowndes, 1682).

11. Anthony Earl of Shaftesbury, *Characteristics of Men, Manners, Opinions, Times* IV, I, III, 2 edited by John M. Robertson (Indianapolis: Bobbs-Merrill, 1964).

12. Francis Hutcheson, *An Inquiry Concerning the Original of Our Ideas of Virtue or Moral Good* VII, 5 in D.D. Raphael (ed.), *British Moralists*, vol. 1 (Oxford: Clarendon Press, 1969).

13. Jeremy Bentham, *An Introduction to the Principles of Morals and Legislation* II, 1-3, 11, 18 (London: Athlone Press, 1970).

14. Martin Luther, *The Bondage of the Will* IV, pp. 180-1 in *Luther's Works*, vol. 33 edited by Philip S. Watson (Philadelphia: Fortress Press, 1972); *Lectures on Romans*, Scholia IX, 6 in *Luther's Works*, vol. 25 edited by Hilton C. Oswald (St. Louis: Concordia Publishing House, 1972).

15. John Calvin, *Institutes of the Christian Religion* II, VIII, 5; III, XXIII, 2 translated by Henry Beveridge (Grand Rapids, MI: Eerdmans, 1962).

16. James Usher, *A Body of Divinity; or, The Sum and Substance of Christian Religion,* 8th ed. (London: Printed by R.J. for Jonathan Robinson, A.&J. Churchill, J. Taylor & J. Wyatt, 1702), pp. 61, 82.

17. William Perkins, *An Exposition of the Symbole or Creed of the Apostles* in *Workes*, vol. 1 (London: John Legatt, 1616), pp. 278, 288, 294.

18. John Preston, *Life Eternall or, A Treatise of the Knowledge of the Divine Essence and Attributes*, 4th ed., I, Eighth Sermon, Second Attribute of God (London: E. Purslowe, 1634).

19. Samuel Willard, *A Compleat Body of Divinity in Two Hundred and Fifty Expository Lectures on the Assembly's Shorter Catechism* (Boston: B. Green & S. Kneeland, 1726), Sermon XXIV, November 5, 1689. See also Sermon LIV, August 8, 1692.

20. See, for example, W. von Leyden, *Introduction* to John Locke's *Essays on the Law of Nature*, p. 51; Robert A. Green & Hugh MacCallum, *Introduction* to Nathaniel Culverwell's *An Elegant and Learned Discourse of the Light of Nature* (Toronto: University of Toronto Press, 1971), p. xxiv; Alessandro Passerin

d'Entreves, *Natural Law* (London: Hutchinson's University Library, 1951), pp. 69, 71.

21. See, for example, D. Goldstick, "Monotheism's *Euthyphro* Problem," *Canadian Journal of Philosophy* 3 (1974): 585-9 at 587; D.A. Rees, "The Ethics of Divine Commands," *Proceedings of the Aristotelian Society* 57 (1956-7): 83-106 at 83.

22. See, for example, Anthony Flew, "The *Religious Morality* of Mr. Patterson Brown," *Mind* 74 (1965): 578-81 at 579; Rees, "The Ethics of Divine Commands," p. 83; Robert Merrihew Adams, "A Modified Divine Command Theory of Ethical Wrongness" in Gene Outka & John P. Reeder, Jr. (eds.), *Religion and Morality* (Garden City, NY: Anchor Press, Doubleday, 1973), p. 320; Philip L. Quinn, "Religious Obedience and Moral Autonomy," *Religious Studies* 11 (1975): 265-81 at 271; Quinn, *Divine Commands and Moral Requirements* (Oxford: Clarendon Press, 1978), p. 36; Outka & Reeder, *Introduction* to *Religion and Morality*, p. 1; Eric D'Arcy, "*Worthy of Worship*: A Catholic Contribution" in Outka & Reeder (eds.), *Religion and Morality*, p. 192.

23. William Ockham, *Quaestiones in Librum Secundum Sententiarum*, q. 15, Solutio Dubiorum, ad 3m edited by Gedeon Gal, O.F.M., and Rega Wood (St. Bonaventure, NY: St. Bonaventure University, 1981), p. 352 = *Super 4 Libros Sententiaum* II, q. 19, O (Lyon, 1494-6).

24. Cudworth, *Treatise Concerning Eternal and Immutable Morality* I, I, 5.

25. Francisco Suarez, *De Legibus* II, VI, 4 in James Brown Scott (ed.), *Selections from Three Works of Francisco Suarez, S.J.*, vol. 2 translated by Gwladys L. Williams, Ammi Brown & John Waldron (Oxford: Clarendon Press, 1944).

26. The writing of the name in Latin has varied. In a number of biographical sources, the name is written as *Novocastro*. See Peter Rodulphe (Petrus Rodulphius/Radulphius), *Historiarum Seraphicae Religionis* (Venice, 1586), 307 cited in Titus Szabo, *Introduction* to *De Conceptione Virginis Gloriosae* by Andreas de Novo Castro, in *Bibliotheca Franciscana Scholastica Medii Aevi*, XVI (Quaracchi: Collegium S. Bonaventurae, 1954), p. 105, n. 4; A. Possevin (Possevinus), *Apparatus Sacer* (Venice, 1606), I, 85 cited in Szabo, *Introduction*, p. 105, n. 5; Quetif-Echard, *Scriptores Ordinis Praedicatorum* (Paris: 1719-23; reprint New York: Burt Franklin, 1959), I, 740; C. Oudin (Oudinus), *Commentarius de scriptoribus Ecclesiae antiquis* (Leipzig, 1722), III, c. 699 cited in Szabo, *Introduction*, p. 105, n. 8; John Albert Fabricius, *Bibliotheca Latina Mediae et Infimae Aetatis* (Padua: Joannem Manfre, 1754), I, 96; H. Hurter, *Nomenclator Literarius Theologiae Catholicae* (Innsbruck: 1906-26; reprint New York: Burt Franklin, 1962), II, 392; John Hyacinth Sbaralea, *Supplementum et Castigatio ad Scriptores Trium Ordinum S. Francisci* (Rome: Nardecchia, 1908), I, 37; G. Fussenegger, *Lexicon fur Theologie und Kirche* (Freiburg: Herder, 1957), 518. Another variant found in the literature is Andreas *Novocastrensis*. See LeMire (Miraeus), *Bibliotheca ecclesiastica* (Antwerp, 1639), p. 267 cited in Hubert Elie, *Le Complexe Significabile* (Paris: J. Vrin, 1936), p. 240; Wharton, *Appendix ad Historiam Litterariam Gulielmi Cave* (Basel: Joh. Rudolph Im-Hoff, 1744), p. 4; Thomas Tanner, *Bibliotheca Britannico-Hibernica* (London, 1748; reprint Tuscon, AR: Audax Press, 1963), 41. And yet another variant is Andreas de *Castro Novo*. See Peter of Alva and Astorga, *Monumenta antiqua Seraphica pro Immaculata Conceptione V. Mariae* (Louvain, 1665), 121a cited in Szabo, *Introduction*, p. 104, n. 3. Several variants are even found in *Primum Scriptum Sententiarum*, the 1514 Parisian printed edition of Andreas's commentary on the first book of the *Sentences*. The form Andreas de *Novo Castro* is used on the title page and in the incipit and colophon, while the parliamentary permission to print the text speaks of Andre de *Castro Novo* and introductory poetry uses the name Andreas de *Castro*. Perhaps more weight should be given to the form of the name used on the title page and in the incipit and colophon. The author in question is likewise responsible for a treatise *De Conceptione Virginis Gloriosae*, and the modern editor of this treatise, Titus Szabo, has pointed out that two manuscript copies of it which explicitly identify the author do so as *Andreas de Novo Castro*; see Szabo, *Introduction*, pp. 104, n. 3; 120-23; 127.

27. See Appendix A.

28. See Appendix B.

29. *Primum Scriptum Sententiarum* (Paris: Granjon, 1514), fol. 251rb-262ra.

30. For a survey of proponents of an ethics of divine commands, see Janine Marie Idziak (ed.), *Divine Command Morality: Historical and Contemporary Readings* (New York & Toronto: Edwin Mellen Press, 1980).

31. William J. Courtenay, *Adam Wodeham* (Leiden: Brill, 1978), p. 139.

32. For more generous assessments of Andreas's contributions to yet other areas of philosophy and theology, see Hubert Elie, *Le Complexe Significabile* (Paris: J. Vrin, 1936); Titus Szabo, *Introduction* to the edition of *De Conceptione Virginis Gloriosae* by Andreas de Novo Castro, O.F.M. in *Bibliotheca Franciscana Scholastica Medii Aevi*, XVI (Quaracchi: Collegium S. Bonaventurae, 1954), p. 112, n. 4 & 5; Katherine H. Tachau, "The *Quaestiones in Librum Primum Sententiarum* of Andreas de NovoCastro, O.F.M., *Archives d'Histoire Doctrinale et Litteraire du Moyen Age* 67 (1992): 289-318 at 291, n. 5.

33. Title question, *Primum Scriptum Sententiarum*, d. 48, q. 1. All references to *Primum Scriptum Sententiarum*, d. 48, q. 1-2 may be found in the present volume.

34. Title question, *Primum Scriptum Sententiarum*, d. 48, q. 2.

35. Andrew of Neufchateau, *Primum Scriptum Sententiarum*, d. 48, q. 1, a. 1, Kinds of Good.

36. *Ibid.*

37. *Ibid.*

38. *Ibid.*

39. *Ibid.* For the distinction between *moral* and *non-moral* senses of good, see William K. Frankena, *Ethics*, pp. 9-11.

40. See the relevant definitions in Andrew of Neufchateau, *Primum Scriptum Sententiarum*, d. 48, q. 1, a. 1, Kinds of Good.

41. *Ibid.*

42. *Ibid.*

43. Note that the subject of the second question of distinction 48 is the evil of fault specifically.

44. Andrew of Neufchateau, *Primum Scriptum Sententiarum*, d. 48, q. 2, statement of question & a. 1.

45. *Ibid.*, d. 48, q. 1, a. 1, Reply to the question, concl. 1.

46. *Ibid.*, d. 48, q. 1, a. 1, Reply to the question, concl. 1.

47. *Ibid.*, d. 48, q. 1, a. 2, concl. 2.

48. *Ibid.*, d. 48, q. 1, a. 2, title of article.

49. *Ibid.*, d. 48, q. 2, a. 2, concl. 1.

50. *Ibid.*, d. 48, q. 1, a. 1, Reply to the question, introduction & concl. 4; d. 48, q. 1, a. 2, concl. 4. Cf. d. 48, q. 1, a. 1, Reply to the question, concl. 2 & 3.

51. *Ibid.*, d. 48, q. 2, a. 2, concl. 2.

52. A *metaethical* divine command theory concerns the meaning of fundamental moral terms, holding that e.g., "right" and "wrong" *mean*, respectively, commanded and forbidden by God. A *normative* divine command theory holds that divine commands and prohibitions constitute the *standard* of right and wrong, a position compatible with analyzing the meaning of fundamental ethical terms without reference to God.

53. Andrew of Neufchateau, *Primum Scriptum Sententiarum*, d. 48, q. 1, a. 1, Kinds of Good.

54. *Ibid.*

55. *Ibid.*

56. *Ibid.*

57. *Ibid.*

58. Quinn, *Divine Commands and Moral Requiremetns*, p. 30. We quote the "simple theory." The remainder of the monograph develops theories which are more sophisticated logically.

59. Philip Quinn, "Divine Command Ethics: A Causal Theory" in Idziak (ed.), *Divine Command*

Morality: Historical and Contemporary Readings, p. 311.

    60. *Ibid.*, p. 312.

    61. *Ibid.*, p. 311.

    62. Andrew of Neufchateau, *Primum Scriptum Sententiarum*, d. 48, q. 1, a. 2, concl. 2.

    63. *Ibid.*, d. 48, q. 1, a. 2, concl. 3, 12m.

    64. *Ibid.*, d. 48, q. 1, a. 2, concl. 3, ad 4m.

    65. *Ibid.*, d. 48, q. 2, a. 2, concl. 1, ad 2m.

    66. *Ibid.*, d. 48, q. 1, a. 1, Reply to the question, concl. 1.

    67. See, for example, Frankena, *Ethics*, p. 28: "One such monistic kind of rule deontology with a long and important history is the Divine Command theory, also known as theological voluntarism...". See also James F. Childress & John Macquarrie (eds.), *The Westmister Dictionary of Christian Ethics* (Philadelphia: Westminster Press, 1986), s.v. Voluntarism.

    68. "Il ne nous reste plus qu'a tirer la conclusion de cette longue etude de la philosophie juridique d'Ockham. ...L'univers juridique d'Ockham est, au contraire, essentiellement une dispersion. Mais cette dispersion est conforme a la logique des principes poses comme lois de l'existant. ...*Deuxieme loi de l'existant:* la volonte est l'attribut essentiel de tout etre raisonnable. L'essence de Dieu est la liberte absolue de sa volonte. L'essence de l'homme est l'autonomie de son libre arbitre. Il est donc parfaitement logique d'aboutir a une philosophie juridique qui reduit tout le droit a la volonte: volonte arbitraire de Dieu pour le droit divin et le droit naturel, volonte libre de l'homme pour le droit humain." Georges de Lagarde, *La Naissance de l'Esprit Laique au Declin du Moyen Age*, vol. 6 *Ockham: La Morale et le Droit* (Paris: E. Droz, 1946), pp. 211-2.

    "L'attribut essentiel de l'etre raisonnable, tel que le concoit Jean Gerson, est la volonte. C'est elle aussi qui est l'essence meme de Dieu, qui est avant tout une Volonte; c'est elle aussi qui sera par consequent la source premiere de toute moralite." Louis Vereecke, "Droit et Morale Chez Jean Gerson," *Revue Historique de Droit Francais et Etranger* 32 (1954): 413-27 at 418.

    69. In the contemporary literature this objection to an ethics of divine commands has been mentioned by Baruch A. Brody, "Morality and Religion Reconsidered" in Baruch A. Brody (ed.), *Readings in the Philosophy of Religion* (Englewood Cliffs, NJ: Prentice-Hall, 1974), pp. 592-3; A.C. Ewing, "The Autonomy of Ethics" in Ian Ramsey (ed.), *Prospect for Metaphysics* (London: George Allen & Unwin, 1961), p. 39; Patterson Brown, "Religious Morality," *Mind* 72 (1963): 235-44 at 241; Carl F. H. Henry, *Christian Personal Ethics* (Grand Rapids, MI: Eerdmans, 1957), p. 210. But this objection is by no means unique to the contemporary literature. Within British modern philosophy it is articulated by Ralph Cudworth, *Treatise Concerning Eternal and Immutable Morality* I, I, 5; Joseph Glanvill, *A Letter Concerning George Rust's A DISCOURSE OF TRUTH* in Glanvill, *Two Choice and Useful Treatises* (London: James Collins & Sam. Lowndes, 1682), no pagination; and Richard Price, *A Review of the Principal Questions in Morals* I, 3. This point has also been picked up by some medievalists. Georges de Lagarde describes Ockham's moral system as *arbitrary and irrational*; see *La Naissance de l'Esprit Laique au Declin du Moyen Age* 6:59, 61, 63, 91, 112-3. Elzearius Bonke gives a similar characterization of Ockham's ethics in "Doctrina Nominalistica de Fundamento Ordinis Moralis Apud Gulielmum de Ockham et Gabrielem Biel," *Collectanea Franciscana* 14 (1944): 57-83 at 58. Indeed, the medieval divine command moralist Andrew of Neufchateau shows an awareness of this line of objection in *Primum Scriptum Sententiarum*, d. 48, q. 2, a. 2, concl. 1, 6m.

    70. Andrew of Neufchateau, *Primum Scriptum Sententiarum*, d. 48, q. 1, a. 2, concl. 3.

    71. *Ibid.*, d. 48, q. 1, a. 2, concl. 3 ff.

    72. *Ibid.*, d. 48, q. 1, a. 2, concl. 3.

    73. *Ibid.*, d. 48, q. 1, a. 2, concl. 3.

    74. See reference notes for *ibid.*, d. 48, q. 1, a. 2, concl. 3, This is confirmed by the verse of Matthew... .

75. *Ibid.*, d. 48, q. 1, a. 2, concl. 3, Moreover, the created will behaves in this way...; see the reference note for this text for the source of this argument in Bradwardine.

76. Bernard Landry, *Duns Scotus* (Paris: Felix Alcan, 1922), p. 266.

77. Francis Oakley, *The Political Thought of Pierre d'Ailly* (New Haven: Yale University Press, 1964), pp. 19-20; "Medieval Theories of Natural Law: William of Ockham and the Significance of the Voluntarist Tradition," *Natural Law Forum* 6 (1961): 65-83 at 82.

78. C. Ruch, *Dictionnaire de Theologie Catholique* (1905), s.v. Biel, Gabriel, col. 819.

79. Frederick Copleston, *A History of Philosophy*, vol. 3, pt. 1 (Garden City, NY: Doubleday Image, 1963), p. 215.

80. Andrew of Neufchateau, *Primum Scriptum Sententiarum*, d. 48, q. 1.

81. *Ibid.*, d. 48, q. 2.

82. *Ibid.*, d. 48, q. 1, Reply to the question, concl. 1.

83. *Ibid.*, d. 48, q. 1, a. 2, concl. 2.

84. *Ibid.*, d. 48, q. 1, The answer seems to be no...; d. 48, q. 1, Reply to the question, Therefore it is asked...; d. 48, q. 1, Reply to the question, concl. 1 & First Proof; d. 48, q. 1, Reply to the question, concl. 4, 3m & 5m; d. 48, q. 1, a. 2, concl. 2, 5m; d. 48, q. 1, a. 2, concl. 3, Moreover, it <otherwise> follows... & Moreover, doing *b*... & Moreover, for no outward activity...; d. 48, q. 1, a. 2, concl. 3, ad 3m & ad 9m, ad confirm. & ad 10m, ad confirm. & ad 12m, ad 2m; d. 48, q. 1, a. 2, concl. 4, 3m, confirm. & 8m & 9m, Confirmation: When it is said... & 9m, Again, it can be argued...; d. 48, q. 2, contra; d. 48, q. 2, a. 2, concl. 2, 9m.

85. *Ibid*, d. 48, q. 1, a. 2, concl. 3.

86. *Ibid.*, d. 48, q. 1, a. 2, concl. 3. The *liberty of contradiction* is the power enjoyed by the will to choose to will or to refrain from willing; see *Dictionnaire de Theologie Catholique* (1926), s.v. Liberte, col. 661-3.

87. *Ibid.*, d. 48, q. 1, a. 2, concl. 3.

88. *Ibid.*, d. 48, q. 1, a. 2, concl. 3.

89. *Ibid.*, d. 48, q. 1, a. 2, concl. 3.

90. *Ibid.*, d. 48, q. 1, a. 2, concl. 3.

91. George Rust, *A Discourse of Truth* XIV.

92. *Ibid.*, XVI.

93. *Natural law* is mentioned in *Primum Scriptum Sententiarum*, d. 48, q .1, a. 1, Kinds of Good; d. 48, q. 1, a. 1, Reply to the question, concl. 1, moral good; d. 48, q. 1, a. 2, concl. 1, Confirmation: According to the Master...; d. 48, q. 1, a .2, concl. 3, ad 12m; d. 48, q. 1, a. 2, concl. 4, 8m; d. 48, q. 2, a. 2, concl. 1, ad 4m; d. 48, q. 2, a. 2, concl. 2.

94. *Ibid.*, d. 48, q. 1, a. 1, Reply to the question, concl. 4, 3m.

95. *Ibid.*, d. 48, q. 1, a. 1, Reply to the queston, concl. 4, ad 3m.

96. *Ibid.*, d. 48, q. 2, a. 2, concl. 2, ad 1m.

97. *Ibid.*, d. 48, q. 2, a. 2, concl. 1, ad 2m.

98. Compare the following remarks of Francisco Suarez about Ockham: "This is the view one ascribes to William of Occam (on the *Sentences*, Bk. II, qu. 19, ad 3 and 4), inasmuch as he says that no act is wicked save in so far as it is forbidden by God, and that there is no act incapable of becoming a good act if commanded by God; and conversely...; whence he assumes that the whole natural law consists of divine precepts laid down by God, and susceptible of abrogation or alteration by him. And if any one insists that such a law would not be natural but positive, the reply is, that it is called natural because of its congruity with the nature of things, and not with the implication that it was not externally enacted by the command of God." In Scott (ed.), *Selections from Three Works of Francisco Suarez, S.J.*, 2:190.

99. Andrew of Neufchateau, *Primum Scriptum Sententiarum*, d. 48, q. 2, a. 2, concl. 1, 8m.

100. *Ibid.*, d. 48, q. 2, a. 2, concl. 1, ad 8m.

101. See also *ibid.*, d. 48, q. 2, a. 2, concl. 2, ad 5m.

102. *Ibid.*, d. 48, q. 2, a. 2, concl. 1, ad 2m. Compare the following remarks of the divine command moralist William Paley: "The case is this: by virtue of the two principles, that God wills the happiness of his creatures, and that the will of God is the measure of right and wrong, we arrive at certain conclusions; which conclusions becomes rules; and we soon learn to pronounce actions right or wrong, according as they agree or disagree with our rules, without loooking any farther...". *The Principles of Moral and Political Philosophy* II, IX.

103. For the mention of *right reason* in the statement of objections, see Andrew of Neufchateau, *Primum Scriptum Sententiarum*, d. 48, q. 1, Reply to the question, concl. 4, 1m & 2m & 5m & 6m; d. 48, q. 2, a .2, concl. 1, 2m; d. 48, q. 2, a. 2, concl. 2, 4m & 11m. For use of the concept of right reason in lines of argument expressing Andrew's own position, see *Primum Scriptum Sententiarum*, d. 48, q. 1, Kinds of Good, definitions of *moral* and *supernatural* goodness; d. 48, q. 1, Reply to the question, concl. 4, Moreover, it can deviate... & ad 2m; d. 48, q. 1, a. 2, concl. 2, ad 2m; d. 48, q. 1, a. 2, concl. 3, ad 2m & ad 10m; d. 48, q. 1, a. 2, concl. 4, ad 8m, ad Bernardum; d. 48, q. 2, a. 2, concl. 2, ad 4m & ad 5m.

104. *Ibid.*, d. 48, q. 1, Reply to the question, concl. 1. Although the evidence is overwhelmingly in favor of regarding Andrew as upholding a *voluntaristic* version of divine command ethics, here is one of the aberrant texts in which Andrew speaks of *both* the divine intellect and the divine will as the foundation of morality.

105. William Ockham, *Scriptum in Librum Primum Sententiarum*, d. 41, q. 1, "But from the very fact that the divine will wills this, right reason dictates that it is to be chosen." Edited by Girard Etzkorn & Francis E. Kelley (St. Bonaventure, NY: St. Bonaventure University, 1979), p. 610 = *Super 4 Libros Sententiarum* I, d .41, q. 1, K (Lyon, 1494-6).

106. See Appendix A, n. 49.

107. Specifically, Gregory of Rimini's views on the *complexe significabile* are mentioned by Andrew in *Primum Scriptum Sententiarum*, Prologue, q. 1: "Some also argue against the stated conclusions, demonstrating as follows that no such complexly signifiable is any thing or entity: Every entity is a substance or quality or quantity or something else which can be signified through one of the predicates according to Gregory, bk. 1, dist. 28, q. 1..." (fol. 2ra). See also Tachau, "The *Quaestiones in Librum Primum Sententiarum* of Andreas de NovoCastro, O.F.M.," pp. 294, 296-8.

108. See Andrew of Neufchateau, *Primum Scriptum Sententiarum*, d. 48, q. 1, reference notes 27, 29, 31-5, 40, 42-3, 52; d. 48, q. 2, reference notes 8, 11, 12.

109. Anselm, *Proslogium* 11 in *Opera Omnia* edited by Francis Salesius Schmitt (Edinburgh: Thomas Nelson & Sons, 1946), 1:109. Citation: Andrew of Neufchateau, *Primum Scriptum Sententiarum*, d. 48, q. 1, a. 2, concl. 2.

110. Pseudo-Cyprian, *De Singularitate Clericorum* 16 in *Corpus Scriptorum Ecclesiasticorum Latinorum* (Vienna: 1866--), III-3:190. Citation: Andrew of Neufchateau, *Primum Scriptum Sententiarum*, d. 48, q. 1, a. 2, concl. 2; see also reference note 21.

111. Anselm, *Cur Deus Homo* I, 8 in *Opera Omnia*, ed. Schmitt 2:59. Citation: Andrew of Neufchateau, *Primum Scriptum Sententiarum*, d. 48, q. 1, a. 2, concl. 2.

112. Augustine, *De Peccatorum Meritis et Remissione et De Baptismo Parvulorum* II, 16, 23 in *Corpus Scriptorum Ecclesiasticorum Latinorum* 60:95-6. Citation: Andrew of Neufchateau, *Primum Scriptum Sententiarum*, d. 48, q. 2, a. 2, concl. 1.

113. Augustine, *Contra Faustum* XXII, 27 in *Corpus Scriptorum Ecclesiasticorum Latinorum* 25:621. Citation: Andrew of Neufchateau, *Primum Scriptum Sententiarum*, d. 48, q. 2, a. 2, concl. 1; see Reference Notes to Distinction 48, Question 2, n. 8.

114. Ambrose, *De Paradiso* 8, 39 in *Corpus Scriptorum Ecclesiasticorum Latinorum* 32-1:296.

Citation: Andrew of Neufchateau, *Primum Scriptum Sententiarum*, d. 48, q. 2, a. 2, concl. 1; see Reference Notes to Distinction 48, Question 2, n. 8.

115. Augustine, *Enarrationes in Psalmos*, Ps. XXXV, 16 in *Corpus Christianorum*, series Latina, 38:334 (Turnholt: Brepols, 1954--). Citation: Andrew of Neufchateau, *Primum Scriptum Sententiarum*, d. 48. q. 2, a. 2, concl. 1.

116. Citation: Andrew of Neufchateau, *Primum Scriptum Sententiarum*, d. 48, q. 1, a. 2, concl. 2.

117. Hugh of St. Victor, *De Sacramentis* I, IV, I translated by Roy J. Deferrari (Cambridge, MA: Mediaeval Academy of America, 1951). This translation is based on an unpublished critical edition prepared by Brother Charles Henry.

118. Thomas Aquinas, *De Veritate*, q. 23, a. 6 in *Opera Omnia* 22-3, Commissio Leonina (Rome: Editori Di San Tommaso, 1975); translation by Robert W. Schmidt, S.J., *Truth* (Chicago: Henry Regnery, 1954).

119. Martin Luther, *The Bondage of the Will* IV, p. 181.

120. John Calvin, *Institutes of the Christian Religion* III, 23.

121. Jerome Zanchius, *Observations on the Divine Attributes*, The Will of God, Position 7 in *The Doctrine of Absolute Predestination*, translated by Augustus Montague Toplady (London: Sovereign Grace Union, 1930), pp. 50-2.

122. John Preston, *Life Eternall or, A Treatise of the knowledge of the Divine Essence and Attributes*, 4th ed. cor., I, Sermon VIII, Second Attribute of God.

123. William Perkins, *An Exposition of the Symbole or Creed of the Apostles* in *Workes* 1:278.

124. Carl F.H. Henry, *Christian Personal Ethics* (Grand Rapids, MI: Eerdmans, 1957), chap. 8; Emil Brunner, *The Divine Imperative* (Philadelphia: Westminster Press, 1947), II, chap. 6.

125. Andrew of Neufchateau, *Primum Scriptum Sententiarum*, d. 48, q. 2, a. 2, concl . 2.

126. *Ibid.*, d. 48, q. 1, a. 2, concl. 4, 8m.

127. Zanchius, *Observations on the Divine Attributes*, The Justice of God, Position 3, pp. 72-3; James Usher, *A Body of Divinity; or, The Sum and Substance of Christian Religion*, 8th ed., p. 51.

128. Andrew of Neufchateau, *Primum Scriptum Sententiarum*, d. 48, q. 1, a. 2, concl. 2, 2m. In this objection the same point is made about a madman and about someone who has an act of willing infused into his will by God alone. For the most part, Andrew's responses to objections from counterintuitive consequences are perfunctory.

129. *Ibid.*, d. 48, q. 2, a. 2, concl. 2, 10m.

130. *Ibid.*, d. 48, q. 1, a. 2, concl. 2, 5m & 6m. Of the same ilk is d. 48, q. 1, a. 2, concl. 2, 4m.

131. *Ibid.*, d. 48, q. 2, a. 2, concl. 2, 8m.

132. *Ibid.*, d. 48, q. 2, a. 2, concl. 1, 5m.

133. *Ibid.*, d. 48, q. 2, a. 2, concl. 1, 7m.

134. *Ibid.*, d. 48, q. 1, a. 2, concl. 4, 5m.

135. *Ibid.*, d. 48, q. 2, a. 2, concl. 2, 11m.

136. *Ibid.*, d. 48, q. 1, a. 2, concl. 2, 1m; d. 48, q. 2, a. 2, concl. 2, 9m.

137. *Ibid.*, d. 48, q. 1, a. 2, concl. 4, 9m; d. 48, q. 2, a. 2, concl. 1, 4m; d. 48, q. 1, a. 2, concl. 2, 1m.

138. *Ibid.*, d. 48, q. 2, a. 2, concl. 1, 4m; d. 48, q. 2, a. 2, concl. 2, 12m.

139. *Ibid.*, d. 48, q. 1, a. 2, concl. 3, 12m. Within the framework of an ethics of divine commands, Andrew attempts to explain the existence of degrees of good and evil (1) by showing how we can make sense of the notion of God *unequally* approving two things (*ibid.*, d. 48, q. 1, a. 2, concl. 4, ad 9m), (2) by appealing to the number of ways in which an action diverges from the divine decree (*ibid.*, d. 48, q. 2, a. 2, concl. 2, ad 12m), and (3) by appealing to the consequences of actions (*ibid.*, d. 48, q. 2, a. 2, concl. 2, ad 12m). Andrew flirts with the notion that the degree of divinely established punishment determines the degree of evil (*ibid.*, d. 48, q. 2, a. 2, concl. 1, ad 4m), but seems to reject it (*ibid.*, d. 48, q. 2, a. 2, concl. 2, ad 12m); see also *ibid.*, d. 48, q. 2, a.

2, concl. 1, 3m.

140. *Ibid.*, d. 48, q. 2, a. 2, concl. 1, 2m.

141. *Ibid.*, d. 48, q. 2, a. 2, concl. 1, 8m. Andrew's reply to this objection is noteworthy in assigning an epistemological role to natural law within the framework of an ethics of divine commands; see the *Introduction* to the present book, sect. III.

142. Quinn, *Divine Commands and Moral Requirements*, pp. 62-3.

143. Andrew of Neufchateau, *Primum Scriptum Sententiarum*, d. 48, q. 2, a. 2, concl. 2, 3m. Andrew's reply to this objection is noteworthy in bringing in the concept of natural law; see also the Introduction to the present book, sect. III.

144. *Ibid.*, d. 48, q. 1, a. 2, concl. 4, 3m. Andrew's reply to this objection is not especially helpful.

145. Cudworth, *Treatise Concerning Eternal and Immutable Morality* I, II, 3.

146. Chubb, *The Comparative Excellence and Obligation of Moral and Positive Duties*, pp. 15, 20.

147. Price, *a Review of the Principal Questions in Morals* I, 3.

148. Andrew of Neufchateau, *Primum Scriptum Sententiarum*, d. 48, q. 1, a. 2, concl. 4, 6m.

149. *Ibid.*, d. 48, q. 1, a. 2, concl. 4, 3m.

150. *Ibid.*, d. 48, q. 1, a. 2, concl. 4, 7m.

151. *Ibid.*, d. 48, q. 1, a. 2, concl. 4, 4m.

152. *Ibid.*, d. 48, q. 1, a. 2, concl. 4, 2m.

153. *Ibid.*, d. 48, q. 2, a. 2, concl. 2, 4m.

154. *Ibid.*, d. 48, q. 1, a. 2, concl. 4, 1m.

155. *Ibid.*, d. 48, q. 2, a. 2,, concl. 2, 7m.

156. William Ockham, *Super 4 Libros Sententiarum* II, q. 19, O in *Opera Plurima* (Lyon, 1494-6) = *Quaestiones in Librum Secundum Sententiarum*, q. 15, Solutio Dubiorum , ad 3m edited by Gedeon Gal, O.F.M. & Rega Wood. (St. Bonaventure, NY: St. Bonaventure University, 1981), p. 352. While the early printed edition formerly standard among scholars gives the reading "hatred of God," the recent critical edition reads only "hatred" and lists "hatred of God" as a textual variant. Nevertheless, using the recent critical edition, a good case can yet be made for understanding the hatred spoken of in the stretch of text in question as referring to the act of hating God specifically. First, the passage constitutes a reply to an objection offered against Ockham's claim, made earlier in the question, that God can totally cause in the will the act of hating God. Second, with few exceptions, the terminology found throughout the question is *hatred of God* explicitly.

157. Andrew of Neufchateau, *Primum Scriptum Sententiarum*, d. 48, q. 2. It should be recalled that Andrew specifies *evil of fault* as the opposite of *supernatural goodness*; see *ibid.*, d. 48, q. 1, a. 1, Kinds of Good.

158. *Ibid.*, d. 48, q. 2, contra.

159. *Ibid.*, d. 48, q. 2, a. 2, concl. 2, ad 5m.

160. Unlike Andrew of Neufchateau, Gerson does not explicitly address the issue of an ethics of divine commands, but mentions the theory only in passing in the course of discussing other issues. Most notably, see *De Vita Spirituali Animae*, Lect. I, corr. 10 in Mgr. Glorieux (ed.), *Oeuvres Completes*, vol. 3 (Paris: Desclee, 1962); *De Consolatione Theologiae* II, Prosa II in Glorieux (ed.), *Oeuvres Completes*, vol. 9 (Paris: Desclee, 1973). The former text dates from 1395, and the latter from 1418. The text of Andrew of Neufchateau, which seems to represent the high point of the medieval dispute on an ethics of divine commands, dates from the second half of the fourteenth century, perhaps as early as 1358-59; see Appendix A.

161. Gerson, *De Vita Spirituali Animae*, Lect. I, corr. 10.

162. Suarez, *De Legibus* II, VI, 11, translation taken from Scott (ed.), *Selections from Three Works of Francisco Suarez, S.J.*, vol. 2.

163. *Ibid.*

164. Jacques Almain, *Moralia* III, 15 (Paris: Jehan Petit, 1526).

165. *Ibid.*

166. Nathaniel Culverwell, *An Elegant and Learned Discourse of the Light of Nature*, pp. 50-1.

167. *Ibid.*, p. 51.

168. Cudworth, *Treatise Concerning Eternal and Immutable Morality* I, I, 5.

169. Auguste Pelzer, "Les 51 articles de Guillaume Occam censures, en Avignon, en 1326," *Revue d'histoire ecclesiastique* 18 (1922): 240-70, nos. 5, 35.

170. Denifle & Chatelain, *Chartularium Universitatis Parisiensis* (Paris: Fratrum Delalain, 1889-97), II, 1124.

171. Stegmueller, "Die zwei Apologien des Jean de Mirecourt," *Recherches de Theologie Ancienne et Medievale* 5 (1933): 40-78, 192-204, Apologia Altera, nos. 13, 29.

172. Francesco Ehrle (ed.), *I Piu Antichi Statuti Della Facolta Teologica Dell'Universita Di Bologna* (Bologna: Universita Di Bologna, 1932), nos. 5, 31, 32, 39.

173. Andrew of Neufchateau, *Primum Scriptum Sententiarum*, d. 48, q. 2, a. 2, concl. 2, ad 5m.

174. *Ibid.*, d. 48, q. 2, a. 2, concl. 2, ad 5m.

175. *Ibid.*, d. 48, q. 2, a. 2, concl. 2, ad 5m. The statement of the argument explicitly includes a supporting reason (viz., premise (2)) which Andrew takes from Anselm.

176. *Ibid.*, d. 48, q. 1, a. 1, Reply to the question, concl. 4.

177. *Ibid.*, d. 48, q. 1, a. 2, concl. 4.

178. *Ibid.*, d. 48, q. 2, a. 2, concl. 2.

179. *Ibid.*, d. 48, q. 1, a. 1, Reply to the question, concl. 4; d. 48, q. 1, a. 2, concl. 4.

180. *Ibid.*, d. 48, q. 1, a. 1, Reply to the question, concl. 4.

181. *Ibid.*, d. 48, q. 1, a. 2, concl. 4.

182. *Ibid.*, d. 48, q. 2, a. 2, concl. 2.

183. *Ibid.*, d. 48, q. 2, a. 2, concl. 2, ad 5m.

184. Thomas Bradwardine, *De Causa Dei* I, 26 (London: John Billius, 1618; reprint Frankfurt am Main: Miverva GMBH, 1964), pp. 255-6.

185. Gregory of Rimini, *Lectura Super Primum et Secundum Sententiarum* II, d. 38-41, q. 1, a. 2, contra, edited by A. Damasus Trapp, OSA & Venicio Marcolino, vol. 6 (New York: Walter De Gruyter, 1980).

186. See also *ibid.*

187. Andrew of Neufchateau, *Primum Scriptum Sententiarum*m d. 48, q. 2, a. 2, concl. 2, ad 5m.

188. *Ibid.*, d. 48, q. 1, a. 1, concl. 4, ad 1m; d. 48, q. 1, a. 2, concl. 2, ad 2m; d. 48, q. 2, a. 2, concl. 2, ad 6m.

189. Almain, *Moralia* III, 16.

190. Suarez, *De Legibus* II, 15, 4; translation from Scott (ed.), *Selections from Three Works of Francisco Suarez, S.J.*, vol. 2.

191. Andrew of Neufchateau shows an awareness of the move of claiming that what is intrisically evil is not an act of hating God simpliciter, but rather, a will *voluntarily and freely* choosing to hate God; see *Primum Scriptum Sententiarum*, d. 48, q. 2, a. 2, concl. 2, 5m. However, he mentions this move within the context of presenting the objection that the hatred of God is intrinsically evil, and it is discussed from the point of view of disqualifying it as a possible evasion of the objection. For the reported line of argumentation claims that the position that a *freely chosen* act of hating God is wrong either is reducible to the position that the act is evil in itself or leaves open the possibility that the act be freely chosen *licitly*. The latter alternative is clearly discordant with the spirit of the objection. That Andrew is here simply reporting, and not endorsing, a line of argumentation is indicated by the fact that the first alternative is unacceptable to him.

192. Ockham, *Quaestiones in Librum Secundum Sententiarum*, q. 15, pp. 341-2 = *Super 4 Libros Sententiarum* II, q. 19, F (Lyon, 1494-6).

193. *Ibid.*, pp. 342-3.

194. John of Mirecourt, *Sententiae* II, q. 2, concl. 6 ff. (Bibliotheque Nationale MS. Lat. 15883, fol. 11vb).

195. John Brammart, *Lectura Super Primo Sententiarum*, d. 5, (MS. Wilhering 87, 25rb32-40).

196. Gabriel Biel, *Collectorium Circa Quattuor Libros Sententiarum* I, d. 42, q. 1, a. 3, dubium 3; edited by Wilfred Werbeck & Udo Hofmann (Tubingen: J.C.B. Mohr (Paul Siebeck), 1973).

197. Almain, *Moralia* III, 16.

198. Denifle & Chatelain, *Chartularium Universitatis Parisiensis* I, 473, no. 63.

199. Andrew of Neufchateau, *Primum Scriptum Sententiarum*, d. 48, q. 2, a. 2, concl. 2, ad 5m.

200. Ockham, *Quaestiones in Librum Secundum Sententiarum*, q. 15, pp. 342-3 = *Super 4 LibrosSententiarum* II, q. 19, F (Lyon, 1494-6). See also Ockham, *Quaestiones in Librum Quartum Sententiarum*, q. 10-11 edited by Rega Wood & Gedeon Gal, O.F.M. (St. Bonaventure, NY: St. Bonaventure University, 1984), p. 198 = *Super 4 Libros Sententiarum* IV, q. 8 & 9, E (Lyon, 1494-6).

201. Andrew of Neufchateau, *Primum Scriptum Sententiarum*, d. 48, q. 2, a. 2, concl. 2.

202. *Ibid.*

203. *Ibid.*, d. 48, q. 2, a. 2, concl. 2, ad 5m.

204. This point is an extrapolation from the following comment in *ibid.*, d. 48, q. 2, a. 2, concl. 2, ad 5m: "Proof of the antecedent: Otherwise, God could not infuse into me the act of hating sin and the act of repentance and contrition by which I would detest my former life of sin or a sinful act if he should propose something unsuitable in a temptation, since such an act is good and, according to some, cannot be performed except by God assisting with a special impulse."

205. Stegmuller, "Die zwei Apologien des Jean de Mirecourt," Apologia Altera, no. 29.

206. Andrew of Neufchateau, *Primum Scriptum Sententiarum*, d. 48, q. 2, a. 2, concl. 2, ad 5m.

207. *Ibid.*

208. In his *Nominalist Glossary*, Heiko A. Oberman defines the *absolute power of God* (*potentia dei absoluta*) as the power of God "subject only to the law of non-contradiction, which leaves the actually chosen order out of consideration." The *ordinate/ordained power of God* (*potentia dei ordinata*), on the other hand, is explained as "the order established by God and the way in which God has chosen to act in his *opera ad extra*, i.e., over against the contingent order outside himself." *The Harvest of Medieval Theology* (Durham, NC: Labyrinth Press, 1983), p. 473.

209. Andrew of Neufchateau, *Primum Scriptum Sententiarum*, d. 48, q. 2, a. 2, concl. 2, ad 5m.

210. *Ibid.*, d. 48, q. 1, a. 2, concl. 4; d. 48, q. 2, a. 2, concl. 2.

211. *Ibid.*, d. 48, q. 2, a. 2, concl. 2, ad 5m.

212. *Ibid.*, d. 48, q. 2, a. 2, concl. 2, ad 5m.

213. Cf. William J. Courtenay's explanation of John of Mirecourt's use of the phrase *sine assertione*: "Finally, he indicates that his conclusions in this question are not proposed assertively. Whether this disclaimer, occasionally used by Mirecourt, represents a device to protect him from heresy hunters or a careful statement of procedure should become evident as we follow his argument. In any case, it stands here as a warning to the reader not to take the obvious verbal sense of each conclusion as being the definitive statement of Mirecourt." William J. Courtenay, "John of Mirecourt and Gregory of Rimini on Whether God Can Undo the Past," *Recherches de Theologie ancienne et medievale* 39 (1972): 224-56.

214. Andrew of Neufchateau, *Primum Scriptum Sententiarum*, d. 48, q. 2, a. 2, concl. 2.

215. *Ibid.*, d. 48, q. 1, a. 1, Reply to the question, concl. 4; d. 48, q. 1, a. 2, concl. 4; d. 48, q. 2, a. 2, concl. 2.

216. *Ibid.*, d. 48, q. 1, a. 1, Reply to the question, concl. 4.

217. *Ibid.*, d. 48, q. 2, a. 2, concl. 2, ad 6m.

218. *Ibid.*, d. 48, q. 2, a. 2, concl. 2, 6m & ad 6m.

219. Ockham, *Quaestiones in Librum Secundum Sententiarum*, q. 15, pp. 352-3 = *Super 4 Libros Sententiarum* II, q. 19, O (Lyon, 1494-6).

220. L. Baudry (ed.), *Tractatus de Principiis Theologiae attribue a G. l'Occam*, 8-9 (Paris: J. Vrin, 1936).

221. *Ibid.*, Introduction, pp. 15-6.

222. Gregory of Rimini, *Lectura Super Primum et Secundum Sententiarum* I, d. 42-4, q. 1, a. 2, concl. 2 & contra, edited by A. Damasus Trapp, OSA & Venicio Marcolino, vol. 3 (New York: Walter De Gruyter, 1984).

223. Peter of Ailly, *Quaestiones Super Libros Sententiarum* I, q. 14, a. 3, T in *Quaestiones Super Libros Sententiarum cum quibusdam in fine adjunctis* (Strassburg, 1490; facsimile reprint Frankfurt: Minerva, 1968).

224. Denifle & Chatelain, *Chartularium Universitatis Parisiensis* II, 1124.

225. Andrew of Neufchateau, *Primum Scriptum Sententiarum*, d. 48, q. 2, a. 2, concl.. 2, 6m.

226. Almain, *Moralia* III, 15.

227. Suarez, *De Legibus* II, 15, 5.

228. Andrew of Neufchateau, *Primum Scriptum Sententiarum*, d. 48, q. 2, a. 2, concl. 2, ad 6m.

229. *Ibid.*

230. *Ibid.*

231. *Ibid.*, d. 48, q. 2, a. 2, concl. 2, 6m.

232. Peter of Ailly, *Quaestiones Super Libros Sententiarum* I, q. 4, a. 3, U.

233. See n. 208 above.

234. Peter of Ailly, *Quaestiones Super Libros Sententiarum* I, q. 4, a. 3, U.

235. *Ibid.*

236. Robert Merrihew Adams, "A Modified Divine Command Theory of Ethical Wrongness," pp. 320-4; Philip L. Quinn, *Divine Commands and Moral Requirements*, pp. 58-61; Graeme de
Graaff, "God and Morality" in Ian T. Ramsey (ed.), *Christian Ethics and Contemporary Philosophy* (New York: Macmillan, 1966), pp. 32-3; A.C. Ewing, "The Autonomy of Ethics" in Ian T. Ramsey (ed.), *Prospect for Metaphysics* (London: George Allen & Unwin, 1961), p. 39; William K. Frankena, *Ethics*, pp. 29-30; Eric D'Arcy, "*Worthy of Worship*: A Catholic Contribution," pp. 200-1. This type of objection is also mentioned by Cudworth, *Treatise Concerning Eternal and Immutable Morality* I, I, 5.

237. Adams, "A Modified Divine Command Theory of Ethical Wrongness," pp. 320-4.

ANDREW OF NEUFCHATEAU, O.F.M.

PRIMUM SCRIPTUM SENTENTIARUM

DISTINCTION 48

QUESTIONS 1 & 2

DISTINCTIO 48

Circa distinctionem quadragesimam octavam, in qua Magister tractat de rectitudine voluntatis creatae per conformitatem ad divinam et quomodo voluntas creata interdum vult male idem Deus vult, quaero:

Utrum omne bonum aliud a Deo sit contingenter bonum ex ordinatione libera divinae voluntatis?

Quod non: Quia aliquod est malum non contingenter ex ordinatione libera divinae voluntatis, quia secundum Augustinum, primo *De Libero Arbitrio* cap. quarto, *aliquod est malum non quia prohibetur, sed ideo prohibetur quia est malum* [1]; igitur similiter de bono.

Contra: Sicut prima entitas ad alias entitates, sic prima bonitas ad alias bonitates; sed prima entitas est causa contingens et libera omnium aliarum entitatum et propter quam unumquodque ens est tale ens; igitur... .

Primo, distinguendum de bono; secundo, ad quaesitum.

\<PRIMUS ARTICULUS\>

DE PRIMO

Bonum dicitur dupliciter, scilicet *bonum in se et absolute*, et *bonum alteri*. Haec distinctio habetur septimo *Ethicorum* cap. decimoquarto [2].

Primo modo omne ens est bonum, quia *bonum et ens convertuntur*, primo *Ethicorum* [3], et secundum Augustinum, *omne quod est, inquantum est, bonum est* [4]. Bono sic sumpto non contrariatur malum per se et proprie. Et ratio boni sic sumpti non videtur ratio obiective appetibilis et allectivi, sed esse appetibile videtur per modum passionis consequi rationem boni formalem; ideo enim *a* est appetibile quia bonum, et est magis appetibile quam *b* quia magis bonum. Ratio huius boni sic sumpti videtur esse in hoc quod res habet formaliter aliquem gradum perfectionis. Et non videtur dici omnino univoce de ente simpliciter perfecto, quod est bonum per essentiam, et de ente secundum quid perfecto, quod est bonum secundum participationem et mutationem boni per essentiam. Iuxta illud *Marci* decimo: *Nemo est bonus nisi solus Deus* [5].

Bonum autem *alicui alteri* est quadruplex, scilicet *bonum naturale, utile, delectabile, honestum*. Et licet hae bonitates vel earum aliquae sint interdum idem subiecto materialiter, sunt tamen rationes distinctae et interdum separantur subiecto.

Bonum naturale alteri dicitur aliquid spectans ad illius alterius integritatem substantialem, ut homini bonum est habere unum oculum vel aurem. Dicitur etiam illud quod est generativum vel

DISTINCTION 48

Concerning the forty-eighth distinction in which the Master discusses the rectitude of the created will through its conformity to the divine will and how the created will sometimes wills wrongly the same thing that God wills, I raise the following question:

Is all good other than God contingently good from the free decree of the divine will?

The answer seems to be no. For something which is evil is not so contingently from the free decree of the divine will because, according to Augustine in *The Free Choice of the Will* I, chap. 4, *something is evil not because it is prohibited, but rather, it is prohibited because it is evil* [1]. Therefore, in like manner in the case of good.

On the other hand, just as the first entity is related to other entities, so is the first goodness related to other good things. But the first entity is the contingent and free cause of all other entities and that on account of which each being is such a being. Therefore...

First, distinctions will be drawn concerning *good*. Second, the reply to the question will be given.

ARTICLE 1

THE VARIOUS KINDS OF GOOD

We speak of *good* in two senses, namely, *good in itself and absolutely*, and *good for the sake of another*. This distinction is made in the *Ethics* VII, chap. 14 [2].

In the first sense every being is good because *good and being are convertible* according to the *Ethics*, I [3], and because, according to Augustine, *everything which is, in so far as it exists, is good* [4]. What is evil through itself and properly speaking is not opposed to good taken in this way. And the quality of good taken in this way does not seem to be an objectively desirable and enticing quality, but being desirable seems to follow the formal quality of the good after the manner of a passion. For *a* is desirable because it is good, and it is more desirable than *b* because it is a greater good. The quality of the good taken in this way seems to lie in the fact that the thing formally possesses some degree of perfection. And it does not seem to be predicated entirely in the same sense of a simply perfect being, which is essentially good, and of a being which is perfect in a certain respect, which is good through participation and change in the essentially good. About this we find in *Mark* 10: *No one is good except God alone* [5].

On the other hand, *good for the sake of some other* is of four kinds, namely, *natural, useful, pleasant* [a], and *noble* [b] *good*. And although these types of goodness (or some of them) sometimes have the same subject materially, they are nevertheless distinct concepts and sometimes

conservativum eius, vel contrarii impeditivum. Dicitur etiam de eo quod facit ad perfectionem secundariam et ad bene esse illius, et est illi apte conveniens. Et licet multa huiusmodi possint reduci ad bonum utile quia disponunt ad finem, tamen aliam rationem boni videntur habere quia quaedam talium amaremus etiam si vitae et fini non essent necessaria vel utilia; patet primo *Metaphysicae* [6].

Malum huic bonitati oppositum est privatio eorum quae spectant ad secundariam perfectionem rei et ad bene esse et pulchritudinem et integritatem illius.

Bonum utile dicitur de eo quod valet ad aliquod bonum acquirendum et confert rei ad acquirendum finem; et tali bono utili utendum est quia referendum in aliud. Et hoc proprie et stricte convenit soli enti rationali secundum Augustinum, *83 Quaestiones* quaest. 32 [7]. Solius enim rationalis creaturae est proprie referre id quod utendum est ad illud quo fruendum est. Hoc bonum etiam dicitur *bonum commodi*.

Malum oppositum huic bono dicitur quod est alicui damnum vel nocivum, vel finis impeditivum disconveniens.

Bonum delectabile est illud quo potentia vitalis formaliter delectatur, sive per modum operationis actualis sive per modum passionis consequentis operationem. Malum huic oppositum dicitur illud quod est afflictivum vel delectationis impeditivum et privativum.

Bonum honestum et iustum non convenit proprie inanimatis neque brutis secundum Anselmum, *De Veritate* cap. duodecimo [8]. Et hoc est triplex, scilicet *bonum ex genere, bonum morale, bonum supernaturale vel theologicum et caritativum* quod est bonum simpliciter et meritorium.

Bonum ex genere est actio voluntaria et libera conveniens operanti ex natura actus et obiecti, et est perfectibilis et apta determinari per circumstantias morales convenientes et conformabiles [d] prudentiae. Unde nec includit circumstantiam deformem, ut mentiri, nec est omnino indifferens ad bonum et ad malum morale simpliciter, sicut levare festucam, sed iam habet aliquid de genere boni moralis et iam includit aliquam rectitudinem et aliqua circumstantias determinatas, puta conveniens obiectum et conveniens genus actus, ita quod est bonum morale et honestum secundum quid et diminute et incohative, ut subvenire indigenti et compati idem. Et dicitur *bonitas ex genere* quia sicut genus est quasi potentiale respectu specierum et determinabile per differentias, sic haec bonitas est quasi materialis et potentialis respectu bonitatis moralis simpliciter et quasi formalis per ulteriores circumstantias debitas; potest tamen vitiari per circumstantiam consequenter additam.

Malum ex genere dicitur actio libera disconveniens operanti ex natura actus et obiecti, et iam vitiatur per aliquam circumstantiam, ut auferre alienum et nocere innocenti. Tamen sicut bonum ex genere potest quandoque vitiari per adiunctionem accidentalis circumstantiae, ut intentionis, sic actio quae dicitur mala ex genere potest in casu per adiunctionem alicuius determinationis corrigi et quasi contra malitiam trahi; ut occidere proximum dicitur malum ex genere cum sit etiam prohibitum in Decalogo, tamen occidere hominem ignorantia invicibili vel auctoritate legis non est malum. Tale tamen agere sibi relictum circumscripta huiusmodi circumstantia videtur malum quia talis actus est respectu materiae indebitae.

Notandum aliquod bonum ex genere potest dici tripliciter: aut illud quod est genus bonorum, ut virtus et iustitia dicitur bonum ex genere; aut quod per nullum circumstantiam potest fieri malum, ut diligere Deum ex caritate et secundum caritatem; aut actio conveniens respectu materiae et obiecti agentis, ut dare eleemosynam indigenti. Et ex opposito malum ex genere potest dici tripliciter: aut quod est genus malorum, ut iniustitia; aut quod per nullam circumstantiam potest bene fieri, ut

have different subjects.

We call *natural good for the sake of another* something pertaining to the integrity of that thing's substance, as it is a good for a human being to have an eye or an ear. It is also said to be that which is productive or conservative of substantial integrity, or an impediment to the opposite. We also speak of it as that which contributes to the secondary perfection and the well-being of that thing and is properly suited to it. And although many goods of this type can be reduced to a useful good because they are directive to an end, they nevertheless seem to have another quality of good because we would love certain ones even if they were not necessary or useful to life and to an end. This is evident in the *Metaphysics* I [6].

The evil opposed to this kind of goodness is the privation of those things which pertain to the secondary perfection of a thing and to its well-being and beauty and integrity.

We call *useful good* that which is of use for acquiring some good and assists a thing in the acquisition of an end. And one must make use of such useful good because it must be referred to something else. According to Augustine in *83 Questions*, q. 32, this good is properly and strictly found only in a rational being [7]. For it properly belongs to a rational creature alone to refer that which must be used to that which is to be enjoyed. This good is also called *commodious good* [c].

The evil opposed to this kind of good is that which is injurious or harmful to something, or an impediment unsuitable for the acquisition of an end.

Pleasant good is that by which vital power is formally found pleasurable, whether after the manner of an actual operation or after the manner of a passion following an operation. We call the evil opposed to this that which is an affliction or an impediment to and privative of pleasure.

Noble and just good is not, properly speaking, found in inanimate things or in animals according to Anselm in *On Truth*, chap. 12 [8]. And this good is threefold, namely, *generic good, moral good,* and *supernatural or theological and charitable good*, which is simply good and meritorious.

Generic good is voluntary and free action which is suitable to the agent by the nature of the act and the object, and it is perfectible and fit to be determined by moral circumstances suitable and conformable [d] to prudence. So it neither includes a deviant circumstance (as does lying) nor is it entirely indifferent to moral good and evil simply (as is picking up a straw), but it already possesses something of the genus of moral goodness and already includes some degree of rectitude and some determined circumstances, namely, being suitable to the object and to the genus of the act. Thus it is a moral and noble good in a certain respect and in a lesser degree and rudimentarily, as is giving assistance to an indigent person and feeling compassion for him. And it is called *generic good* because just as a genus is as it were in a state of potentiality with respect to species and determinable by differences, so this goodness is as it were material and potential with respect to moral goodness simply, and as it were formal, through further due circumstances. It can, however, be vitiated by a circumstance which is subsequently added.

We call *generic evil* free action which is unsuitable to the agent by the nature of the act and the object, and it is already vitiated by some circumstance, as is stealing another's property and harming an innocent person. Nevertheless, just as generic good can sometimes be vitiated by the addition of some accidental circumstance (as that of intention), so an action which is said to be a generic evil can be corrected in a special case through the addition of some stipulation and be as it were drawn away from evilness. For example, killing one's neighbor is said to be a generic evil since

mentiri, adulari; aut actus disconveniens voluntati quantum ex natura obiecti et talis actus, unde obiectum materiale dicitur quasi genus subiectum ex quo actus talis trahit deformitatem.

Bonitas moralis dicitur tripliciter. Primo, convenientia seu conformitas liberae actionis vel cessationis vel habitus ad rectam rationem dictantem de circumstantiis eligibilis et fugibilis [e] prout nobis innotescit in lumine naturali rationis naturalis [f], seu dicitur integritas [g] eorum quae secundum rectam rationem naturalem debent inesse voluntati in sua actione vel cessatone vel habitu. Et accipio *rationem naturalem* pro prudentia morali ut ea usi sunt philosophi. Et hoc modo usi sunt philosophi gentiles *bonitate morali* vel *vita*, scilicet pro vivere conformiter dictamini doctrinae moralis humanitus et naturaliter acquisitae. Et hoc modo contingit actionem bonam moralem esse simpliciter vitiosam, quia contingit illam habere circumstantiam specialiter lege Dei prohibitam. Quaedam autem spectantia ad actiones humanas falsa et haeretica sunt quae tamen magis apparentia sunt in lumine naturali quam eius oppositum.

Alio modo dicitur conformitas actionis vel vitae ad rectam rationem dictantem de circumstantiis specialibus absque falsitate contraria veritati Catholicae et absque speciali circumstantia respectu talis actionis specialiter prohibita. Et intelligo de ratione recta naturaliter acquisibili, circumscribendo legem specialem a Deo revelatam et traditam. Et hoc modo bonitas moralis [h] est communis ad actiones bonas simpliciter et meritorias vitae aeternae et ad quascumque actiones in homine peccatore vel infideli. Licet enim in tali sit quaedam circumstantia lege Dei prohibita, scilicet privatio caritatis, tamen haec circumstantia non est specialis circumstantia respectu talis actionis secundum speciem vel genus prohibita specialiter; immo est circumstantia generalis quae requiritur ad actiones supernaturales et etiam naturales quia tenetur semper esse in caritate. Infidelis autem potest habere dictamen absque falsitate, ut quod *a* est agendum propter iustitiam et ordinationem iustitiae servandum et propter bonum se ipsum [i] et propter observantiam iuris naturalis quod est ius divinam et quia recta ratio hoc dictat aut etiam propter Deum ut rectorem omnium, absque inclusione falsi vel circumstantiae specialiter prohibitae in tali actione. Et hoc modo nulla actio vitiosa bona est moraliter. Bonitas igitur moralis praeficit bonitatem ex genere, et ad istam est illa potentialis sicut ista est in potentia ad bonitatem meritoriam et caritativam.

Malitia moralis opposita est carentia circumstantiae debitae et secundum dictamen rationis requisitae, vel appositio circumstantiae disconvenientis quam ratio dictat debere non inesse.

Bonitas supernaturalis seu theologica et caritativa [j], quae est bonitas simpliciter et in viatore est meritoriae gloriae, dicitur conformitas voluntatis ad rectam rationem plene dictantem de circumstantiis requisitis secundum fidem Catholicam et legem Dei nobis traditam, vel dicitur conformitas creatae voluntatis in agendo vel vivendo ad divinam voluntatem ut praeceptivam vel persuasivam et approbativam. Et haec bonitas est perfectiva legis vel bonitatis moralis, et addit ad illam sicut ratio recta, comprehendens circumstantias debitas secundum fidem Catholicam, addit ad dictamen rectae rationis secundum legem et ius naturae, et sicut ius divinum, secundum Catholicam veritatem, addit ad ius naturale.

Malitia opposita est *malitia culpae et iniustitiae*, quae est carentia circumstantiae debitae vel appositio indebitae contra legem Dei praeceptivam vel consultivam.

Notandum quod bonitas et rectitudo quam habuit Adam ante casum erat minor quam bonitas supernaturalis et gratuita viatoris praesentis, quia propter talem viator est dignus vita aeterna et conceptus per gratiam gratum facientem. Erat tamen maior quam bonitas pure moralis in via non solum quia meliora erant naturalia, sed etiam quia intellectus et voluntas adiuvabantur quibusdam

it is even prohibited in the Decalogue. Nevertheless, to kill a human being out of invincible ignorance or by the authority of the law is not evil. Yet such activity left to itself, with this kind of circumstance excluded, seems evil because such an act has to do with a matter that is undue.

It should be noted that something can be called a generic good in three ways. It is either that which is the genus of goods, as virtue and justice are called generically good; or that which cannot become evil through any circumstance, as loving God out of charity and according to charity; or an action which is suitable with respect to its matter and with respect to the object of the agent, as giving alms to the poor. And the opposite generic evil is threefold. It is either that which is the genus of evils, as injustice; or that which cannot be done rightly through any circumstance, as lying or flattery offered in a cringing manner; or an act which is unsuitable to the will as far as the nature of the act and the object, and so we say that the material object is as it were the generically one subject from which such an act draws its deviation.

Moral goodness is spoken of in three ways. First, it is the agreement or conformity of free action or of the cessation of action or of a habit to right reason prescribing about the circumstances of what ought to be chosen and what ought to be avoided [e] as they are known to us in the natural light of natural reason [f]. Or it is said to be the totality [g] of those circumstances which, according to natural right reason, ought to be present in the will in its action or cessation of action or in a habit. And I take *natural reason* as moral prudence, as philosophers have used this term. And pagan philosophers have used *moral goodness* or *moral life* in this sense, namely, as living conformably to the dictate of moral philosophy which is humanly and naturally acquired. And in this sense it happens that a morally good action is simply vicious because it happens that the action has some circumstance specifically prohibited by the law of God. But some things pertaining to human actions are false and heretical which yet are more apparent in the natural light <of human reason> than the opposite.

In another way, moral goodness is said to be the conformity of action or of life to right reason prescribing about particular circumstances without falsehood contrary to Catholic truth and without any particular circumstance specifically prohibited with respect to such an action. And I understand this with regard to right reason naturally acquired, excluding the particular law revealed and delivered by God. And in this sense moral [h] goodness is common to actions which are simply good and meritorious of eternal life, and to whatever actions are in a human being who is a sinner or an infidel. For although there is in such action a certain circumstance prohibited by the law of God, namely, a privation of charity, this circumstance is not a particular circumstance specifically prohibited with regard to such an action according to species or genus. On the contrary, it is a general circumstance which is required for supernatural and even for natural actions, for one is always obliged to be in a state of charity. But an infidel can have a dictate without falsity, as that *a* ought to be done for the sake of justice and serving the decree of justice and for the sake of the good itself [i] and for the sake of observing the natural law which is a divine law and because right reason dictates it, or even for the sake of God as the ruler of all things. He can have it without the inclusion of falsehood <contrary to Catholic truth> or of a circumstance specifically prohibited in such an action. And in this sense no vicious action is morally good. Therefore moral goodness takes precedence over generic goodness, and the latter is in a state of potentiality with respect to the former just as the former is in a state of potentiality with respect to meritorious and charitable goodness.

The opposing *moral evilness* is the lack of a circumstance which is due and required according to the dictate of <right> reason, or the addition of an unsuitable circumstance which

donis supernaturalibus et quia tanta bonitas non stabat cum peccato mortali. Et sic illa bonitas posset reduci ad istam vel ad bonitatem moralem.

Et sic ergo patet de primo.

<DE SECUNDO>

Quaeritur ergo an omne bonum aliud a Deo, sive bonum in se sive bonum alteri, sit bonum ex libera ordinatione divinae voluntatis, et sic consequenter quod ipse possit esse vel alteri inesse et non esse taliter bonum.

Primo igitur videtur de bonitatibus aliis a supernaturali et meritoria seu caritativa et gratuita; secundo, specialiter de ista quoad primum.

PRIMA CONCLUSIO: Omne bonum creatum, sive in se et absolute [l] sive alicui alteri bonum, ideo est sic bonum quia divina voluntas libere vult et ordinat ipsum tale bonum.
Probatur primo de bono in se et absolute [m], quia omne creatum ideo habet formaliter talem gradum perfectionis quia Deus libere dat ei talem entitatem.
Quoad bonum alicui alteri [n], patet idem, quia a quo per se et principaliter habet unumquodque quod sit ens tale, ab eo habet quod sit natum esse conveniens primo alteri.
Consimiliter de bono utili et delectabili. De bono etiam iusti ex genere, a Dei enim voluntate

<right> reason dictates ought not to be present.

Supernatural goodness or *theological and charitable goodness* [j], which is simple goodness and is meritorious of glory for the viator, is said to be the conformity of the will to right reason prescribing completely about the circumstances required according to the Catholic faith and the law of God delivered to us. Or we say that it is the conformity of the created will in acting or living to the divine will as preceptive or persuasive and approving. This goodness is the perfecting of the moral law or moral goodness. And it adds to that just as right reason, in including the circumstances that are due according to the Catholic faith, adds to the dictate of right reason according to the law of nature [k], and just as the divine law adds to the natural law according to Catholic truth.

The opposing evil is the *evilness of fault and injustice*, which is the lack of a circumstance which is due or the addition of an undue circumstance contrary to the preceptive or consultative law of God.

It should be noted that the goodness and rectitude which Adam had before the Fall was less than the goodness of the present viator which is supernatural and conferred by grace. For, on account of such goodness, the viator is worthy of eternal life and conceived through the grace which makes one pleasing to God. Adam's goodness was, however, greater than purely moral goodness on earth not only because natural things were better, but also because the intellect and will were aided by certain supernatural gifts and because goodness of such a degree did not remain with mortal sin. And so that goodness could be reduced to the former or to moral goodness.

And so the answer to the first topic of inquiry is evident.

REPLY TO THE QUESTION

Therefore it is asked whether all good other than God, whether good in itself or good for the sake of another, is good from the free decree of the divine will, and consequently, whether it can exist or be present in another and fail to be good in that way.

This question will first be considered for types of goodness other than supernatural and meritorious or charitable and conferred by grace. Second, it will be considered specifically for the latter type of good with respect to the first type.

FIRST CONCLUSION: All created good, whether good in itself and absolutely [l] or good for the sake of some other, is this kind of good because the divine will freely wills and decrees it to be such good.

This conclusion is proved first of good in itself and absolutely [m]. For everything created has such a degree of perfection formally because God freely gives it such entity.

With respect to good for the sake of some other [n], the same is evident. For what per se and principally makes each one such a being, also designs it to be primarily suitable for another.

et ordinatione est quod talis actus sit [o] conveniens operanti ex natura actus talis et [p] obiecti.

De bono etiam morali probatur idem, quia ideo est sic bonum quia conforme prudentiae et rationi rectae morali secundum ius naturale; sed talis ratio ideo est recta quia divinus intellectus et voluntas sic dictat et ordinat et approbat. Et ideo ita est in re sicut ratio naturalis dictat de eligibili et fugibili quia Deus dictat ita esse in re cum sit prima regula omnis alterius rectitudinis; et huius bonitatis Deus est causa effectiva et finalis et quasi formalis et exemplaris et regulativa et mensurativa.

SECUNDA CONCLUSIO: Illud quod in se et absolute est bonum non potest esse non bonum huiusmodi bonitate. Patet, quia non potest esse non tale.

TERTIA CONCLUSIO: Illud quod est bonum naturale alteri non potest ei convenire quin sit ei bonum naturale.

Probatur, quia esse taliter bonum convenit ei tanquam per se passio, scilicet esse naturaliter perfectivum talis entitatis vel esse naturaliter perfectibile tali entitate; ergo repugnat quod sit maior vel melior perfectio naturalis.

Confirmatur, quia aliter esset possibile de quolibet ut esset finis ultimus et summum bonum cuiuslibet vel quod esset summa miseria cuiuslibet; et quod videre Deum et frui Deo cum delectatione et securitate non esset summum bonum hominis, immo nec bonum hominis; et quod summa tristitia in anima et [q] summus cruciatus in corpore aeternaliter non esset malum naturale homini; et quod videre festucam esset summa beatitudo hominis, magis quam videre Deum et frui eo.

Correspondenter potest dici de bono delectabili. Bonum vero delectabile potest dici quod delectat formaliter et intrinsece, vel quod delectat causaliter vel materialiter et extrinsece, puta effective vel objective. Primo modo non potest inesse potentiae vitali quin delectet. Secundo autem modo, licet possit esse praesens potentiae et non delectare quia impeditur, tamen natum est secundum aptitudinem, circumscripto omni impedimento et posito actu in anima, delectare.

Correspondenter de bono utili et commodo. Licet enim possit esse non utile actu et non conferre actu ad acquisitionem finis, tamen circumscripto impedimento, natum est, quantum est ex se, esse medium conveniens ad aliqualiter attigendum talem finem.

Consimiliter de bono ex genere. Licet possit vitiari per concomitantiam circumstantiae indebitae, ut est intentionalis perversitas vel disconvenientia loci et temporis quia [r] potest pro tempore prohiberi; tamen, circumscripto accidentaliter in factivo, non potest inesse operanti quin sit ei bonum secundum quid vel secundum aptitudinem.

Similarly, in the case of useful and pleasant good. Likewise in the case of the just good generically, for such an act being [o] suitable to the agent by the nature of the act and [p] the object comes from the will and decree of God.

The same is likewise proved of moral good. For it is this kind of good because it is conformed to prudence and to moral right reason according to natural law; but such reason is right because the divine intellect and will so dictates and decrees and approves. And therefore it is so in fact as natural reason prescribes about what ought to be chosen and what ought to be avoided because God prescribes that it be so in fact since he is the first rule of all other rectitude. And God is the effective and the final and as it were the formal and the exemplary and the regulative and the measuring cause of this goodness.

SECOND CONCLUSION: That which is in itself and absolutely good cannot fail to be good with this kind of goodness.

This is evident because it cannot fail to be such a thing.

THIRD CONCLUSION: That which is a natural good for the sake of another cannot be found in it without being a natural good for it.

Proof: Being good in this way is found in it as if a per se passion; namely, it is either naturally perfective of such an entity or naturally perfectible in such an entity. Therefore, it is inconsistent that its natural perfection be greater or better.

Confirmation: Otherwise, it would be possible that anything whatever be the final end and highest good of anything else, or its greatest misery. And it would be possible that seeing and enjoying God with pleasure and security not be the highest good of a human being, or even a human good at all. And it would be possible that eternally the greatest sadness in the soul and [q] the worst torment in the body not be a natural evil for a human being. And it would be possible that seeing a straw be the greatest beatitude of a human being, greater than seeing God and enjoying God.

Correspondingly, in the case of the pleasant good. We can call pleasant good what gives pleasure formally and intrinsically or what gives pleasure causally and materially and extrinsically, for example, effectively and objectively. In the first way, it cannot be present in a vital power without giving pleasure. In the second way, however, it can be present to a <vital> power and fail to give pleasure because of an impediment. Nevertheless, it is designed with the aptitude to give pleasure when the act is posited in the soul and when every impediment is excluded.

Correspondingly, in the case of useful and commodious good. It may not actually be useful, and it could fail actually to assist in the acquisition of an end. Nevertheless, excluding any impediment, it is in itself designed to be a suitable means for attaining such an end in some way.

Similarly, in the case of generic good. It can be vitiated by an undue circumstance accompanying it, such as a perverse intention or unsuitability of place and time since [r] it can be prohibited for a time. Nevertheless, excluding such a circumstance which may accidentally be present in producing it, it cannot be present in an agent without being good for him in a certain respect or by aptitude.

QUARTA CONCLUSIO: Omne ens finitum creaturae rationali bonum bonitate morali, non maiori, potest inesse creaturae rationali et non esse ei sic bonum. Et accipio *bonitatem moralem* ut supra, scilicet sicut usi sunt philosophi in philosophia morali.

Probatur primo, quia potest causari totaliter ab ipso solo Deo in homine; igitur non erit tunc homini bonum morale. Nullus enim actus facit hominem moraliter bonum si respectu illius non se habet libere et active secundum Anselmum, *De Casu Diaboli* cap. decimoquarto [9].

Item, Deus potest annihilare omnem actionem intellectus conservando quicquid est in voluntate; igitur non erit actio vel operatio virtuosa moraliter, immo nec operatio a proposito.

Praeterea, talis actus potest elici a dormiente et somniante vel ebrioso vel furioso vel subrepto et inadvertenter sine deliberatione vel ex passione antecedente vel contra conscientiam pro tunc. Si autem nullus actus est sic essentialiter bonus, igitur nec habitus ex huiusmodi actibus generatus vel generabilis, quia non est magis essentialiter bonus cum etiam maneat in homine qui sit noviter malus.

Praeterea, potest esse deformis praecepto divino dictamini rectae rationis; igitur non est bonus moraliter perfecte.

Antecedens probatur, quia Deus potest praecipere Sorti ut eligeret [s] talem actum cum determinata circumstantia et condicione quam potest Sortes omittere, ita tali loco et tempore vel tanta intensione et duratione praecise. Item, potest Deus illum Sorti prohibere pro tali loco et tempore, vel praecipere alium actum imcompossibilem elici toto conatu.

Praeterea, aliquae circumstantiae requisitae ad bonitatem [t] moralem actus non necessario concomitantur [u] huiusmodi actum; potest enim fieri non ubi vel quando vel sicut vel quare oportet, circumstantiae enim sunt extrinsice actui.

Dices, aliquis actus potest omnes circumstantias ad bonitatem moralem requisitas habere pro obiecto; ideo non possunt deesse illi actui animae inexistenti. Contra hoc: non impedit propositum, quia oportet quod, si locus et tempus etc., non solum sint obiecta actus sed etiam quod sint condiciones actus et operantis, puta quod actus eliciatur convenienti loco et tempore et fine et gradu etc., et quod causetur a voluntate libera scienter et ex deliberatione et prudentia inexistente operanti. Has autem condiciones non necesse est inesse actui, quicquid habeat pro obiecto.

Praeterea, talis actus, secundum naturalem entitatem et aeque intensus, potest in uno tempore vel homine esse magis bonus quam in alio; igitur [v] non ex se essentialiter et necessario habet huiusmodi bonitatem.

CONTRA:

SIT *b* nomen alicuius virtutis moralis, ut iustitiae, tunc sic: impossibile est *b* inesse Sorti quin sit virtus moralis; igitur quin sit bonum ei morale.

FOURTH CONCLUSION: Every finite being which is good for a rational creature with moral goodness, not a greater, can be present in a rational creature and fail to be such a good for him. And I understand *moral goodness* as previously explained, namely, as philosophers have used it in moral philosophy.

The first proof is this. It can be caused in a human being totally by God himself alone. Therefore, it will not then be a moral good for a human being. For, according to Anselm in *The Fall of the Devil*, chap. 14, no act makes a human being morally good if he does not behave freely and actively in performing it [9].

Again, God can annihilate every action of the intellect while preserving whatever is in the will. Therefore, the action or operation will not be morally virtuous, indeed not even purposely an operation.

Moreover, such an act can be elicited by someone sleeping and dreaming, or by a drunkard, or by a madman, or surreptitiously and inadvertently without deliberation, or by a preceding passion, or contrary to conscience for that time. But if no act is essentially good with this type of goodness, then neither is a habit produced or producible by such acts. For the habit is no more essentially good since it even remains in a human being who has recently become evil.

Moreover, it can deviate from the dictate of right reason by a divine precept; therefore, it is not perfectly good morally.

Proof of the antecedent: God can command Socrates to choose [s] such an act in connection with a determined circumstance and condition which Socrates can omit, as that it be done at such a place and time or with precisely so much intensity and duration. Again, God can prohibit it to Socrates for such a place and time, or command another act which is incompatible with it to be elicited with all his might.

Moreover, some circumstances required for the moral goodness [t] of an act do not necessarily accompany [u] such an act. For it can be done not where or when or as or why it ought, for these circumstances belong to the act extrinsically.

But you will say that some act can have for its object all the circumstances required for moral goodness; therefore, they cannot be absent from that act existing in the soul. In opposition it may be said that it does not constitute an impediment to what we propose to prove. For it is necessary that, supposing place and time etc., these not only be objects of the act but also conditions of the act and of the agent, namely, that the act be elicited at a suitable place and time and with a suitable end and degree etc., and that it be caused by a free will knowingly and by deliberation and prudence existing in the agent. It is not necessary, however, that these conditions be present in an act, whatever it may have for an object.

Moreover, such an act can, at one time or in one human being, be a greater good than in another, taking the act according to its natural entity and assuming it is equally intense in both cases. Therefore [v], it does not have this kind of goodness of itself, essentially and necessarily.

OBJECTIONS:

LET *b* be the name of some moral virtue, such as justice. Then it is impossible that *b* be present in Socrates without being a moral virtue, and therefore, without being a moral good for him.

Antecedens probatur multipliciter:

Primo, quia habitus causatus ex actibus virtuosis conformibus rectae rationi et inclinativus in actus morales virtuosos conformes prudentiae morali est virtuosos moraliter; sed *b* necessario est huiusmodi.

Probo: impossibile est enim quin fuerit causatus ex actibus huiusmodi quia hoc iam transiit in praeteritum ut supponitur. Est etiam essentialiter inclinativus in actus similes illis ex quibus genitus est quia inclinat per modum naturae, et ex natura sua ei convenit per modum per se passionis quod sit ita inclinativus et habilitativus.

Secundo, probatur antecedens: sicut virtus intellectualis ad veritatem [w], sic virtus moralis ad bonitatem; sed aliqua virtus intellectualis est essentialiter et necessario vero, et habet veritatem ex natura habitus et obiecti; igitur...

Tertio, omnis species habet vel habere potest aliquod per se individuum de quo per se et essentialiter praedicatur; igitur et virtus moralis; igitur aliquis singularis habitus est per se et essentialiter virtus moralis.

Quarto, *b* non potest fieri habitus vitiosus vel non virtuosus; ergo est essentialiter et necessario virtuosus.

Antecedens probatur, tum quia individuum non transit de specie in speciem, igitur nec habitus de virtute in vitium vel non virtutem; tum quia secundum Augustinum, 2 *De Libero Arbitrio* cap. 31, *virtutes ut iustitia, prudentia, fortitudo, temperantia sunt summa bona; nec istis aliquis male utitur quia recta ratione male uti nemo potest* [10]; tum quia *b* non fiet habitus vitiosus vel non virtuosus per hoc quod sit in dormiente vel phrenetico, nec per hoc quod causetur totaliter a Deo, quia habitus supernaturaliter infusi qui sunt virtuosi sunt in illis.

SECUNDO principaliter, *b* actus bonus moraliter aut est per se et ex natura sua bonus moraliter, et propositum, aut propter aliud sibi coniunctum, puta *c*; tunc *c* non est malum nec indifferens cum *b* sit bonum propter ipsum; aut igitur *c* est ex se essentialiter bonum et virtuosum moraliter, et propositum, aut propter aliud, et processus in infinitum.

Confirmatur: sicut omne verum per accidens reducitur ad aliquod verum per se et prius, pari ratone de bono.

Confirmatur: actio non ex se sed accidentaliter et consequenter bona et ex se indifferens ad bonum et non bonum, not sit simpliciter et determinate bona nisi per alium actum et habitum ex se et intrinsece bonum; quia si per aliud ex se indifferens ad bonum et non bonum, igitur non magis est hoc determinate bonum per illud quam econtra. Nihil autem est moraliter bonum nisi procedat a voluntate creata.

Confirmatur: actus hominis exterior, quia est tantum bonus propter aliud et denominatione extrinseca et accidentali, ideo oportet praecedere alium actum interiorem primo et principaliter bonum; igitur si iste sit tantum bonus propter aliud et denominatione extrinseca accidentali, sequitur quod oportet dare alium actum priorem et principalius bonum; unde actus interior non esset magis per se et intrinsece bonus et virtuosus quam operatio exterior, quia uterque consequenter et per accidens.

Confirmatur: si *b* actus voluntatis sit bonus accidentaliter et denominatione extrinseca ex aliquod cui coniungitur, maxime videtur quod ex ratione recta cui ut regulae conformatur; sed hoc non, quia actus voluntatis foret bonus et virtuosus ex eo quod est pure naturalis [x]. Nec est in

The antecedent is proved in a number of ways.

First, a habit caused by virtuous acts conformed to right reason and inclining towards virtuous moral acts conformed to moral prudence is morally virtuous; but *b* is necessarily of this type.

I prove this as follows. It is impossible that *b* should not have been caused by such acts since, according to supposition, this has now become part of the past. It is also essentially inclined towards acts similar to those by which it was produced because it inclines in a natural manner, and being so inclined and adapted is found in it by nature after the manner of a per se passion.

Second, just as intellectual virtue is related to truth [w], so moral virtue is related to goodness. But some intellectual virtue is essentially and necessarily true, and gets its truth form the nature of the habit and the object. Therefore...

Third, every species has or can have something which is itself individual with respect to which it is predicated per se and essentially. Therefore, this is also true of moral virtue. And therefore, some particular habit is through itself and essentially a moral virtue.

Fourth, *b* cannot become a habit which is vicious or not virtuous; therefore it is essentially and necessarily virtuous.

Proof of the antecedent: First, an individual does not cross over from one species into another; therefore, neither does a habit change from something virtuous into something vicious or not virtuous. Second, according to Augustine in *The Free Choice of the Will* II, chap. 31, *virtues such as justice, prudence, fortitude, and temperance are highest goods; nor does anyone use them badly because no one can use right reason wrongly* [10]. Third, *b* will not become a habit which is vicious or not virtuous from the fact that it is in someone asleep or in a madman nor from the fact that it is totally caused by God, because supernaturally infused habits which are virtuous are in them.

SECOND, a morally good act, *b*, either is morally good through itself and by its nature, and this is what is to be proven; or it is morally good on account of something else joined to it, for instance, *c*. Then *c* is neither evil nor indifferent since *b* is good on account of it. Therefore either it is the case that *c* is morally good and virtuous of itself essentially, and this is what is to be proven; or it is the case that *c* is morally good and virtuous on account of something else, which leads to an infinite regress.

Confirmation: Just as everything which is accidentally true is reduced to something which is true through itself and first, in like manner in the case of good.

Confirmation: An action which is not good of itself but which is accidentally and consequentially good and is of itself indifferent to being good and failing to be good, is not simply and determinately good except through another act and habit which is good of itself and intrinsically. For if it were good through something else of itself indifferent to being good and failing to be good, then no more is the former determinately good through the latter than the contrary. Nothing is morally good, however, unless it proceeds from a created will.

Confirmation: Because an exterior act of a human being is only good on account of something else and by extrinsic and accidental denomination, it is necessary that another, interior act precede it which is first and principally good. Then if that act is only good on account of something else and by extrinsic, accidental denomination, it follows that it is necessary to introduce another act which is prior and more fundamentally good. So an interior act would no more be good and virtuous through itself and intrinsically than an exterior operation because each one is good and virtuous

potestate voluntatis, scilicet veritas dictaminis intellectualis. Et voluntas esset recta et homo rectus a rectitudine intellectus, primo et propter rectitudinem intellectus; primo igitur intellectus esset laudabilis et virtuosus.

TERTIO principaliter, sequitur quod stando in lumine naturali, omnes actus creaturae rationalis sunt indifferentes et nullus esset per se ex natura rei bonus vel malus.

Consequens est contra communem doctrinam; sunt enim quidam actus indifferentes sed non omnes, et quia periret ius naturale si nihil esset iustum ex natura rei sed ex libera et voluntaria ordinatione extrinseca.

Consequentia patet, quia nullus actus vel habitus est in nobis naturaliter acquisibilis quin possit esse rectus et non rectus; et ita iuvare iustum et dignum non magis ex natura rei esset bonum et rectum quam iuvare malum et indignum.

QUARTO, quod est demonstrabile de aliquo ut passio convenit ei non contingenter; sed esse eligibile vel fugibile moraliter est demonstrabile de aliqua actione humana.

Probo, quia stando praecise in lumine naturali, non habito respectu ad divinum intelligere et velle, philosophia moralis ex ceteris principiis demonstrat hoc esse eligibile et hoc esse melius et eligibilius illo; et procedit per media necessaria sumpta ex rationibus et naturis rerum.

Confirmatur: unicuique animali sunt aliqua per se et ex natura rei appetibilia et prosequibilia et [y] convenientia suae naturae; ergo non minus animali rationali ut rationale est.

QUINTO, aliquod dictamen prudentiae moralis et consilii practici de eligibili et fugibili est essentialiter et necessario rectum ex natura actus et obiecti; ergo electio et actio voluntatis illi conformis est necessario bona moraliter.

Antecedens patet, quia veritas principiorum moralium non subiacet libertati voluntatis, ut quod voluntas debet vivere conformiter rationi rectae et divinae voluntati, et quod Deus est diligendus debite, etc.

Consequentia probatur, tum quia sicut verum ad intellectum, ita bonum ad voluntatem. Tum quia si regula sit recta, regulatum illi conformatum est rectum; contradictio igitur videtur quod iudicium dictans sic esse volendum sit rectum et quod voluntas volens conformiter non velit recte.

SEXTO, actio conformis recto dictamini est bona moraliter; sed aliqua electio est actio conformis necessario recto dictamini.

Probo: pura electio qua voluntas eliciet esse volendum et vivendum conformiter recta rationi [z] et ut debet et conformiter voluntati divinae, sit igitur *b* huiusmodi electio; tunc impossibile est

consequentially and accidentally.

Confirmation: If an act of the will, *b*, is good accidentally and by extrinsic denomination from something to which it is joined, most of all it seems that it would be good from right reason to which it is conformed as a rule. But this is not the case since an act of the will would be good and virtuous because it is purely natural [x]. Neither is this in the power of the will, viz., the truth of an intellectual dictate. And a will would be upright and a human being would be upright from rectitude of the intellect first and on account of rectitude of the intellect. Therefore, the intellect would first be praiseworthy and virtuous.

THIRD, it follows that, standing in the natural light <of human reason>, all acts of a rational creature are indifferent and that none would be good or evil through itself by its nature.

The consequent goes against common teaching, because certain acts are indifferent but not all of them, and because natural law would be destroyed if nothing were just by its nature but from a free and voluntary extrinsic decree.

The inference is evident, because no act or habit is naturally acquirable by us which cannot be right and not right; and so to support what is just and worthy would no more be good and right by its nature than to support what is evil and unworthy.

FOURTH, what is demonstrable of something as a passion is not contingently found in it; but to be worthy of choice or deserving of avoidance morally is demonstrable of some human action.

I prove this as follows. Standing precisely in the natural light <of human reason> and without regard to the divine understanding and volition, moral philosophy demonstrates that this is worthy of choice and that this is better and worthier of choice than that from other principles. And it proceeds through necessary means of proof taken from the qualities and natures of things.

Confirmation: For every single animal, there are some things which are desirable and deserving of pursuit through themselves and by nature and [y] which are suitable to its nature. Therefore no less is this true for a rational animal as it is rational.

FIFTH, some dictate of moral prudence and of practical counsel concerning what ought to be chosen and what ought to be avoided is essentially and necessarily right from the nature of the act and the object. Therefore a choice and action of the will conformed to it is necessarily good morally.

The antecedent is evident because the truth of moral principles is not subject to the liberty of the will, as, for example, that the will ought to live conformably to right reason and the divine will, that God must be duly loved, etc..

Proof of the inference: First, just as truth is related to the intellect, so good is related to the will. Second, if a rule is right, the subject of the rule is right when conformed to it. Therefore it seems to be a contradiction that a judgment prescribing that one ought so to will be right and that a will willing conformably not will rightly.

SIXTH, an action conformed to a right dictate is morally good; but some choice is an action necessarily conformed to a right dictate.

I prove this as follows. Let *b* be a pure choice wherein a will resolves to be willing and living conformably to right reason [z] and as it ought and conformably to the divine will. Then it is

voluntatem [a*] habendo *b* non recte velle secundum *b*. Probo, quia si voluntas in habendo *b* non recte vult, igitur non est rectum et bonum voluntatem velle conformiter rectae rationi et divinae voluntati; igitur nec verum est dictamen dictans sic esse volendum et vivendum; igitur non est bonum nec rectum conformari sed deformari illis, quod est contradictio.

Confirmatur: si voluntas in habendo *b* non recte nec bene vult, igitur in habendo *b* non vult conformiter rectae rationi et divinae voluntati; igitur per *b* non vult vivere recte et conformiter rationi, quod est oppositum casus.

AD PRIMUM negatur antecedens.

Ad primam probationem [b*]: licet causatus fuit ex actibus virtuosis et ex his sequatur quod fuit virtuosus aliquando, non tamen sequitur quod necessario sit nunc virtuosus quia potest esse in furioso privato usu rationis et liberi arbitrii simpliciter, immo in moraliter malo. Sicut enim habitus vitiosus non statim totaliter deletur secundum suam naturalem realitatem in homine noviter iustificato et converso, ita econtra *b* habitus secundum aliquem gradum stat in homine agente vitiose vel proponente agere contrarie illi habitui. Et cum dicitur quod inclinat in similes, dicendum quod licet inclinet, quantum est ex se, in similes secundum naturalem realitatem actuum, non tamen est necessario inclinans in similes quoad moralem bonitatem vel malitiam, quia possible est ut actus similes secundum entitatem physicam non sint modo virtuosi. Esto etiam quod natus esset, quantum est ex se, inclinare et adiuvare voluntatem ad similes actus moraliter. Si voluntas vellet bene agere, non tamen est virtus quia voluntas est modo vitiosa et depravata per alios actus vel impeditur impedimento repugnante simpliciter bonitati morali, ut furiae permansivae.

Ad secundam probationem: non est simile, quia veritas covenit enuntiationi ex conformitate ad sic esse in re sicut significatur, ideo si impossibile est aliter esse in re, impossibile est enutiationem illam non esse veram; sed bonitas convenit actioni vel habitui voluntatis non ex hoc solum quod est circa tale obiectum, sed ex hoc quod conformatur divinae voluntati praecipienti vel persuadenti et approbanti vel recto dictamini practico de actione et singularibus circumstantiis dictanti.

Ad tertiam conceditur quod omne praedicabile quod est species potest dici per se et in quid de aliquo subiecto inferiori per modum individui, et ita est de virtute; sed contingit quod nulla res est vel potest esse quin de illa sub proprio et quidditativo conceptu demonstrata dicatur contingenter illud praedicabile, sicut de hoc praedicabili *simile* vel *creans* vel *agens*.

Ad quartam probationem negatur antecedens.

Ad primam probationem conceditur quod subiectum nullum per se contentum per modum individui in linea praedicamentali sub praedicato specifico potest esse alterius speciei essentialis; sed possibile est quod de eadem seu pro eadem re singulari verificetur nunc contingenter aliquid praedicabile specifice accidentale et postea non verificetur sed praedicabile oppositum, sicut idem transit de recto ad curvum et de simile ad dissimile.

Ad aliam probationem potest dici quod virtute manente virtute, nemo male utitur agendo conformiter illi et non agendo deformiter illi nec alteri virtuti, sed quia contingit *b* esse secundum suam naturalem realitatem et non esse virtutem, ideo contingit Sortem uti *b* non virtuose; contingit etiam Sortem agere non omnino conformiter ipsi *b* sed tamen secundum quid. Verbi gratia [c*], Sortes habituatus ad actus temperantiae virtuosos postmodum [b*] animo depravatus; adhuc, sub

impossible that the will [a*] in having *b* does not will rightly in accordance with *b*. I prove the latter as follows. If the will in having *b* does not will rightly, then it is not right and good for the will to will conformably to right reason and the divine will. And therefore, that dictate is not true which prescribes that one ought so to will and live. And therefore, to be conformed to them is neither good nor right, but rather, to deviate from them, which is a contradiction.

Confirmation: If the will does not will rightly or correctly in having *b*, then it does not will conformably to right reason and the divine will in having *b*. Therefore, it does not will to live rightly and conformably to <right> reason through *b*, which is the opposite of the case.

REPLY TO THE FIRST OBJECTION: The antecedent is denied.

Reply to the first proof [b*]: Although the habit was caused by virtuous actions and from these it will follow that it was virtuous at one time, it does not follow, however, that it is necessarily virtuous now because it can be in a madman who is simply deprived of the use of reason and of free will, and indeed it can be in someone who is morally evil. For just as a vicious habit is not completely destroyed immediately according to its natural reality in a human being who is recently justified and converted, so conversely a habit *b* remains to some degree in a human being who acts viciously or intends to act in a manner contrary to that habit. And when it is said that the habit inclines towards similar acts, it must be affirmed that although the habit in itself inclines towards acts which are similar according to the natural reality of the acts, it does not necessarily incline towards acts which are similar with respect to moral goodness or evilness because it is possible that actions which are similar according to physical entity not be virtuous just now. Let it even be the case that it was in itself designed to incline and to help the will towards acts which are similar morally. If the will should will to act correctly, this is not a virtue, however, because the will can just now be vicious and depraved by virtue of other acts or it can be hindered by an impediment which is simply inconsistent with moral goodness, as, for example, the impediment of persistent madness.

Reply to the second proof: The case is not similar, because truth is found in a statement from the conformity of what is signified to what is so in fact. Therefore, if it is impossible that it be otherwise in fact, it is impossible that that statement not be true. But goodness is found in an action or habit of the will not from the fact alone that it concerns such an object, but from the fact that it is conformed to the divine will commanding or persuading and approving, or to a right, practical dictate prescribing about action and particular circumstances.

Reply to the third proof: It is conceded that every predicable which is a species can be said per se and essentially of some subject which is inferior after the manner of an individual, and so it is in the case of virtue. But it happens that there is not or cannot be anything such that the predicable is not said contingently of it demonstrated under its proper and essential concept, as in the case of the predicable *similar* or *creating* or *acting*.

Reply to the fourth proof: The antecedent is denied.

Reply to the first proof <of the antecedent>: It is conceded that no subject per se, contained after the manner of an individual in the line of the predicaments under the predicate of a species, can belong to another essential species. But it is possible that, of or for some particular thing, some accidental predicable of a species is now contingently shown to be true but afterwards is not shown to be true, but the opposite predicable is, just as the same thing passes from straight to curved and

hypothesi, agit actus temperantiae sed non virtuose, et ad istos inclinatur et facilitatur magis ex habitu temperantiae praeacquisitae ex actibus virtuosis. Vel potest dici quod virtutibus moralibus formatis per caritatem et subservientibus caritati nemo male utitur. Unde Augustinus ibidem dicit quod *virtutes sunt bona quibus recte vivitur et quibus vita recta et honesta constat* [11].

Ad aliam probationem patet supra quod contingit *b* fieri non virtutem ex aliis causis. Potest ulterius dici quod *b* non desinit simpliciter esse virtus ex eo quod est in dormiente, quia somnus est passio naturaliter et regulariter adveniens et conveniens humanae naturae ad bonum naturae fatigabilis et recedens de ebrioso. Aut potest dici quod saltem secundum quid desinit *b* esse virtus quia est impedimentum vitiosum vel innaturale et disconveniens naturae. De furia autem permansiva adhuc potest magis idem dici. Si vero sit incurabilis et perpetua, videtur quod *b* simpliciter non est virtus. Nec est simile de caritate infusa, quia ex ordinatione divina facit etiam infantem baptizatum iustum et virtuosum.

AD SECUNDUM dicendum quod *b* non est moraliter bonum per se essentialiter ex gratia talis actus respectu talis obiecti, sed quia conformatur secundum certas circumstantias dictamini intellectus et ordinationi divinae voluntatis et rectae rationi inexistenti operanti. Et hoc contingit illi actui non necessario quia possible esset rectam rationem dictare alio tempore alias circumstantias, vel possibile est eundem actum vel similem variari secundum aliam circumstantiam. Et conceditur quod aliquid propter quod *b* dicitur moraliter bonum est bonum moraliter vel bonitate eminentiori, scilicet voluntas divina. Contingit etiam quod aliquid, per conformitatem ad quod dicitur *b* bonum moraliter, non est proprie bonum nec malum moraliter neque proprie indifferens et potentiale ad utrumque, sed est rectum rectitudine iudicativa et dictativa de agibili eligibile vel fugibile.

Ad confirmationem: licet consequens posset concedi ratione boni increati, negatur tamen consequentia, quia *album* vel *simile* vel *aequale* per accidens non oportet reduci at tale per se. Ad antecedens patet ex dictis.

AD TERTIUM principale negatur consequentia, quia Deus instituit ius naturale et certas leges secundum quas multi actus regulariter sunt boni simpliciter, quidem boni ex genere; sed referendo ad potentiam Dei absolutam, conceditur consequens.

AD QUARTUM negatur minor ut esset ad propositum. De nullo enim actu singulari sub conceptu absoluto demonstratur esse bonum moraliter, sed de subiecto non absoluto, quod contingenter diceretur de hoc actu singulari demonstratum [e*] per pronomen vel per conceptum

from similar to dissimilar.

Reply to the following proof: With a virtue remaining a virtue, no one uses it wrongly in acting conformably to it and in not acting in a way deviating from it or from another virtue. But because it happens that *b* exists according to its natural reality and fails to be a virtue, it therefore happens that Socrates uses *b* in a way that is not virtuous. It likewise happens that Socrates acts in a way not entirely conformable to *b*, but yet conformable in a certain respect. For example [c*], take the case of Socrates habituated to virtuous acts of temperance who is presently [d*] depraved in his heart. Thus far, on our hypothesis, he performs acts of temperance but not virtuously, and he is inclined to them and helped more towards them by the habit of temperance antecedently acquired from virtuous acts. Or it can be said that no one wrongly uses moral virtues formed by charity and subservient to charity. So Augustine says in the same place that *the virtues are goods by which we live rightly and by which a righteous and honest life endures* [11].

Reply to the following proof: It is evident above that it happens that *b* becomes what is not a virtue from other causes. It can further be said that *b* does not simply cease to be a virtue because it is in someone asleep, because sleep is a passion which comes to and is suitable to human nature naturally and regularly for the good of a nature subject to fatigue, and which withdraws from the drunkard. Or it can be said that *b* ceases to be a virtue at least in a certain respect because there is an impediment which is vicious or unnatural and unsuitable to its nature. Concerning persistent madness, however, thus far more of the same can be said. But if it is in fact incurable and perpetual, it seems that *b* simply is not a virtue. The case is not similar wiht regard to infused charity because it makes even a baptized infant just and virtuous by divine decree.

REPLY TO THE SECOND OBJECTION: *B* is not morally good through itself essentially by the grace of such an act with respect to such an object, but because it is conformed to the dictate of the intellect and the decree of the divine will and right reason existing in the agent in accordance with certain circumstances. And this does not necessarily happen to the act because it is possible that right reason dictate other circumstances at another time, or that the same act or a similar one differ according to another circumstance. And it is conceded that something on account of which *b* is called morally good is good morally or with a more eminent goodness, namely, the divine will. It likewise happens that something by conformity to which *b* is said to be morally good is, strictly speaking, neither good nor evil morally nor indifferent and potentially either, but is right with a rectitude which is judicative and prescriptive about action worthy of choice or deserving to be avoided.

Reply to the confirmation: Although the consequent can be conceded by reason of uncreated good, the inference is denied because *white* or *like* or *equal* accidentally need not be reduced to what is such through itself. The reply to the antecedent is evident from what has been said.

REPLY TO THE THIRD OBJECTION: The inference is denied because God established natural law and certain laws according to which many acts regularly are simply good and certain ones are generically good. But in referring to the absolute power of God, the inference is conceded.

REPLY TO THE FOURTH OBJECTION: The minor is denied as it pertained to what is to be proven. For being morally good is demonstrated of no particular act under an absolute concept, but it is demonstrated of a subject under a concept which is not absolute. We would contingently

proprium quidditativum.

Ad confirmationem conceditur consequens de aliquibus bonis, scilicet de bonis naturalibus, sed ultra hoc habet homo bona iusti et honesti; sed hoc not habet sicut inanimata vel irrationabilia quae habent bona sibi naturalia.

AD QUINTUM: si antecedens intellegatur de dictamine singulari, mere categorico, completo et ultimato de elicitione talis actus secundum substantiam, negatur antecedens; immo tale contingit esse non rectum vel non verum in intellectu humano, vel esse non tale iudicum ut in intellectu divino. Si vero antecedens intellegatur de dictamine universali vel non mere categorico et ultimate determinativo de eligendo talem entitatem absolutam actus sed implicite condicionali et de eligendo actum sub talibus condicionibus, ut quod Deus est super omnia diligendus quando et ubi et sicut oportet, vel oboediendum est Deo, vel vivendum est bene, negatur consequentia summendo consequens in sensu divisionis, quia contingit *b* actum conformari tali iudicio et interdum non conformari.

Ad primam probationem consequentiae patet supra.

Ad secundam: assumptum est verum, sed non probat propositum quia illud quod est regulabile per huiusmodi regulam potest idem numero secundum absolutam entitatem regulari actualiter et conformiter illi.

AD SEXTUM negatur minor.

Ad probationem dicendum quod si *b* sit nomen absolute significans illam entitatem secundum id quod est realiter, possibile est *b* actum inesse voluntati et non esse bonum moraliter; et contingit voluntatem in agendo *b* non conformiter operari dictamini rectae rationis inexistentis operanti et dictantis sufficienter ad hoc ut sit bonitas moralis.

Ad improbationem consequentia negatur.

Ad confirmationem conceditur prima consequentia et negatur secunda si ly *recte* et *conformiter* determinent ly *vivere* et non determinent ly *vult* et si sit condicio obiecti, non actus; in antecedente autem est condicio actus.

\<SECUNDUS ARTICULUS\>

SECUNDUS ARTICULUS de bonitate iusti et honesti supernaturali seu theologica et caritativa et gratuita quae communiter ponitur in viatore meritoria vitae aeternae, et ponitur maior bonitate morali prout bonitas moralis accipitur in philosophia morali humanitus adinventa et ut bonitate morali usi sunt philosophi et ut est minor bonitate existentis in gratia quam ponent Catholici

speak of this particular act being morally good demonstrated [e*] through a pronoun or through its own essential concept.

Reply to the confirmation: The consequent is conceded in the case of some goods, namely, natural goods. But beyond this a human being has just and noble goods. And he does not have them as do inanimate or irrational beings which have goods natural to them.

REPLY TO THE FIFTH OBJECTION: If the antecedent is understood of a particular, purely categorical, complete and final dictate about eliciting such an act according to its substance, the antecedent is denied. Indeed it happens that such a dictate fails to be right or true in the human intellect, or is not that judgment as it is in the divine intellect. But if in fact the antecedent is understood of a dictate which is universal or which is not purely categorical and finally determinative with respect to choosing the absolute entity of an act, but is implicitly conditional and about choosing an act under certain conditions (as, for example, that God ought to be loved above all things or that God ought to be obeyed or that one ought to live rightly when and where and as one ought); then the inference is denied in taking the consequent in the sense of division. For it happens that act *b* is conformed to such a judgment but sometimes is not conformed to it.

Reply to the first proof of the inference: The reply is evident above.

Reply to the second proof: What is accepted <as a basis for the conclusion> is true, but it does not prove what is to be proven. For that which is regulable by such a rule can actually be regulated the same way with regard to the individual according to its absolute entity and conformably to it.

REPLY TO THE SIXTH OBJECTION: The minor is denied.

Reply to the proof: If *b* is a name absolutely signifying that entity according to that which it really is, it is possible that act *b* be present in the will and not be morally good. And it happens that the will, in doing *b*, does not operate conformably to the dictate of right reason existing in the agent and prescribing sufficiently for it to be moral goodness.

Reply to the disproof: The inference is denied.

Reply to the confirmation: The first inference is conceded and the second is denied if *rightly* and *conformably* determine *to live* and do not determine *will* and if it is a condition of the object and not of the act. In the antecedent, however, it is a condition of the act.

ARTICLE 2

The SECOND ARTICLE concerns the just and noble goodness which is supernatural or theological and charitable and conferred by grace, and which is commonly placed in the viator meriting eternal life. This goodness is asserted to be greater than moral goodness as moral goodness is taken in moral philosophy which is humanly devised and as philosophers have used moral goodness,

et secundum quam homo dicitur bonus simpliciter; de huiusmodi bonitate.

PRIMA CONCLUSIO: Bonitatis [f*] iusti et honesti maioris bonitate morali ratio formalis non per se est ratio meritorii gratiae [g*] vel vitae aeternae sed est ratio prior, ita quod prius secundum naturalem intellegentiam est actum esse bonum tali bonitate quam esse meritorium gratiae vel vitae aeternae.

Probatur, quia contingit huiusmodi [h*] bonitatem reperiri sine ratione meritorii, ut in actibus bonorum in patria.

Item, sine contradictione possibile est Deum dare praecepta alicui creaturae rationali cui, quamvis observet illa, non dabit vitam aeternam, quia de rigore districto iustitiae nulli quantumcumque bono tenetur dare in fine vitam aeternam.

Item, pone quod Sortes et Plato aequaliter bene vixerint usque ad mortem implendo praecepta sibi data, ita ut fuerint aequaliter boni: possibile erit Deum dare in fine isti beatitudinem et non dare illi; igitur actus illius fuerunt tanta bonitate boni et tamen non aeque meritorii actualiter [i*] et formaliter vitae aeternae, quia Deus istum non acceptavit nec ordinavit ad hoc.

Praeterea, intellectus potest iudicare talem bonitatem esse eligibilem et oppositum esse fugibile absque respectu ad praemium ulterius vel ad punitionem consequentem [j*]; igitur talis bonitas non per se et essentialiter consistit in ratione meritorii.

Antecedens probatur primo, per Bernardum [k*], *De Diligendo Deo: Deus non sine praemio diligitur, Deus etsi absque intuitu praemii sit diligendus* [12]; secundo, per Augustinum, 21 *Civitate* cap. 15, dicentem: *Si (quod absit) tanti boni,* scilicet aeternae mercedis, *spes* [l*] *nulla esset, adhuc malle debuimus in vitiorum conflictationis molestia* [m*] *remanere quam vitiorum in nos dominationem* [n*], *non eis resistendo, permittere* [13].

Praeterea, prius secundum naturalem intellegentiam est hunc actum esse malum et vitiosum malitia opposita quam esse demeritorium punitionis et quam deputari ad poenam ulteriorem; igitur similiter de bonitate opposita respectu praemii ulterioris.

Consequentia probatur, quia actus bonus non magis est per se meritorius praemii quam malus sit demeritorius poenae.

Antecedens probatur, tum quia ideo a Deo deputatur ad poenam quia est mala, et ideo ad maiorem poenam quia magis mala. Tum quia in remissione culpae tollitur totaliter malitia culpae, et tamen non totaliter aufertur demeritum et reatus poenae et obligatio ad poenam sed commutatur maior in minorem quia aeterna in temporalem. Similiter in remissione culpae venialis remanet deputatio ad poenam temporalem; non autem in remissione culpae sit commutatio maioris culpae in minorem culpam.

Praeterea, bonitas moralis non est formaliter acceptatio vel ordinatio ad praemium ulterius, virtuosus enim agit bonum gratia boni; igitur pari ratione de bonitate maiori supernaturali.

Confirmatur, quia secundum Magistrum libro 2 dist. 24, *homo in statu innocentiae erat rectus et poterat aliquando vivere, non tamen proficere in merito vitae aeternae per sola dona tunc accepta* [14]; et idem dicit de angelis ibidem [15] et dist. 5, cap. 5 [16]. Illa autem bonitas, licet possit reduci ad moralem, tamen est gradus bonitatis perfectior bonitate morali quam posuerunt philosophi, quae est naturaliter acquisibilis nec exigit adiutorium supernaturale nec respicit praecepta et monitiones divinae voluntatis data specialiter ultra commune ius naturae.

and as moral goodness is less than the goodness of existing in grace which Catholics posit and according to which a human being is called simply good. The article concerns this kind of good.

FIRST CONCLUSION: The formal quality of just and noble goodness [f*] (which is greater than moral goodness) is not per se the quality of being meritorious of grace [g*] or of eternal life but is a prior quality, so that, according to natural understanding, it comes first that an act be good with such goodness than that it be meritorious of grace or of eternal life.

Proof: It happens that such [h*] goodness is found without the quality of being meritorious, as, for example, in the acts of good persons in heaven.

Again, it is possible, without contradiction, that God give precepts to some rational creature to whom God will not give eternal life although he observes those precepts. For, by the strict rule of justice, God is bound to give eternal life in the end to no good, however great.

Again, suppose that Socrates and Plato have lived equally well up until death in fulfilling the precepts given to them so that they have been equally good. It will be possible that, in the end, God give beatitude to the former but not to the latter. Therefore, the acts of the latter were good with so much goodness and yet they were not actually [i*] and formally equally meritorious of eternal life because God neither accepted him for nor ordered him to this end.

Moreover, the intellect can judge that such goodness is worthy of choice and that the opposite deserves to be avoided without regard to ulterior reward or to consequent [j*] punishment. Therefore such goodness does not, through itself and essentially, constitute the quality of being meritorious.

The antecedent is proved first by Bernard [k*] in *On Loving God*: *God is not loved without a reward, although God ought to be loved without consideration of reward* [12]. Second, the antecedent is proved by Augustine's statement in *The City of God*, XXI, chap. 15: *If (God forbid) there were no hope* [l*] *of so great a good,* namely, of an eternal reward, *still we should prefer to remain in the troublesome state of the conflict of the vices* [m*] *than to permit, by not resisting them, the dominion* [n*] *of the vices in us* [13].

Moreover, according to natural understanding, it comes first that this act be evil and vicious with the opposing evilness than that it be deserving of punishment and assigned to ulterior punishment. Therefore, similarly with regard to the opposing goodness with respect to ulterior reward.

Proof of the inference: A good act is no more meritorious of reward through itself than an evil act is deserving of punishment.

Proof of the antecedent: First, it is assigned to punishment by God because it is evil, and therefore to a greater punishment because it is a greater evil. Second, the evilness of fault is totally taken away in the remission of a fault and yet the demerit and the guilt of punishment and the obligation to punishment are not totally taken away, but a greater is changed into a lesser because the eternal is changed into the temporal. Similarly, assignment to temporal punishment remains in the remission of a venial fault. It is not the case, however, that in the remission of the fault a greater fault is changed into a lesser one.

Moreover, moral goodness does not formally constitute an acceptance or decree for an ulterior reward, for the virtuous person does good for the sake of good. Therefore, in like manner, with respect to the greater, supernatural goodness.

Praeterea, bonitas actionis et servitii respectu domini temporalis non per se et formaliter est acceptatio illius ad praemium a domino; igitur similiter in proposito.

Antecedens patet, quia princeps talem actum iam praeteritum potest noviter acceptare ad praemium vel ad maius praemium.

CONTRA conclusionem: illud secundum quod formaliter *b* est bonum magis et, quo circumscripto, *b* foret minus bonum non est extra bonitatem ipsius *b* nec posterius bonitate huiusmodi; sed esse meritorium gratiae [o*] et acceptari a Deo ad beatitudinem est huiusmodi.

Probo, quia tam habitus quam actus caritatis est magis diligibilis et eligibilis ex hoc quam si non foret huiusmodi; ergo...

Respondeo: *b* non est secundum hoc formaliter magis bonum secundum bonitatem iusti et honesti, licet ex hoc dicatur magis bonum bonitate utilis vel delectabilis. Item, esto quod illud foret circumstantia augens bonitatem; tamen, illa circumscripta, habetur bonitas simpliciter iusti et maior bonitate morali quam ponunt philosophi.

SECUNDA CONCLUSIO: Omne quod est viatori bonum iusti simpliciter et meritorii ideo est ei sic bonum quia divina voluntas libere vult et ordinat illud esse taliter bonum, et eo formaliter est sic bonum quo est conforme divinae voluntati ut praeceptivae vel persuasivae et consultivae vel approbanti et complacenti et acceptanti.

Probatur, quia omnis bonitas et rectitudo secundaria et posterior ideo est talis rectitudo quia est conformis primae et summae rectitudini, quia est regulabilis primo per illam et illa est prima regula et mensura omnis alterius rectitudinis. Unde 10 *Metaphysicae: In unoquoque genere est dare primum quod est maxime tale et mensura aliorum* [17].

Confirmatur: aut ordinatio divinae voluntatis cum dictamine intellectus divini est prima regula, ratio et mensura rectitudinis et iustitiae actuum nostrorum aut non sed recta ratio in intellectu creato, aut quodlibet istorum est aeque prima [p*] regula rectitudinis in voluntate nostra, aut huius nulla est prima regula nec causa prior. Si primum, propositum. Si secundum, contra: quia velle et iudicare divinum essent magis dirigibilia et regulabilia per intellectum humanum quam econtra, cum tamen intellectus noster sit defectibilis et per consequens regulabilis per intellectum indefectibilem. Si tertium, contra: quia sicut non sunt 2 prima entia, ita 2 primae causae et regulae bonitatis; et quia

Confirmation: According to the Master, bk. II, dist. 24, *a human being in the state of innocence was righteous and once was able to live <in this state> yet not to progress in the merit of eternal life through the only gifts then received* [14]. And he says the same thing about angels in the same place [15] and in dist. 5, sect. 5 [16]. But that goodness, although it can be reduced to moral goodness, yet is a degree of goodness more perfect than the moral goodness which philosophers have posited, which can be acquired naturally and neither requires supernatural help nor considers precepts and admonitions of the divine will specifically given beyond the common law of nature.

Moreover, the goodness of action and service with respect to a temporal lord does not, through itself and formally, constitute the acceptance of that for a reward from the lord. Therefore, similarly in what we propose to prove.

The antecedent is evident because a sovereign can accept anew such an act now past for a reward or for a greater reward.

OBJECTION to the conclusion: That in accordance with which *b* is formally a greater good and, where excluded, *b* would be a lesser good, is not outside of the goodness of *b* itself nor posterior to such goodness. But to be meritorious of grace [o*] and accepted by God for beatitude is of this type.

I prove this as follows. A habit, just as much as an act of charity, is more lovable and worthy of choice from this than if it would not be of this kind. Therefore...

I reply in the following way. *B* is not, in accordance with this, formally a greater good according to just and noble goodness, although from this it is said to be a greater good than useful or pleasurable goodness. Again, let us allow that that would be a circumstance increasing goodness. Nevertheless, with that circumstance excluded, simply just goodness is possessed and a goodness greater than the moral goodness which philosophers posit.

SECOND CONCLUSION: Everything which is a simply just and meritorious good for a viator is this kind of good for him because the divine will freely wills and decrees it to be good in this way, and it is formally this kind of good because it is conformed to the divine will as preceptive or as persuasive and consultative or as approving and being pleased and accepting.

Proof: All secondary and posterior goodness and rectitude is such rectitude because it is conformed to the first and highest rectitude, since it is regulated first by that and that is the first rule and measure of all other rectitude. So it is said in the *Metaphysics* X: *In one genus there is granted to be a first which is such in the highest degree and the measure of the others* [17].

Confirmation: Either the decree of the divine will with the dictate of the divine intellect is the first rule, reason and measure of the rectitude and righteousness of our acts or it is not, but rather, right reason in the created intellect is; or it is the case that either one of them is equally the first [p*] rule of rectitude in our will; or it is the case that neither is the first rule and prior cause of this rectitude. If the first is the case, we have what we propose to prove. If the second alternative is chosen, the following may be said in opposition to it. The divine volition and judgment would more be subject to guidance and regulation by the human intellect than the contrary, when it is the case,

rectitudo creata non magis esset regulabilis et mensurabilis per increatam quam econtra. Si quartum, contra: quia voluntas nostra est defectibilis, igitur regulabilis et dirigibilis per regulam priorem propter conformitatem ad quem dicatur recta et propter deformitatem, non recta [q*].

Praeterea, Anselmus, *Proslogii* 11: *Id solum iustum est quod vis, et iniustum quod non vis* [18]; et primo *Cur Deus Homo* cap. 8: *Sufficere nobis debet ad rationem voluntas* [r*] *Dei cum aliquid facit, licet non videamus cur velit. Voluntas namque Dei numquam est irrationabilis* [19].

Item, Hugo, primo *De Sacramentis* parte 4 cap. 1: *Prima omnium rerum causa est voluntas creatoris, quae est ex semetipsa iusta. Nec enim idcirco iuste voluit quia futurum iustum fuit quod voluit, sed quod voluit idcirco iustum fuit quia ipse voluit.* Sequitur: *Cum ergo quaeritur quare iustum est quod iustum est, convenientissime* [s*] *respondetur: quoniam secundum Dei voluntatem est, quae sancta est et iusta est. Cum vero quaeritur quare et ipsa Dei voluntas iusta est, hoc sanius respondetur: quoniam primae causae nulla causa est* [20].

Item, Augustinus [21], *De Singularitate Clericorum* cap. 4: *Dei mandata ita sunt observanda, ut si aliquid* [t*] *iusserit quod secundum homines iniustum esse videatur, iustum credatur et fiat; eius enim voluntas est sola et vera iustitia. Si enim totum quod gerimus ad hoc solum gerimus, ut Domino placeamus, profecto* [u*] *id solum erit iustum, quicquid voluerit et iusserit et probaverit Deus* [22].

CONTRA:

Sequitur quod creatura rationalis posset ex puris naturalibus agere actus aeque bonos et ita bene sicut cum gratia vel donis supernaturalibus.

Consequens est falsum, quia posset ex puris naturalibus aeque bene vivere et tam laudabilis et tanto bono digna esse, quod videtur error Pelagii.

Consequentia probatur, quia creet Deus *b* creaturam rationalem in puris naturalibus dando sibi certa praecepta vel consilia, tunc huiusmodi creatura posset ista praecepta vel consilia observare absque omissione vel transgressione alicuius circumstantiae contentae in praecepto; igitur posset conformari voluntati divinae totaliter secundum omnem circumstantiam contentam in praecepto vel consilio, absque alia deformitate [w*] secundum aliam circumstantiam; igitur aeque conformatur divinae voluntati sicut voluntas habens caritatem et observans huiusmodi praeceptum; igitur esset aeque recta. Si enim duo conformarentur eidem regulae sine aliqua deformitate ab illa, sequitur quod illa aeque conformantur tali regulae, et consequenter sunt aeque recta. Per idem arguitur quod actus viatoris vel existentis in puris naturalibus posset esse aeque bonus sicut actus boni quia aeque conformari divinae voluntati praecipienti vel consulenti, puta si praecipiatur elicere *b* actum in tali gradu, vel isti in tanto gradu et illi in alio certo gradu.

Confirmatur: per idem sequitur quod omnes actus simpliciter boni et iusti sunt aeque boni et

however, that our intellect is defectible and consequently subject to regulation by an indefectible intellect. If the third alternative is chosen, the following may be said in opposition to it. First, just as there are not two first beings, so there are not two of the first cause and rule of goodness. Second, created rectitude would no more be regulable and measurable by the uncreated than the contrary. If the fourth alternative is chosen, the following may be said in opposition to it. Our will is defectible, and therefore subject to regulation and guidance by a prior rule. On account of conformity to this rule, our will may be called upright; and on account of deviation from it, not upright [q*].

Moreover, Anselm states in the *Proslogion* 11: *That alone is just which you will, and unjust which you do not will* [18]. And in *Why God Became Man*, bk. I, chap. 8, he says: *The will [r*] of God ought to suffice us as a reason when he does anything, although we do not see why he wills to do it. For the will of God is never irrational.* [19]

Again, Hugh states in *On the Sacraments*, bk. I, pt. 4, chap. 1: *The first cause of all things is the will of the creator, which is just from itself. For he did not will justly because what he willed was about to be just, but what he willed was just because he himself willed it.* There follows: *When, therefore, it is asked why that is just which is just, the most appropriate [s*] response is: because it is according to the will of God, which is holy and just. When, however, it is asked why too the will of God itself is just, this is more reasonably responded: because there is no cause of the first cause* [20].

Again, Augustine [21] says in *On the Singleness of Clerics*, chap. 4: *The commands of God are so to be observed that, if he shall have ordered something [t*] which appears to be unjust according to human beings, it may be believed to be just and be done, for his will is the sole and true justice. For if all that we carry out we carry out to this end alone, that we be pleasing to God, surely [u*] that alone will be just, whatever God shall have willed and ordered and approved.* [22]

OBJECTIONS:

It follows that a rational creature could perform acts equally good and as uprightly out of purely natural capacities [v*] as with grace or supernatural gifts.

The consequent is false because he could live equally uprightly and be as praiseworthy and deserving of so much good out of purely natural capacities, which seems to be the error of Pelagius.

Proof of the inference: Let God create a rational creature, *b*, in a state of purely natural capacities, giving him certain precepts and counsels. Then such a creature could observe those precepts or counsels without the omission or transgression of any circumstance contained in the precept. Therefore he could be totally conformed to the divine will according to every circumstance contained in the precept or counsel, without other deviation [w*] according to another circumstance. And therefore, he is equally conformed to the divine will as the will which has charity and observes such a precept. And therefore, his will would be equally upright. For if two things should be conformed to the same rule without any deviation from it, it follows that they are equally conformed to such a rule, and consequently, that they are equally right. It is argued through the same considerations that the act of a viator and of someone existing with purely natural capacities could be equally good as a good act because they are equally conformed to the divine will commanding or counseling, as, for example, if he is commanded to elicit an act, *b*, to such a degree, or towards this

iusti quia aeque conformes suae regulae, in conformitate ad quam stat formalis bonitas. Ex quo enim nulla est deformitas vel obliquitas, ab illa sequitur quod aeque recti sunt. Sicut enim regulabile corporale ad regulam materialem, sic proportionabiliter de spirituali. Et quia si non perfecte et totaliter conformantur regulae primo actus *a* et actus *b* sed *a* conformatur illi secundum aliam condicionem secundum quam non conformatur *b* eidem, sequitur quod in voluntate divina est distinctio, quia secundum aliquid sui est illa regula conformis *a* secundum quod non est conformis ipsi *b*.

SECUNDO principaliter, si ratio boni et iusti consistat formaliter in conformitate ad divinam voluntatem et ordinationem, sequeretur quod in rebus inanimatis et brutis sit bonum iusti, quia vivunt et operantur et se habent conformiter ordinationi et dispositioni voluntatis divinae et ut Deus vult.

Item, furiosus vellet iuste et virtuose quia conformiter divinae voluntati, pone quod sine culpa incurrerit furiam.

Item, si a solo Deo infunderetur actus volendi in voluntate, illa vellet conformiter divinae voluntati et tamen non esset iusta in sic volendo secundum Anselmum, *De Casu Diaboli*, 14 [23].

TERTIO, si quicquid est bonum eo formaliter est huiusmodi quo est a Deo volitum et ei placitum, igitur quicquid Deus vellet, eo ipso sequeretur illud esse istum quia ratio iusti ei conveniret.

Consequens est contra Anselmum, primo *Cur Deus Homo* cap. 12, dicentem: *Quod autem dicitur quia quod vult iustum est et quod non vult non est iustum, non illud intelligendum est ut, si Deus velit quodlibet inconveniens, iustum sit, quod ipse vult. Non enim sequitur: Si Deus vult mentiri, iustum esse mentiri* [24].

QUARTO arguitur sic: hanc actionem esse malam est a Deo volitum et ordinatum; igitur esset simpliciter bonum et iustum.

Consequens est falsum, quia talem actum esse et fieri esset bonum, et facere tale opus esset bonum et iustum quia includitur in illo vel est per se et necessario annexum.

Antecendens probatur, quia taliter agere ideo est malum quia Deus instituit et ordinavit quod tale agere foret malum, et taliter agere non habet unde sit malum nisi ex divino statuto; ab eius autem ordinatione habet *b* actio quod sit mala a quo habet quod sit prohibita.

QUINTO, si prima et tota ratio quare *b* est bonum et iustum sit libera ordinatio et approbatio divinae voluntatis, sequitur quod Sortem esse reprobatum [x*] sit bonum et iustum.

Probatur consequentia, quia hoc est a Deo volitum et institutum; Deus enim ab aeterno hunc reprobavit et reprobandum instituit.

Falsitas consequentis probatur, tum quia non est bonum iusti ipsi Sorti nec alicui alteri; tum

one to such a degree and towards that one to another degree.

Confirmation: It follows through the same considerations that all acts simply good and just are equally good and just because they are equally conformed to their rule, in conformity to which formal goodness consists. For from the fact that there is no deviation or obliquity, it follows that they are equally right. For just as a corporeal thing subject to regulation is related to a material rule, so correspondingly with respect to the spiritual. Further, if act *a* and act *b* are not first completely and totally conformed to the rule but *a* is conformed to it according to some other condition while *b* is not, it follows that there is a distinction in the divine will. For that rule is conformed to *a* but not to *b* according to something of itself.

SECOND, if the quality of being good and just consists formally in conformity to the divine will and decree, it would follow that there is just good in inanimate beings and in animals because they live and operate and behave conformably to the decree and prescription of the divine will and as God wills.

Again, a madman would will justly and virtuously because he wills conformably to the divine will, assuming that he has incurred madness without fault.

Again, if an act of willing were infused into the will by God alone, that will would will conformably to the divine will and yet it would not be just in so willing according to Anselm in *The Fall of the Devil* 14 [23].

THIRD, if whatever is good is such formally because it is willed by God and is pleasing to him, then whatever God would will, it would follow from that very fact that it is just because the quality of being just would be found in it.

The consequent is contrary to Anselm's statement in *Why God Became Man*, bk. I, chap. 12: *But with respect to the statement that what he wills is just and what he does not will is not just, that must not be understood to mean that, if God should will anything unsuitable, it is just, because he wills it. For the inference does not follow: If God wills to lie, then lying is just.* [24]

FOURTH, it is argued as follows. That this action is evil is willed and decreed by God; therefore it would be simply good and just.

The consequent is false, because it would be good that such an act exist and be done, and it would be good and just to do such a work because this is included in that or it is connected through itself and necessarily.

Proof of the antecedent: To act in such a way is evil because God established and decreed that such activity would be evil, and to act in such a way does not have a *whence* it is evil except *from the divine statute*. But an action *b* has its evil status from his decree, wherefrom it has its prohibited status.

FIFTH, if the first and entire reason why *b* is good and just is the free decree and approval of the divine will, it follows that Socrates being reprobated [x*] is good and just.

Proof of the inference: This is willed and established by God, for from eternity God reprobated him and established that he should be reprobated.

Proof of the falsity of the consequent: First, it is not a just good for Socrates himself nor for

quia Sortem esse peccatorum et finaliter impaenitentem esset bonum et iustum quia hoc includitur in illo vel per se et necessario est annexum.

SEXTO, sequitur quod miseria Gehennae est damnato summum bonum, et ita ei summe bene esset secundum bonitatem iusti et honesti.

Probatio consequentiae: quia ipsum sic pati et esse miserum est conforme ordinationi voluntatis divinae quae instituit hunc modum punitionis.

AD PRIMUM negatur consequentia. Voluntas enim donis supernaturalibus adiuta potest in aliquas actiones in quas non posset sine illis vel non aeque perfecte et eisdem modis, ceteris paribus; tamen non est impossibile Deo absolute quod aliqua actio voluntatis non habentis dona supernaturalia sit in creatura aeque bona sicut quaedam alia actio voluntatis habentis huiusmodi dona.

Ad confirmationem [y*] negatur alia consequentia. Nec est simile de corporali et spirituali rectitudine. Rectitudo enim corporalis consistit in praesentia [z*] fortitudinis seu in nonexitu medii ab extremis, ideo simpliciter rectum non suscipit magis et minus; sed rectitudo spiritualis in creatura rationali consistit in conformitate actionis vel voluntatis et vitae ad divinam ordinationem secundum varias circumstantias quibus convenit differentia, secundum magis et minus, et secundum plures vel pauciores, et secundum quamlibet inaequaliter conformari. Contingit quaedam enim circumstantiae possunt adesse quae non requiruntur, et per consequens earum privatio non causaret deformitatem; tamen maiorem rectitudinem et bonitatem.

Ad alia per idem.

AD SECUNDUM negatur consequentia, quia bonitas iustitiae consistit in conformitate agentis liberi ad divinam voluntatem ut praeceptivam vel consultivam, ita ut quasi per modum materialis praesupponitur voluntatis activitas libera et recta ratio in intellectu et quasi per modum formalis additur *conformiter ad divinam voluntatem*, non tantum ut generaliter determinantem [a**], ordinantem et disponentem sed ut praecipientem vel persuadentem. Licet autem Deus dicatur disponere de rebus quae subsunt eius dominio, tamen proprie loquendo praeceptum vel consilium non datur inanimatis vel brutis; ideo nec in eis reperitur bonum iusti et honesti prout huiusmodi bonitate usi sunt philosophi et utuntur theologi.

Eodem modo de furioso, quia non habet liberi arbitrii usum nec capax est rationis. Eodem modo si Deus se solo infundat actum, quia tunc voluntas non se habet ut activum liberum nec ratio antecedens ut causa.

AD TERTIUM: accipiendo in consequente ly *quicquid* proprie, conceditur consequentia, et improbatio peccat per figuram dictionis [b**] mutando *quid* in *quale* vel *quasi quale*; sed accipiendo *quicquid* large, negatur consequentia, intelligendo consequens quod illud esset sic absolute iustum quod non sequitur ipsum esse iniustum. Et quaedam enim sunt quae ex sua impositione et formali

anyone else. Second, Socrates being a sinner and finally impenitent would be good and just because this is included in that or it is connected through itself necessarily.

SIXTH, it follows tht the misery of Gehenna is the highest good for someone damned, and so it would go extremely well for him according to just and noble goodness.

Proof of the inference: That he suffer and be miserable in this way is conformed to the decree of the divine will which established this method of punishment.

REPLY TO THE FIRST OBJECTION: The inference is denied. For a will assisted by supernatural gifts is capable of some actions of which it would not be capable without them, or not with equal perfection and in the same ways, other things being equal. Nevertheless, it is not impossible for God absolutely that some action of a will which does not have supernatural gifts be just as good in a <rational> creature as a certain other action of a will having such gifts.

Reply to the confirmation [y*]: The other inference is denied. And the cases of corporeal and spiritual rectitude are not similar. For corporeal rectitude consists in the presence [z*] of fortitude or in not departing from the mean by extremes. Therefore, the simply right is not susceptible of *more* and *less*. But spiritual rectitude in a rational creature consists in the conformity of action or of the will and life to the divine decree according to the various circumstances by which a difference is found, viz., according to more and less, and according to the more or the fewer, and according to whatever circumstances unequal conformity occurs. For it happens that certain circumstances can be present which are not required, and consequently, the privation of them would not cause deviation. Nevertheless, <affixing these circumstances makes for more conformity, and so for> greater rectitude and goodness.

Reply to the other points: Through the same considerations.

REPLY TO THE SECOND OBJECTION: The inference is denied. Just goodness consists in the conformity of a free agent to the divine will as preceptive or consultative, so that free activity of the will and right reason in the intellect are presupposed as it were by the material mode, and there is added, as it were by the formal mode, *conformably to the divine will*, not only as generally determining [a**], decreeing, and disposing but as commanding or persuading. And although God is said to make disposition of the things which are under his dominion, nevertheless, a precept or counsel is not, properly speaking, given to inanimate beings or to animals. Therefore, neither is just and noble good found in them, as philosophers have used and theologians use this kind of goodness.

The same response can be given about a madman, because he does not have the use of free will and is not capable of reason. And the same response can be given if God infuses an act by himself, because then the will does not behave as a free, active principle, nor antecedent reason, as a cause.

REPLY TO THE THIRD OBJECTION: In taking *whatever* in the consequent properly, the inference is conceded, and the disproof errs by a figure of speech [b**] in changing *what* into *what kind of* or as it were *what kind of*. But in taking *whatever* in a broad sense, the inference is denied, understanding the consequent as saying that that would be so absolutely just that it does not follow

significatione implicant circumstantiam indebitam et malitiam et defectum, et tale attributum Deo infert illud esse iustum aut esse iniustum. Infertur enim esse iustum quia antecedens accipit Deum velle illud, et sequitur ipsum esse iniustum ex formali significatione terminorum. Vult enim Anselmus quod non cuiuslibet inconvenientis attributio ipsi Deo infert illud esse iustum sic absolute quin etiam sequatur absolute illud esse iniustum.

AD QUARTUM: si antecedens intellegitur de volitione et ordinatione antecedenti et simplici et absoluta, negatur antecedens, quia hoc implicaret quod Deus vult et ordinat mala agere; est igitur antecedenter [c**] et absolute notum et prohibitum. Si vero antecedens intellegitur de velle et ordinatione consequenti et quasi condicionali et praesuppositiva, conceditur antecedens. Et sub uniformi hypothesi, conceditur consequens, quia si talis actio sit acta [d**] ab homine, iustum est quod ipsa censeatur esse mala et quod imputatur homini ad culpam; sed iustitia a qua hoc iustum dicitur non est iustitia existens formaliter homini sic agenti sed inexistens legislatori in eo quod sic ordinat, et ab eadem iustitia dicitur lex iusta et mandatum iustum.

AD QUINTUM per idem.

AD SEXTUM negatur consequentia.
Ad probationem patet ex dictis.

TERTIO CONCLUSIO: Nullum agere creaturae rationalis simpliciter bonum et iustum ideo divina voluntas vult et ordinat esse bonum et iustum quia illud in se ex natura rei sit bonum et iustum, aut quia primo sit ab intellectu divino praedictatum et praeiudicatum ita ut non divina voluntas ut voluntas sed dictamen divini intellectus sit prima ratio et regula vel mensura ipsius agere boni et iusti simpliciter.
Probatur haec conclusio per auctoritates suprapositas quae velle divinum assignant pro praescientia [25] vel prima et principali causa omnis alterius iusti [26].
` Confirmatur per illud *Matthaei* 11, *Ita, Pater, quoniam sic fuit placitum ante te* [27], et per illam parabolam *Matthaei* 19 de operariis in vinea [28], ubi dicitur, *An non licet mihi quod volo facere?* [29]
Praeterea, sequitur quod Deus necessitaretur praecipere vel consulere Sorti agere *b*.
Consequens est falsum; potest enim eum absolvere ab hoc, immo prohibere vel disconsulere pro quocumque finito tempore determinato.
Probatio consequentiae [e**]: si ideo divina voluntas vult et ordinat quod Sortem agere *b* sit bonum quia divinus intellectus hoc prius dictat et praeiudicat esse bonum, igitur Deus ideo ordinat quod *b* sit agendum a Sorte et praecipit et consulit Sortem *b* agere quia Deus praedictat et praeiudicat; aut igitur divinus intellectus necessario iudicat in tanquam necessario verum, aut contingenter et ut verum contingens. Si secundum, igitur haec [f**] reducitur et resolvitur ultimate in liberam ordinationem divinae voluntatis, et propositum. Si primum, igitur voluntas divina

that it be unjust. For there are certain ones which imply an undue circumstance and evilness and defect from their imposition and formal signification. And such being attributed to God yields the inference that it is just, or rather, that it is unjust. For it is inferred that it is just because the antecedent accepts that God wills it, and it follows that it is unjust from the formal signification of the terms. Indeed Anselm intends that the attribution of anything unsuitable to God himself does not yield the inference that it is just so absolutely that it does not also follow that it is unjust absolutely.

REPLY TO THE FOURTH OBJECTION: If the antecedent is understood of a volition and decree which is antecedent and simple and absolute, the antecedent is denied. For this would imply that God wills and decrees that we do evil things. It is therefore antecedently [c**] and absolutely known and prohibited. But if the antecedent is understood of a volition and decree which is consequent and as it were conditional and makes a presupposition, the antecedent is conceded. And supposing the same interpretation, the consequent is conceded. For if such an action is performed [d**] by a human being, it is just that it be considered to be evil and that it be imputed to him as a fault. But the justice by which this is said to be just is not a justice existing formally in the human being so acting, but a justice existing in the legislator inasmuch as he so decrees. And it is by the same justice that a law is called just and a command is said to be just.

REPLY TO THE FIFTH OBJECTION: Through the same considerations.

REPLY TO THE SIXTH OBJECTION: The inference is denied.
Reply to the proof: The response is evident from what has been said.

THIRD CONCLUSION: For no activity of a rational creature which is simply good and just is it the case that the divine will wills and decrees it to be good and just because it is good and just in itself by its nature. In other words, because first it is antecedently dictated and judged to be good and just by the divine intellect, so that it is not the divine will as will but the dictate of the divine intellect which is the first reason and rule or measure of his activity which is simply good and just.

This conclusion is proved by the aforementioned authorities who assign the divine will to foreknowledge [25] or to being the first and principal cause of all else that is just [26].

This is confirmed by the verse of *Matthew* 11, *Yes, Father, because so it was pleasing before you* [27], and by the parable in *Matthew* 19 concerning laborers in the vineyard [28] where it is said, *Am I not allowed to do what I want to do?* [29].

Moreover, it <otherwise> follows that God would be necessitated to command or counsel Socrates to do *b*.

The consequent is false, for God can release him from this action, or even prohibit or counsel against it for any determined finite period of time whatever.

Proof of the inference [e**]: If the divine will wills and decrees that Socrates doing *b* is good because the divine intellect first dictates and antecedently judges this to be good, then God decrees that *b* ought to be done by Socrates and commands and counsels Socrates to do *b* because God antecedently so dictates and judges. Then either the divine intellect necessarily judges this inasmuch as it is necessarily true, or judges this contingently as a contingent truth. If the second is the case,

necessitatur sic ordinare nisi non [g**] conformetur iudicio divini intellectus.

Confirmatur: si ideo voluntas divina vult et ordinat quod *b* sit agendum a Sorte et quod Sortem agere *b* sit bonum quia intellectus divinus praedictat et praeiudicat ex ratione dictante propter quid, sit illud propter quid *c esse d*; aut igitur *c esse d* est necessario verum et necessario ab intellectu divino iudicatum et dictatum, aut contingenter. Si secundum, habetur propositum, quia ultimatum propter quid [h**] non erit nisi *quia divina voluntas hoc vult*, quia ipsa est prima ratio omnis contingentiae. Si primum, igitur necessario vult Deus *c esse d*, et per consequens *b esse agendum a Sorte* vel divina voluntas non erat recta. Et si dicatur quod *b esse agendum* vel *b agere esse bonum* vel *c esse d* sit necessarium sub condicione et ex suppositione, quaeritur de huiusmodi suppositione an sit verum necessarium vel contingens ut falsum.

Praeterea, omne dictamen singulare et distinctum et absolutum et ultimatum de agere *b* potest esse non verum et non ut est in intellectu creato, vel non esse iudicium huiusmodi in intellectu divino; igitur contingens et liberum est quod agere *b* sit bonum et iustum; igitur prima ratio huius non est aliud quam velle divinum.

Antecedens probatur, quia sit in intellectu Sortis iudicium naturaliter acquisitum quod *b* est agendum a Sorte pro tali tempore; aut igitur Deus, de potentia absoluta, potest substrahere influentiam respectu actionis voluntatis sine culpa praecedente in Sorte, aut non potest. Si secundum, igitur necessitatur agere extra se. Si primum, igitur *b* non est secundum dictamen rationis agendum a Sorte, quod est propositum.

Praeterea, agere *b* potest esse magis vel minus bonum ex libera ordinatione et determinatione voluntatis divinae primo [i**]; igitur est bonum et iustum simpliciter ab eiusdem voluntatis ordinatione primo [j**].

Consequentia patet, quia ab eadem causa habet primo esse iustum a qua primo habet vel potest habere esse minus iustum.

Antecedens patet, quia potest magis vel minus approbari et acceptari a voluntate divina, cum etiam actus idem vel consimilis possit a Deo nunc praecipi, nunc prohiberi, et per consequens nunc approbari, nunc reprobari; et actus prius indifferens possit noviter fieri bonus et iustus ex ordinatione divinae voluntatis praeceptiva vel consultativa.

Praeterea, si ideo Sortem agere *b* est bonum et iustum quia primo intellectus dictat et praeiudicat ex rationali causa non reducibili in libere velle, sequitur quod aliquod ens secundum ex natura rei est bonum, non ideo quia voluntas divina sic vult sed econtra.

Consequens est falsum, ut patet supra dist. 38 [30].

Consequentia probatur, quia ratio propter quam intellectus divinus dictabat quod *b* agere sit bonum erit reducibilis ad naturam rei creatae, quia non ex ordinatione divinae voluntatis primo; igitur ideo Deus sic dictat et ordinat quia obiectum ex natura rei est tale.

Praeterea, Deus esset subiectus certis regulis ex legibus respectu agibilium non ex sua voluntate nec in sua potestate positis, quia ex parte obiectorum extra et ex natura rei extra per se et necessario erit verum, *Sic agere, sic rectum*, et verum dictamen, *Illud, sic rectum*.

Praeterea, nullum agere Dei ad [k**] extra ideo voluntas divina vult et ordinat quia primo praedictatum et praeiudicatum sit ab intellectu divino quasi ex ratione praemovente et dicente cur sit ita agendum, et non supponente ordinationem liberam voluntatis tanquam secundum naturalem intelligentiam; igitur pari ratione de agere creaturae rationalis.

Consequentia patet, quia agere divinum ad extra non minus est liberum perfecta libertate

then this truth [f**] is ultimately reduced and resolved into the free decree of the divine will, and this is what we propose to prove. If the first is the case, then the divine will is necessitated so to decree lest it not [g**] be conformed to the judgment of the divine intellect.

Confirmation: Suppose the divine will wills and decrees that *b* ought to be done by Socrates and that Socrates doing *b* is good because the divine intellect antecedently dictates and judges this from reason dictating why it is. Let the why be that *c is d.* Then either *c is d* is necessarily true and necessarily judged and dictated by the divine intellect, or this is so contingently. If the second is the case, then we have what we propose to prove because the final why [h**] will be only *because the divine will wills this,* since the divine will is the first reason of all contingency. If the first is the case, then necessarily God wills that *c is d,* and consequently, that *b ought to be done by Socrates,* or else the divine will was not right. And if it is said that *b ought to be done* or that *doing b is good* or that *c is d* is necessary conditionally and suppositionally, it is asked whether such a supposition is a necessary truth or a contingent one as false.

Moreover, every particular and distinct and absolute and final dictate about doing *b* can fail to be true and not as it is in a created intellect, but rather, it can fail to be such a judgment in the divine intellect. Therefore, it is contingent and free that doing *b* is good and just. And therefore, the first reason for this is nothing other than the divine will.

Proof of the antecedent: Let there be a naturally acquired judgment in the intellect of Socrates that *b* ought to be done by Socrates for such a time. Then either God can, with regard to his absolute power, withdraw his influence with respect to an action of the will without a preceding fault in Socrates, or God cannot do this. If the second is the case, then God is necessitated to act outside himself. If the first is the case, then *b* is not to be done by Socrates according to the dictate of reason, which is what we propose to prove.

Moreover, doing *b* can be a greater or lesser good first [i**] from the free decree and determination of the divine will; therefore it is simply good and just first [j**] from the decree of the same will.

The inference is evident because something has the quality of being just first from the same cause from which it has or can have first the quality of being less just.

The antecedent is evident because doing *b* can be more or less approved and accepted by the divine will since the same act or an entirely similar one can be commanded by God at one time and prohibited at another, and consequently, be approved at one time and reprobated at another. Further, an act which was previously indifferent could recently have become good and just from the preceptive or consultative decree of the divine will.

Moreover, if Socrates doing *b* is good and just because first the intellect dictates and antecedently judges this from a rational cause not reducible to a free volition, it follows that some secondary being is good by its nature and not because the divine will so wills, but the contrary.

The consequent is false, as is evident above in dist. 38 [30].

Proof of the inference: The reason on account of which the divine intellect dictates that doing *b* is good will be reducible to the nature of the created thing, since it will not be first from the decree of the divine will. Therefore God so dictates and decrees because the object is such by its nature.

Moreover, God would <otherwise> be subject to certain rules from laws concerning actions which are not enacted by his will and are not in his power. For, on the part of the objects and by the nature of the thing (and these are outside God), it will be true according to itself and necessarily, *Thus*

contradictionis.

Antecedens probatur, quia voluntas divina necessitaretur agere ad extra vel repugnaret et deformaretur rationi praedictanti [31]. Tum quia Deus non posset aliter operari nec meliora facere [32]. Si enim ratio sic dictat, voluntas necessario faciet; si non dictat, non potest facere. Dictare autem non erit liberum ex quo praeintelligitur omni dictamini liberae divinae voluntatis. Tum per exemplum Apostoli de figulo luti respectu vasorum, *Romanorum* 9 [33]. Tum *a* et *b* producibilibus aeque possibilibus, non est ratio quare hoc producatur, non illud, nisi primo quia placet divinae voluntati; igitur pari ratione in agendis, quare hoc est agendum, non illud, et quare iustum est agere hoc a voluntate humana, non illud.

Praeterea, in aliquo casu voluntas creata hoc habet, ut duobus positis in articulo mortis. Si non possum liberare nisi unum, liberabo iuste quem voluero sine ratione praemovente ex parte huius magis quam illius; et eo ipso quo volo liberare istum [l**], actus liberandi istum iustus est. Duorum autem aeque idoneorum dabo isti non illi, et datio respectu istius erit bona et iusta actio et privatio dationis respectu alterius non est iniusta [34].

CONTRA:

SPECIALITER de agere divino, quod Deus nihil agat nisi ex ratione praedictante et praeiudicante, et tanquam dicente propter quid sic agit. Et sic agere vult primo quia Deus omnia agit sapienter et rationabiliter, igitur ex ratione intellectuali [m**] praedictante; sapientia enim est ratio intellectualis. Unde *Sapientiae* 7: *Sapientia attingit a fine usque ad finem, et disponit omnia* [35].

Item, *Ephesiorum* 1, *Deus operatur omnia secundum consilium voluntatis suae* [36], glossa, id est, *secundum voluntatem suam quae est ex ratione* [37], et quia secundum Philosophum, 3 *Ethicorum* cap. 7, *consilium supponit rationem praedictantem* [38].

Item, Deus agit per electionem, igitur ex ratione praedictante.

Antecedens patet, nam praedestinati dicuntur electi.

Consequentia patet, quia *electio supponit iudicium praedictativum*; cap. 6 et 8 [39].

to act, thus right, and a true dictate, *That, thus right*.

Moreover, for no outward [k**] activity of God is it the case that the divine will wills and decrees it because first it is antecedently dictated and judged by the divine intellect as it were from reason antecedently moving and stating why it must be done so, and not supposing a free decree of the will as it were according to natural understanding. Therefore, in like manner with regard to the activity of a rational creature.

The inference is evident because outward divine activity is no less free with complete liberty of contradiction.

Proof of the antecedent: First, the divine will would <otherwise> be necessitated to act outwardly or it would be inconsistent with and deviate from reason antecedently dictating [31]. Second, God could not work otherwise or make better things [32]. For if reason so dictates, the will necessarily will do it; and if reason does not so dictate, the will cannot do it. The dictating, however, will not be free since it is understood prior to every dictate of the free divine will. Third, the antecedent is proved by the example given by the Apostle of the potter of clay with respect to his vessels in *Romans* 9 [33]. Fourth, in the case of two things, *a* and *b*, which are producible and equally possible, there is no reason why this one is produced and not that one except primarily because it pleases the divine will. Therefore, in like manner in the case of actions, why this ought to be done and not that, and why it is just for the human will to do this and not that.

Moreover, the created will behaves this way in some cases, as, for example, in the case of two persons placed under a sentence of death. If I am able to free only one of them, I will justly free him whom I shall have willed to free without reason antecedently moving toward the side of this one more than that one. And from the very fact that I will to free this one [l**], the act of freeing him is just. Between two who are equally suitable, however, I will give to this one and not to that one, and my act of giving to this one will be a good and just action, and the deprivation of a gift to the other is not unjust [34].

OBJECTIONS:

FIRST, concerning divine activity specifically. God may do nothing unless from reason antecedently dictating and judging and as it were stating why it is that he so acts. And God wills so to act in the first place because God does everything wisely and rationally and therefore from intellectual reason [m**] antecedently dictating, for wisdom is intellectual reason. So *Wisdom* 7: *Wisdom reaches from one end of the earth to the other, and arranges all things* [35].

Again, there is the verse in *Ephesians* 1, *God administers all things according to the counsel of his will* [36], on which a gloss comments, that is, *according to his will which comes from reason* [37]. Further, according to the Philosopher in the *Ethics* III, chap. 7, *counsel supposes reason antecedently dictating* [38].

Again, God acts by choice, and therefore from reason antecedently dictating.

The antecedent is evident, for the predestined are called *the chosen* [n**].

The inference is evident because *choice supposes an antecedently dictating judgment*; chaps. 6 and 8 [39].

QUARTO [o**], modus agendi et regendi magis decens et conveniens et honorabilis principanti attribuendus est Deo; sed videtur minus decens et minus honorabile principi et regenti quod agat et velit et ordinet non ex ratione praedictante et quod non habeat aliud propter quid nisi *Sic volo, sic iubeo, sit pro ratione voluntas* [40].

QUINTO, voluntas creata esset rationabilior in volendo et agendo quam divina quia *semper habet cur* secundum Anselmum, *De Veritate* 12 [41].

SEXTO, voluntas nostra esset magis recta praecedendo rationem in volendo quia esset conformior in hoc divinae voluntati [42].

SEPTIMO, divina voluntas vult et agit propter finem, igitur ex ratione praedictante quia finis dicit potissime rationem propter quid.
Antecedens probatur, quia omne agens rationale [p**] agit propter finem proprium, *universa propter semetipsum operatus est Dominus* [q**] [43].

OCTAVO, frustra quaererent doctores rationem et propter quid alicuius agere divini; sufficeret enim dicere quod Deus vult, et esset ultimum et principale propter quid non resolubile [44].

Consequens est falsum, quia secundo *Sententiarum* dist. 1 [r**] quaerit Magister *quare Deus creavit naturam humanam et angelicam* [45]; et dist. 18 *quare creavit virum ante mulierem* [46], et *quare voluit ex uno homine facere totaliter genus humanum* [47], et *quare voluit facere mulierem de costa viri* [48], *quare viri dormientis, non vigilantis* [49]; et dist. 21 *quare Deus redemit hominem, non angelum* [50]; et dist. 23 *quare permisit hominem tentari quem praescivit casurum* [51]. Et multa huiusmodi quaeruntur a sanctis [52].

NONO, ea quae Deus non facit nec vult facere, non facit nec vult facere ex ratione praedictante illa non esse facienda; igitur pari ratione de his quae facit et vult facere.
Antecedens probatur: quaedam enim ideo non vult nec facit quia non esset conveniens suae dignitati. Patet per Augustinum, *De Quaestionibus Veteris et Novae Legis*, et ponitur 1 *Sententiarum* dist. 42: *Omnia quidem potest Deus, sed non facit nec faciet nisi quod convenit eius veritati* [s**] *et iustitiae* [53]. Sequitur: *Potuit Deus cuncta facere simul, sed ratio prohibuit* [54]. Et cap. 5: *Maximum Deum omnia facere posse praeter ea* [t**] *sola quibus eius dignitas laederetur eiusque excellentiae derogaretur* [55].
Confirmatur: Anselmus, 1 *Cur Deus Homo* cap. 10: *In Deo sicut quodlibet parvum inconveniens sequitur impossibilitas, ita quamlibet parvam rationem, si maiori ratione non vincitur, comitatur* [u**] *necessitas* [56]. Et libro 2 cap. 10 reddit causam quare Deus non fecit tot homines impeccabiles (sicut est Christus) quot sunt personae in divinis, dicens sic: *respondeo, quia tunc ratio fieri nullatenus hoc exigebat, sed omnino, quia Deus sine ratione nihil facit, prohibebat* [57].

FOURTH [o**], that mode of acting and ruling which is the more fitting and suitable and honorable for a ruler must be attributed to God. But it seems less fitting and honorable for the sovereign and ruler to act and will and decree in a way that does not come from reason antecedently dictating, and to have no other why except *So I will, so I order, let will serve as the reason* [40].

FIFTH, the created will would be more rational in willing and acting than the divine will because *it always has a why* according to Anselm in *On Truth* 12 [41].

SIXTH, our will would be more upright by preceding reason in volition because it would be more conformed to the divine will in doing this [42].

SEVENTH, the divine will wills and acts for the sake of an end, and therefore from reason antecedently dictating because the end principally states the reason why.
Proof of the antecedent: Every rational [p**] agent acts for the sake of his particular end, and *the Lord* [q**] *has made all things for himself* [43].

EIGHTH, teachers would in vain seek the reason and the why for any divine activity. For it would suffice to say that God wills it, and this would be the final and principal why not susceptible of analysis [44].
The consequent is false because the Master inquires in the second book of the *Sentences*, dist. 1 [r**], *why God created human and angelic nature* [45]; and in dist. 18, *why God created man before woman* [46], and *why God willed to make the human race totally from one human being* [47], and *why God willed to make woman from a rib of man* [48], and *why of a man who was sleeping, not awake* [49]; and in dist. 21, *why God redeemed a human, not an angel* [50]; and in dist. 23, *why God permitted a human to be tempted whom he foreknew would fall* [51]. And many things of this nature are asked by holy people [52].

NINTH, those things which God does not do and does not will to do are not done and not willed on account of reason antecedently dictating that they ought not to be done; therefore, in like manner with respect to those things which he does and wills to do.
Proof of the antecedent: God does not will and does not do certain things because it would not suit his dignity. This is evident from Augustine in *On Questions of the Old and of the New Law*, cited in the first book of the *Sentences*, dist. 42: *Certainly God can do all things, but he does not do nor will he do anything except what suits his truth* [s**] *and justice* [53]. There follows: *God was able to make the whole at the same time, but reason prohibited it* [54]. And in sect. 5: *That the supreme God can do all things except those* [t**] *alone by which his dignity would be damaged and which would detract from his excellence* [55].
Confirmation: Anselm states in *Why God Became Man* I, chap. 10: *In the case of God, just as impossibility follows from any slight unsuitability, so necessity attends* [u**] *any little reason if it is not overridden by a stronger reason* [56]. And in bk. 2, chap. 10 he reports the cause why God did not make as many people impeccable (as is Christ) as there are divine persons, speaking as follows: *I answer, because reason in no way required this to be done at that time, but, since God does nothing without a reason, entirely prohibited it* [57].

DECIMO, ab aeterno aliquos elegit ad beatitudinem ex ratione praedictante quia scilicet praescivit eorum merita, aut saltem aliquos [v**] per voluntatem reprobavit et deputavit ad poenam ex ratione praedictanti quia praevidit mala eorum futura; igitur pari ratione in aliis.

Confirmatur: Deus ideo vult mala punire quia ratio prohibet, et quia non est decens nec conveniens aliter velle per Anselmum, 1 *Cur Deus Homo* cap. 12, dicentem quod ideo *Deus non relinquit peccatum impunitum quia non decet Deum aliquid inordinatum in suo regno dimittere, et quia similiter esset apud Deum peccanti et non peccanti, quod Deo non convenit* [58]. Et infra: *Quamvis Deus praecipiat nobis dimittere peccantibus in nos, nihilominus dimittere peccatores impunitos Deum non decet, nec hoc derogat eius benignitati. Libertas* [w**] *enim non nisi ad hoc quod expedit aut quod decet se extendit, nec benignitas est quae Deo aliquid indecens operatur* [59].

UNDECIMO, divina voluntas quibuscumque peccatoribus miseretur et parcit ex ratione praedictante illud esse iustum ex natura rerum; igitur pari ratione in aliis, aeque enim rationabiliter vult in aliis.

Antecedens probatur per Anselmum, *Proslogii* 9 [x**], dicentem: *Ideo misericors es, quia totus et summe bonus. Et cum videatur, cur bonis bona et malis mala retribuas, illud mirandum est, cur malis et reis bona retribuas* [60]. Sequitur: *de plenitudine bonitatis quia peccatoribus pius es, et in altitudine bonitatis tuae latet qua ratione hoc es* [y**]. *Licet enim bonis bona et malis mala retribuas ex bonitate, ratio tamen iustitiae hoc postulare videtur. Cum vero malis bona tribuis, mirum est cur summe iustus hoc velle potuit* [61]. Et infra cap. sequenti: *Si misericors es quia es summe bonus, et summe bonus non es* [z**] *nisi summe iustus, vere idcirco es misericors quia summe iustus es* [62]. Et infra: *Cum punis malos, iustum es, quia illorum meritis convenit; cum vero parcis malis, istum est, non quia illorum meritis convenit, sed quia bonitati tuae condecens est. Et salvando nos iustus es, non quia nobis reddis debitum, sed quia facis quod decet te summum bonum* [63]. Sequitur: *Iustum quippe est te sic esse iustum, ut iustior nequeas cogitari. Quod nequaquam esses* [a***], *si tantum bonis bona, et non malis mala redderes* [64]. Haec Anselmus.

DUODECIMO principaliter arguitur sic: aliquod agere est melius et laudabilius altero ex natura rei, non ex eo primo quia Deus sic velit et ordinet sed potius econtra, ideo sic Deus vult magis et ordinat quia melius et convenientius est ex natura rei; igitur et de bono simpliciter.

Consequentia patet, quia quod est prima causa et ratio boni etiam est secunda causa et ratio maioris boni.

Antecedens probatur primo, secundum Augustinum, 13 *De* [b***] *Trinitate* cap. 10: *Alius modus reddendi nos et syllogizandi vel sanandi miserias nostras quam per filii Dei incarnationem et passionem fuit Deo possibilis, sed nullus alius fuit miseriae nostrae sanandae convenientior* [65].

TENTH, from eternity God elected some to beatitude on account of reason antecedently dictating because he foreknew their merits. Or at least he reprobated some [v**] by his will and assigned them to punishment on account of reason antecedently dictating because he foresaw their future evils. Therefore, in like manner in other cases.

Confirmation: God wills to punish evils because reason prohibits them, and because it is neither fitting nor suitable to will otherwise according to Anselm who says, in *Why God Became Man* I, chap. 12, that *God does not leave sin unpunished because it is not fitting that God let go something that is disordered in his kingdom, and because God would be dealing with the sinner and the one who does not sin in the same way, something which does not suit God* [58]. And later he says: *Although God commands us to forgive those sinning against us, nevertheless it is not fitting that God let sinners go unpunished, nor does this detract from his benevolence. For liberty* [w**] *pertains only to what is advantageous or what is fitting, nor is that benvolence which produces something unbefitting God* [59].

ELEVENTH, the divine will has mercy on all sinners and spares them from reason antecedently dictating that to be just by its nature. Therefore, in like manner in other cases, for God wills equally rationally in other matters.

The antecedent is proved by Anselm who states in the *Proslogion* 9 [x**]: *Therefore you are merciful because you are completely and supremely good. And while it may be apparent why you repay good things to those who are good and evil things to those who are evil, it is a source of wonder why you repay good things to those who are evil and guilty* [60]. There follows: *It is from the plenitude of your goodness that you are kind to sinners, and in the depth of your goodness is hidden the reason why you are* [y**] *this way. For although out of goodness you repay good things to those who are good and evil things to those who are evil, yet the definition of justice seems to require this. But when you give good things to those who are evil, we wonder why the supremely just one could have willed this* [61]. And later, in the following section: *If you are merciful because you are supremely good, and you are supremely good only because you are* [z**] *supremely just, then truly you are merciful because you are supremely just* [62]. And later: *When you punish those who are evil, it is just, because this suits their deserts; but when you spare those who are evil, it is just, not because this suits their deserts, but because it is befitting to your goodness. And in saving us you are just, not because you give us what is due, but because you do what is befitting to you as supreme good* [63]. There follows: *Surely it is just that you are so just that you cannot be thought to be more just. You would not at all be* [a***] *so if you only repaid good things to those who are good and did not repay evil things to those who are evil* [64]. Anselm states these things.

TWELFTH, it is argued as follows: Some activity is better and more praiseworthy than another by its nature and not first from the fact that God so wills and decrees; rather, the contrary is the case, viz., God so wills and decrees more because it is better and more suitable by its nature. Therefore this is also true in the case of the simply good.

The inference is evident because that which is the first cause and reason for good likewise is the second cause and reason for a greater good.

The antecedent is proved first by the statement of Augustine in *On* [b***] *the Trinity* XIII, chap. 10: *Another means of restoring us and of syllogizing or of allaying our miseries than through*

Ex quo patet quod non ideo iste est convenientior quia Deus magis voluit istum, sed econtra. Secundo, per Anselmum, primo *Cur Deus Homo* cap. 16: *Rationalis creatura futura beata est a Deo praescita in quocumque rationabili et perfecto numero, ita ut nec maiorem nec minorem illum esse deceat; scit enim Deus in quo numero melius eam deceat constituti* [c***], *et in eo illam constituit quem ad hoc* [d***] *decentiorem intellexit* [66]. Tertio, quia ex natura rei, scilicet operationis et obiecti, magis bonum est diligere Deum super omnia quam velle levare festucam, quia per illud magis coniungitur et assimilatur fini ultimo et summo bono; et quia si velle levare festucam esset beatitudo et formale summum bonum [e***] viatoris, igitur levare festucam esset finis ultimus creaturae rationalis et praeponendus Deo quia praevolendus et [f***] praediligendus Deo [g***], et ratio sic dictans foret recta.

AD PRIMUM negatur consequentia. Sufficit quod velle et agere sit conforme recto dictamini rationabili formaliter inexistenti in principio actionis [67].

AD SECUNDUM accipitur consilium non [h***] proprie et stricte pro discursu deliberativo super agendum implicante antecedenter aliquam ignorantiam vel ambiguitatem et obscuritatem, sed pro dictamine intellectuali respectu agibilium. Et dicitur Deus velle ex ratione quia rationabiliter et conformiter rectae rationi formaliter inexistenti [68].

AD TERTIUM: in Deo est non [i***] proprie et stricte electio prout de ea loquitur Philosophus 3 *Ethicorum* sub determinatione ad alteram partem oppositorum post discursum syllogisticum practicum deliberativum et inquisitivum [69], sed large pro libera et recta determinatione voluntatis ad alterum.

AD QUARTUM: procedit de voluntate quae non est prima causa et regula et mensura rectitudinis, sed subiecta legibus superioribus et regulabilis per aliud.

AD QUINTUM negatur consequentia propter idem.

AD SEXTUM negatur consequentia.
Ad probationem: non esset conformior in modo volendi, id est, volendo sicut Deus vult et iubet eam velle, nec conformior voluntati divinae ut oboediens pracipienti, sed conformior per superbam praesumptionem et usurpationem divinae dominationis, quo modo Lucifer voluit esse similis Deo.

AD SEPTIMUM: non sequitur quod primo ex ratione praedictante, quia illa ratio

the incarnation and passion of the Son of God was possible for God, but no other was more suitable for allaying our misery [65]. From this it is evident that it is not the case that that means is more suitable because God willed it more, but the contrary. Second, the antecedent is proved by Anselm in the first book of *Why God Became Man*, chap. 16: *The rational creature who will be happy in heaven is foreknown by God in whatever reasonable and perfect number, so that it is not fitting that that number be greater or lesser. For God knows in what number it is more fitting that the rational creature be created* [c***], *and he created him in that number which he perceived more fitting for this purpose* [d***] [66]. Third, by its nature, specifically, the nature of the operation and the object, it is a greater good to love God above all things than to will to pick up a straw because one is united and assimilated more to the final end and highest good by that act. Further, if willing to pick up a straw were the beatitude and formally the highest good [e***] of a viator, then picking up a straw would be the final end of a rational creature and would deserve to be put before God because it is to be willed and [f***] loved before God [g***], and reason so dictating would be right.

REPLY TO THE FIRST OBJECTION: The inference is denied. It suffices that volition and activity be conformed to a right rational dictate formally present in the begining of the action [67].

REPLY TO THE SECOND OBJECTION: *Counsel* is not [h***] taken properly and strictly as a deliberative discourse upon what is to be done which implies that there is antecedently some ignorance or ambiguity or obscurity, but rather, as an intellectual dictate regarding actions. And God is said to will from reason because he wills rationally and conformably to right reason formally present [68].

REPLY TO THE THIRD OBJECTION: In the case of God choice does not [i***] occur in a proper and strict sense as the Philosopher speaks of it in the *Ethics* III, as a determination to one of two sides of opposites after deliberative and inquisitive practical syllogistic argument [69]. Rather, it occurs in a broad sense, as the free and right determination of the will to one of two things.

REPLY TO THE FOURTH OBJECTION: It proceeds with respect to a will which is not the first cause and rule and measure of rectitude, but which is subject to higher laws and regulated by something else.

REPLY TO THE FIFTH OBJECTION: The inference is denied on account of the same consideration.

REPLY TO THE SIXTH OBJECTION: The inference is denied.
Reply to the proof: It would not be more conformed in the manner of willing, that is, in willing as God wills and orders it to will, nor would it be more conformed to the divine will as obeying the commander, but it would be more conformed by arrogant presumption and usurpation of the divine dominion, in which way Lucifer willed to be similar to God.

REPLY TO THE SEVENTH OBJECTION: It does not follow that <the divine will wills and

praedictativa de fine secundum naturalis intelligentiae ordinem praesupponit determinationem voluntatis de agere *b* et propter huiusmodi finem, ita quod secundum ordinem rationis primo est per intellectum exhibitio ostensiva et pure apprehensiva, secundo determinatio voluntatis de agere *b* sic et propter talem [j***] finem, tertio iudicium et approbatio intellectus.

AD OCTAVAM negatur consequentia. Licet enim inter propositiones significantes divinem agere ad extra et divinum velle et intelligere respectu agibilium sit ordo, et una sit notior et prior secundum intelligentiam quam alia et quasi causalis et convenienter responsiva ad quaestionem propter quod de aliquo [k***], tamen *propter quid ad quod* stabit. Resolutio erit velle divinum, non ratio dictativa, quia taliter et taliter sit volendum et agendum. Et licet aliqua propositio significans Deum velle habeat secundum ordinem rationis aliquam priorem quasi talem significantem divinum intelligere vel naturam rei, tamen haec propositio ulterius reducibilis in aliam propositionem significantem Deum velle ita, ut reducantur iste ordo ultimate in libertatem divini beneplaciti. Unde Hugo, primo *De Sacramentis* parte secunda cap. ultimo: *Cum in Deo sint tria: sapientia, potentia, voluntas; primordinabiles causae a voluntate divina igitur proficiscuntur, per sapientiam diriguntur, per potestantem producuntur. Voluntas enim movet, sapientia disponit, potestans explicat* [70].

Item, licet in forma loquendi doctores videantur quaerere propter quid Deus sic agere voluit et sic agit, tamen realiter est inquirere causam et propter quid alicuius effectus, ut quaerere propter quid creavit hominem est quaerere quae est causa ipsius hominis et [l***] ad quod [m***] Deus ordinat hominem creatum.

AD NONUM negatur antecedens loquendo de rebus factibilibus et per se productionem terminantibus et quas Deus de potentia absoluta potest facere.

Ad probationem primam: illa veritas et iustitia non intelligitur veritas dictaminis praecedentis omnem determinationem liberam divinae voluntatis, sed intellegitur veritas iudicii intellectualis cum iustitia et rectitudine determinatorum divinae voluntatis.

Ad dictum Magistri: intellegitur non de productione alicuius causabilis multipliciter [n***], sed de productione cum circumstantiis deformibus et defectuosis, ut mentiri et facere peccatum.

Ad confirmationem: si sit inconveniens simpliciter ut mentiri, sequitur impossibilitas simpliciter; si autem sit inconveniens secundum leges positas, sequitur impossibilitas secundum leges ordinatas, ut hominem sine fide placere Deo vel finaliter impaenitentem non damnari; sed talis inconvenientiae ratio prima est determinatio libera divinae voluntatis de opposito. Quod autem dicit, *quamlibet parvam rationem* etc., non intelligitur quod aliqua ratio recta dictet hoc a Deo esse faciendum et alia ratio magis recta vel fortior dictet oppositum et quod Deus sequatur fortiorem necessitatus, sed intellegitur quod si simpliciter rationabile est Deum sic facere, sequitur necessario quod Deus sic faciet. Si vero nobis appareat esse rationabile Deo sic esse faciendum, non necessario sequetur Deum sic facere quia rationabile magis est Deum aliter facere; sed huius ratio est determinatio divinae voluntatis.

acts> first from reason antecedently dictating because that antecedently dictating reason concerning the end presupposes, according to the order of natural understanding, a determination of the will about doing *b* and for the sake of such an end. Thus, according to the order of reason, there is first a presentation by the intellect which is demonstrative and concerned purely with apprehension; second, a determination of the will about doing *b* in this manner and for the sake of such [j***] an end; and third, the intellect's judgment and approval.

REPLY TO THE EIGHTH OBJECTION: The inference is denied. For although there is an order among propositions signifying outward divine activity and the divine volition and understanding regarding actions, and one proposition is better known than another and prior to another according to understanding and as it were causally and suitably responsive to the question *why* about something [k***], yet the question *why toward that* will remain. The explanation will be the divine volition, not reason dictating, because so and so ought to be willed and done. And although some proposition signifying the divine volition has, according to the order of reason, some proposition prior to it as it were signifying such divine understanding or the nature of the thing, nevertheless this proposition is further reducible into another proposition signifying that God so wills, so that that order is finally reduced to the freedom of the divine good pleasure. So Hugh states in *On the Sacraments*, bk.I, pt. 2, final chap.: *Since there are three things in God, viz., wisdom, power, and will, the primordial causes therefore proceed from the divine will, are directed by wisdom, and are produced by power. For the will moves, wisdom disposes, and power executes* [70].

Again, although teachers seem to ask in the form of their speech why it is that God willed so to act and does act, yet in reality this is an inquiry about the cause and the why of some effect, so that asking why it is that God created a human being is asking what is the cause of that human being and [l***] toward what [m***] God orders the created human.

REPLY TO THE NINTH OBJECTION: The antecedent is denied in speaking of things which are producible and which complete production through themselves and which God can do with regard to his absolute power.

Reply to the first proof: That truth and justice is not understood to be the truth of a dictate preceding every free determination of the divine will, but it is understood to be the truth of an intellectual judgment together with the justice and rectitude of the determinations of the divine will.

Reply to the statement of the Master: It is understood not of the production of something able to be caused in various ways [n***], but of production with deviant and defective circumstances, as, for example, lying and committing a sin.

Reply to the confirmation: If it is simply unsuitable, as, for example, is lying, what follows is simple impossibility. On the other hand, if it is unsuitable according to the established laws, what follows is impossibility according to the ordained laws, as, for example, that a human being without faith be pleasing to God or that a human being who is finally impenitent not be damned. But the primary reason for such unsuitability is the free determination of the divine will regarding the opposite. What he says, *any little reason*, etc., is not to be taken to mean that some right reason may dictate that this ought to be done by God and that another reason which is more right or stronger may dictate the opposite and that God, being necessitated, follows the stronger. Rather, it is to be taken

AD DECIMUM: non praedestinavit quia praesciret merita, sed reprobavit propter demerita praescita. Sed ratio dictans futuros finaliter impaenitentes fore iuste damnandus ideo recta erat quia divina voluntas hoc libere determinavit quasi pro lege.

Ad confirmationem: conceditur quod de velle divino respectu agibilium formantur propositiones et respectu aliquarum sunt aliae quasi causales priores significantes aliquod iustum et debitum. Et licet hominibus appareat secundum cursum et ordinem regulariter institutum quod talis propositio causalis sit necessaria et immediata, tamen secundum veritatem illa reducibilis est ad aliam propositionem quasi causalem et priorem significantem determinationem et ordinationem liberam divinae voluntatis. Ideo enim indecens est inordinationem peccati dimitti impunitam et non reordinari per poenam quia voluntas divina oppositum instituit pro iustissima lege.

AD UNDECIMUM per idem.

AD DUODECIMUM: loquendo de bono iusto simpliciter, negatur antecedens.

Ad primam probationem: si Deus hunc modum per voluntatem non ordinavisset [o***], non foret conveniens; et si alium ordinasset, ille alius foret conveniens. Sed Augustinus intendit quod ex apparentibus nobis notitias naturaliter acceptibiles et secundum iudicia communiter accepta ex naturis rerum, nullus alius apparet homini efficacior et aptior ad excitandum hominem ad Dei dilectionem et laudem.

Ad secundum: huiusmodi maior decentia non sequitur per se et necessario talem numerum salvandorum [p***]. Deus enim simpliciter posset maiorem instituere, nec indecenter vel irrationabiliter in hoc se haberet; sed huiusmodi maior decentia ultimate reducibilis est in liberam determinationem divinae voluntatis. Licet forte talem numerum concomitetur corresponditer aliqua proprietas quae congrue apparet homini correspondere praecipue multitudini salvandorum inspiciendo ius naturale institutum (si talis numerus et congruens correspondentia [q***] iuxta illam proprietatem numeri revelaretur homini), sed omnia ista subsunt simpliciter liberae ordinationi divinae voluntatis.

Ad tertiam: illud est verum de bonitate naturali vel morali ex genere; illud etiam est verum de bonitate iusta simpliciter secundum leges positas et suppositis certis condicionibus et circumstantiis; sed non simpliciter respectu potentiae Dei absolutae, vel licet ita esset adhuc, prima ratio est ordinatio divinae voluntatis qua voluit unicuique rei dare talem et tantum gradum entitatis.

to mean that if it is simply rational that God so does, it follows necessarily that God will so do. If in fact it appears to us to be rational that it ought so to be done by God, it will not necessarily follow that God so does because it is more rational that God do otherwise. But the reason for this is the determination of the divine will.

REPLY TO THE TENTH OBJECTION: God did not predestine because he foresaw merits, but he reprobated on account of foreseen demerits. But reason dictating that those who will be finally impenitent will be justly damned was right because the divine will freely determined this as it were for a law.

Reply to the confirmation: It is conceded that propositions are formed about the divine will with regard to actions, and that with respect to some there are other propositions which are as it were causal and prior and signifying that something is just and due. And although it may appear to human beings according to the regularly established course and order that such a causal proposition is necessary and immediate, yet in truth that proposition is reducible to another propositon which is as it were causal and prior, signifying a free determination and decree of the divine will. For it is unfitting that the disorder of sin be let go unpunished and not be reordered through punishment because the divine will established the opposite as a law which is most just.

REPLY TO THE ELEVENTH OBJECTION: Through the same considerations.

REPLY TO THE TWELFTH OBJECTION: Speaking of the simply just good, the antecedent is denied.

Reply to the first proof: If God had not decreed [o***] this means by his will, it would not be suitable. And if he should have decreed another means, that other one would be suitable. But Augustine has in mind that according to ideas naturally receivable by us from appearances and according to judgments commonly taken from the natures of things, no other means appears to a human being to be more efficacious and more appropriate for arousing a human being to the love and praise of God.

Reply to the second proof: Such greater fittingness does not follow such a number of the saved [p***] by itself and necessarily. For God could simply establish a greater number, and God would not behave unfittingly or irrationally in doing this. But such greater fittingness is finally reducible into a free determination of the divine will. Although by chance some property may accompany correspondingly such a number, a property which appears to a human being fittingly to correspond particularly to the multiplicity of the saved in examining the natural law which has been instituted (if such a number and the fitting correspondence [q***] of the number with that property were revealed to a human being), yet all these are subject simply to the free decree of the divine will.

Reply to the third proof: That is true in the case of natural or generic moral goodness. That is likewise true in the case of simply just goodness according to the established laws and supposing certain conditions and circumstances. But it is not true simply with respect to the absolute power of God. In other words, although it were so thus far, the primary reason is the decree of the divine will by which God willed to give every single thing such and so great a degree of entity.

QUARTA CONCLUSIO, sine assertione: Omne aliud a Deo quod est viatori formaliter bonum et iustum simpliciter potest de potentia Dei absoluta ei inesse et non esse ei bonum et iustum simpliciter, loquendo de bono et iusto secundum bonitatem theologicam et supernaturalem quae facit hominem simpliciter bonum et iustum.

Probatur primo de actu, quia sit nomen proprium et absolutum illius entitatis *b*, sive illa sit actus diligendi Deum super omnia sive alius; tunc *b* potest a solo Deo causari in voluntate; igitur tunc secundum *b* voluntas non erit iusta nec iniusta, sed secundum Anselmum, *De Casu Diaboli* cap .14 [71]...

Item, *b* potest elici a furioso vel somniante.

Item, potest in casu elici contra conscientiam pro tali loco et tempore.

Item, potest a Deo prohiberi pro certo loco et tempore, vel sub tanto gradu, vel actus alius toto conatu eliciendus praecipi.

Item, potest esse in homine existente in mortali.

Probo: possibile est quod Sortes aliquando peccaverit mortaliter nec Deus ei remiserit peccatum, et tamen *b* est in eius voluntate a quibuscumque causis hoc fiat; nec Deus necessitatur remittere peccatum praeteritum propter positionem illius formae et qualitatis in anima.

Item, *b* potest ex divina voluntate fieri magis vel minus bonus et iustus simpliciter quia etiam actum pure indifferentem potest facere esse iustum et bonum per praeceptum vel consilium, et non per se et necessario habet huiusmodi bonitatem; igitur potest esse non bonus.

Ex his sequitur idem de habitu specialiter, quia potest esse in homine peccator.

CONTRA:

SICUT prima et summa veritas ad alias veritates, sic prima bonitas ad alias bonitates, quia non minus esse verum aliquid a primo vero habet esse verum ab eo quam esse bonum aliud a primo bono habet esse bonum ab illo; sed isto non obstante, aliquid est per se verum ex natura rei sic quod non potest non esse verum, ut hominem esse risibilem et non esse asinum; igitur...

SECUNDO, voluntatem creatam subici et conformari voluntati divinae et velle conformiter divinae ordinationi et sicut Deus vult eam velle est bonum creaturae rationali aliud a Deo et non potest ei inesse et esse non bonum et iustum.

Probo, quia si taliter velle not sit bonum, igitur non est conforme divinae voluntati et ordinationi, igitur taliter velle non est velle conformiter divinae ordinationi; in huiusmodi enim conformitate consistit formaliter rectitudo et iustitia voluntatis creatae.

Confirmatur: tunc voluntatem creatam non subici nec conformari creatoris voluntati esset rectum et iustum; igitur repugnare et deformari esset istum; igitur voluntas creata est recta, non voluntas Dei.

FOURTH CONCLUSION, without assertion: Everything other than God which formally is simply good and just for a viator can, with respect to the absolute power of God, be present in him and fail to be simply good and just for him, speaking of good and just according to the theological and supernatural goodness which makes a human being simply good and just.

This conclusion is proved first of an act. Let the proper and non-relative name of that entity be *b*, whether it be an act of loving God above all things or another act. Then *b* can be caused in the will by God alone. Therefore, the will then will be neither just nor unjust in accordance with *b*, but according to Anselm in *On the Fall of the Devil*, chap. 14... [71].

Again, *b* can be elicited by a madman or by a dreamer.

Again, it can, in a particular case, be elicited contrary to conscience for such a place and time.

Again, God can prohibit it for a certain place and time or on condition of being of so great a degree, or command another act to be elicited with all one's might.

Again, it can be in a human being existing in a state of mortal sin.

I prove this as follows. It is possible that Socrates shall have sinned mortally at some time and that God shall not have remitted his sin and yet that *b* is in his will by whatever causes this may be done. Nor is it the case that God is necessitated to remit that past sin on account of the placement of that form and quality in his soul.

Again, *b* can be made more or less simply good and just by the divine will because God can make even an act which is purely indifferent to be just and good by a precept or counsel, and it does not have such goodness through itself and necessarily. Therefore, it can fail to be good.

From these considerations the same conclusion follows with regard to a habit specifically, because it can be in a human being who is a sinner.

OBJECTIONS:

JUST AS the first and highest truth is related to other truths, so is the first goodness related to other good things. For no less does something being true from the first truth have its status of being true from it than does another being good from the first good take its status of being good from that. But that not withstanding, something is true according to itself by its nature in such a way that it cannot fail to be true, as, for example, that a human being is capable of laughter and is not a donkey. Therefore...

SECOND, that the created will be subject and conformed to the divine will and that it will conformably to the divine decree and as God wills it to will is a good for a rational creature other than God and cannot be present in him and fail to be good and just.

I prove this as follows. If willing in such a way is not good, then it is not conformed to the divine will and decree. And therefore, willing in such a way is not willing conformably to the divine decree, for the rectitude and justice of the created will consists formally in such conformity.

Confirmation: Then the created will not being subject and conformed to the will of the Creator would be right and just. Therefore, to oppose it and deviate from it would be just. And therefore, the created will would be right, not the will of God.

TERTIO, id propter quod omnis alia virtus est virtus et omnis actio hominis bona est bona est ex se essentialiter bonum actus; et virtus oboedentiae [r***] est huiusmodi. Nam Augustinus 8 *Super Genesim* cap. 4: *oboedientiam* [s***] *possum verissime dicere solam esse virtutem omni creaturae rationali agenti sub Dei potestate* [72].

Confirmatur: quod est iustum et praesuppositum omni praecepto vel consilio divino tanquam prius naturaliter non est contingenter iustum quia a Deo libere praeceptum vel ordinatum; sed esse oboediendum Deo et oboedire Deo est huiusmodi .

Probo, quia inconvenienter daret superior praecepta nisi prius verum et rectum esset quod eius voluntati est oboediendum, dationi enim praecepti praesupponitur iusta subiectatio et dominatio; igitur praesupponitur tanquam iustum quod est oboediendum; ideo igitur convenienter datur praeceptum creaturae rationali quia oboediendum est Deo. Quantum igitur impossibile est Deum et creaturam esse et Deum non esse dominum creaturae, tam impossibile est non esse iustum et rectum esse oboediendum Deo et creaturam rationalem debere oboedire Deo. Licitum enim esset creaturae diligere se supra Deum, et contemnendo [t***] et postponendo eius praeceptum non peccaret.

QUARTO, illus est ex se et necessario bonum quod impossibile est convenire homini quin faciat ipsum meliorem; sed aliquod bonum creaturae rationali est huiusmodi. Probo, quia implere mandata Dei et consilia; in hoc enim consistit bonitas et rectitudo voluntatis; igitur quanto magis sic exercetur et conformatur, tanto est magis bona et iusta.

QUINTO, si omnis actus voluntatis creatae est contingenter bonus et accidentaliter, sequitur quod omnis potest esse non solum non bonus sed malus.

Consequentia patet, quia cui contingenter et accidentaliter inest unum oppositum, potest inesse reliquum; et quia, iuxta probationes conclusionis, potest probari a Deo, saltem pro loco et tempore. Actus enim non necessario bonus sed indifferens potest prohiberi, et quia quod est homini possibile et licitum potest ei a Deo praecipi; sed non producere *b* actum pro tali tempore est homini possibile et licitum quia praecepta affirmativa non obligant pro semper; igitur non elicere potest praecipi et elicere prohiberi; igitur talis actus potest esse transgressio, etiam mortalis [u***].

Falsitas consequentis probatur, de actu dilectionis Dei super omnia et de velle oboedire Deo et voluntatem velle sicut Deo placet et sicut Deus vult eam velle, qui actus sit *b*; tunc si [v***] *b* potest esse peccatum et iniustum, sequitur quod quanto quis magis oboediret et consentiret et adhaereret Deo et converteretur ad Deum, tanto magis averteretur a Deo et dissentiret et rebelleret et recederet, et consequenter tanto miserior esset.

Confirmatur falsitas consequentis, quia voluntas per eundem actum frueretur et uteretur Deo, et praeponeret Deum omnibus et postponeret ipsum creaturae et praeponeret [w***] creaturam Deo, et contemneret Deum et ipsum super omnia diligeret. Probo, quia per peccatum mortale praeponitur creatura Deo; in hoc enim distinguitur a mortali veniale secundum Augustinum, *Enchiridion* 69 [73] et 12 *Civitate* cap. 26 [x***] [74].

THIRD, that on account of which every other virtue is a virtue and every good action of a human being is good is a good act of itself, essentially. And the virtue of obedience [r***] is of this type. For Augustine says in *On Genesis* VIII, chap. 4: *I can most truly say that obedience* [s***] *alone is a virtue for every rational creature acting under the power of God* [72].

Confirmation: What is just and presupposed by every divine precept or counsel as naturally prior is not contingently just because freely commanded or decreed by God. But that one ought to obey God and to obey God is of this type.

I prove this as follows. God would unsuitably give higher precepts unless first it were true and right that one ought to obey his will, for giving a precept presupposes a just subjection and lordship. Therefore, it is presupposed as being just that one ought to obey. And therefore, a precept is fittingly given to a rational creature because God ought to be obeyed. Therefore, in so far as it is impossible that God and a creature exist and that God not be the lord of the creature, so it is impossible that it not be just and right that God ought to be obeyed and that a rational creature ought to obey God. For <otherwise> it would be permissible for a creature to love himself above God, and he would not sin in contemning [t***] God's precept and putting it second.

FOURTH, that is good of itself and necessarily which cannot be found in a human being without making him better; but some good for a rational creature is of this type.

I prove this by the case of fulfilling the commands and counsels of God, for the goodness and rectitude of the will consists in this. Therefore, how much the more it is so exercised and conformed, so much the more is it good and just.

FIFTH, if every act of the created will is contingently and accidentally good, it follows that every act can not only fail to be good but also be evil.

The inference is evident. First, that which has one member of opposites present in it contingently and accidentally can have the other one present in it. Second, according to the proofs of the conclusion, this can be proved true by God, at least for a place and time. For an act which is not necessarily good but indifferent can be prohibited. Further, what is possible and licit for a human being can be commanded to him by God. But not to produce an act, *b*, for such a time is possible and licit for a human being because affirmative precepts do not oblige for all times. Therefore, not eliciting *b* can be commanded and eliciting *b* can be prohibited. And therefore, such an act can be a transgression, even a mortal one [u***].

The falsity of the consequent is proved with regard to the act of loving God above all things and with regard to willing to obey God and that the will will as is pleasing to God and as God wills it to will. And let us call this act, *b*. Then if [v***] *b* can be a sin and unjust, it follows that how much the more someone would obey God and be in accord with God and adhere to God and be turned towards God, so much the more would he be turned away from God and be out of harmony with God and rebel against and withdraw from God, and consequently, so much the more miserable would he be.

The falsity of the consequent is confirmed as follows. By the same act, the will would enjoy God and use God, and would put God before everything and put him after a creature and put a creature before [w***] God, and would contemn God and love him above all things. I prove this by the fact that a creature is put before God by mortal sin. For in this lies the distinction between a

SEXTO, habitum iustitiae infusae seu caritatis et gratiae inesse voluntati creatae non potest esse non bonum et iustum illi.

Probo, quia voluntas grata et cara Deo est bona et iusta. Si enim est accepta Deo, igitur se habet sicut placet Deo; igitur iusta et recta est.

Confirmatur: voluntas Sortis nunc bona et recta per habitum iustitiae et caritatis infusae, et Plato; secundum te habeat caritatem et tamen eius voluntas non sit bona et iusta. Contra: quia voluntas Sortis, si est bona, hoc est ex eo quod passive recipit caritatem, non enim se habet active respectu illius; igitur pari ratione voluntas Platonis. Et quia posset fieri transitus talis contradictionis sine mutatione, puta si iste habitus fiat Platoni bonus sicut Sorti.

SEPTIMO, visio et fruitio beati sunt bonum iusti et honesti et eminentiori bonitate quam praecise morali, immo supremum gradum boni iusti creati obtinent; et tamen non est possibile illas [y***] inesse creaturae rationali et non esse ei bonum quia sunt eius formalis beatitudo et nobilissima operatio respectu sui nobilissimi obiecti.

OCTAVO, id quod sic praecipitur quod non ex se essentialiter et necessario est rectum et iustum sed accidentaliter et contingenter ex libera ordinatione voluntatis extrinsece potest dispensationem recipere ut non obliget; sed aliquod praeceptum creaturae est sic rectum ut non recipiat dispensationem.

Probatur per Bernardum [z***], *De Praecepto et Dispensatione* cap. 4, ubi ponit 3 gradus necessitatis in praeceptis quos exprimit per haec verba, *stabile, inviolabile, incommutabile*. Primus gradus necessitatis est praeceptorum statutorum ab homine quae dispensationem in casu recipiunt ab homine, non quocumque sed praelato, ut decreta maiorum. Secundus gradus est praeceptorum Dei ut *Non occides, Non moechaberis, Non furtum facies*; et haec ab homine nullam dispensationem recipiunt sed a Deo tantum, ut Hebraei ex praecepto Dei spoliaverunt Aegyptios et propheta accepit mulierem fornicariam et Samson se ipsum interfecit. Tertius gradus est illius quod sic firmatum est divina aeternaque ratione ut nulla ex causa possit vel etiam ab ipso Deo aliquatenus immutari, ut sunt traditiones de dilectione et virtutibus. Et infra dicit quod talium tanta est immutabilis quod nec ipsi Deo mutare liberum est [75].

Confirmatur in *Canone* [a****] dist. 13, cap. 1, *Adversus ius naturale nulla dispensatio admittitur* [76].

Probatur, quia possibile esset creaturam rationalem non debere nec teneri oboedire et subici Deo, et ita licitum esset ei diligere se ipsam supra Deum et postponere Deum et eius mandata.

venial sin and a mortal sin according to Augustine in the *Enchiridion* 69 [73] and in *The City of God* XII, chap. 26 [x***] [74].

SIXTH, the habit of infused justice or of charity and grace being present in the created will cannot fail to be good and just for it.

I prove this as follows. The will which is beloved by God and dear to him is good and just. For if it is accepted by God, then it conducts itself as is pleasing to God, and therefore, it is just and upright.

Confirmation: Consider the will of Socrates which is now good and upright through the habit of infused justice and charity, and Plato. According to you, Plato may have charity and yet his will may not be good and just. In opposition to this the following may be said. The will of Socrates, if it is good, has this quality because it passively receives charity, for it does not conduct itself actively regarding that. Therefore, in like manner, the will of Plato. Further, the resolution of such a contradiction could be effected without a change, namely, if that habit becomes good for Plato as it is for Socrates.

SEVENTH, the vision and enjoyment of the blessed are a just and noble good and are good with a more eminent goodness than specifically moral goodness. Indeed, they possess the highest degree of created just good. Nevertheless, it is not possible that they [y***] be present in a rational creature and fail to be good for him because they constitute his formal beatitude and most noble operation with respect to his most noble object.

EIGHTH, that which is commanded in such a way that it is right and just not of itself, essentially and necessarily, but rather, accidentally and contingently from the free decree of a will extrinsically, can receive a dispensation so that it does not oblige. But some precept for a creature is right in such a way that it does not receive a dispensation.

This is proved by Bernard [z***] in *On Precept and Dispensation*, chap. 4, where he proposes three degrees of necessity in precepts, which he describes by these words, *stable, inviolable,* and *incommutable*. The first degree of necessity belongs to precepts established by a human being which, in a particular case, receive a dispensation from a human being, not from anyone whomever, but from a prelate, as, for example, the decretals of the forefathers. The second degree belongs to the precepts of God as, for example, *Do not kill, Do not commit adultery, Do not steal*. And these do not receive any dispensation from a human being, but receive it from God alone. For example, the Hebrews plundered the Egyptians and the prophet took a woman who was a fornicator and Samson killed himself according to a precept of God. The third degree belongs to that which has been made firm by the divine and eternal reason in such a way that it cannot be changed to any extent by any cause, or even by God himself. Such, for example, are the teachings about love and the virtues. And later on he says that the immutability of such precepts is so great that God himself is not free to change them [75].

This is confirmed in the *Canon* [a****], dist. 13, sect. 1, *No dispensation is admitted against natural law* [76].

Proof: It would be possible that a rational creature neither ought to obey God nor is bound to obey and to be subject to God. And so it would be licit for him to love himself above God and to

NONO, contra hanc conclusionem et praecedentem: sequitur quod omnia bona et iusta et virtuosa sunt aequaliter bona et virtuosa.

Probo, quia [b****] non ex se formaliter nec ex natura rei, sed praecise ex eo quod antecedenter et contingenter sunt a voluntate Dei libere volita et approbata; si ex parte divinae voluntatis sunt aequaliter volita et approbata, ipsa sunt aequaliter bona; sic erit de quibuscumque bonis virtuosis. Igitur maior patet, quia eadem et aequalis ratio bonitatis. Minor probatur, voluntas enim divina non inaequaliter illa vult et approbat quantum est ex parte sui quia in Dei dilectione esset formaliter distinctio et imperfectio. Ubi enim formaliter inaequalitas, ibi inaequalia; ubi autem inaequalia, ibi distincta.

Confirmatur: posito quod Deus inaequaliter approbat *a* et *b* et quod *a* et *b* inaequaliter approbantur, aut haec inaequalitas est formaliter et primo in divina voluntate aut in *a* et *b*. Si primum, igitur distinguuntur in divina voluntate. Si secundum, contra: quia Deus non est approbans formaliter per aliquid creatum extra se, sed per suum velle; per idem autem formaliter est Deus approbans *a* et *b* et approbantur *a* et *b*. Secundo, quia *a* et *b* essent inaequaliter approbata et bona per denominationem intrinsecam, non ab extrinseco, nec quia Deus illa inaequaliter approbaret, quia inaequalitas dicitur primo de his quibus formaliter inest quam de extrinseco.

Confirmatur: cum dicitur quod Deus inaequaliter approbat *a* et *b* et quod *a* et *b* sunt inaequaliter bona, aut igitur per eandem inaequalitatem aut per aliam et aliam. Si secundum, igitur una est prior et causalis respectu alterius; igitur altera est in divina voluntate formaliter. Si primum, illa non est formaliter et primo in Deo; patet ut prius. Si autem in *a* et *b*, igitur *a* et *b* sunt inaequalia bona formaliter et intrinsece, non per denominationem extrinsecam accidentalem a libera divina approbatione; nec ideo sunt inaequaliter bona quia primum et taliter Deus approbet inaequaliter, sed potius econtra.

Confirmatur: *a* non est praecise tam bonum et tantae bonitatis quia Deus praecise tam approbet, nec *b* est magis bonum quia Deus magis approbet *b*; igitur non sunt simpliciter bona quia Deus simpliciter approbat ea.

Antecedens probatur, quia magis et minus essent formaliter in divina voluntate, igitur distinguuntur.

Si dicatur quamvis divinum velle non habeat in se formaliter inaequalitatem quia est summe simplex, tamen Deus dicitur inaequaliter approbare *a* et *b*, et haec inaequalitas se tenet formaliter ex parte eorum bonorum ad quae acceptatur et ordinatur, scilicet inaequalitas praemiorum, contra: quia ut patet ex prima conclusione, *a* et *b* sunt bona iusti absque respectu ad praemium et prius omni habitudine ad praemium; nihil autem est formaliter tantum bonum per illud quod est naturaliter posterius eius bonitate; igitur *a* et *b* non sunt formaliter inaequaliter bona per inessentialem bonitatem praemiorum. Item, arguitur de illis praemiis inaequaliter bonis sicut argutum est de *a* et *b*: aut enim erit processus in infinitum aut illa praemia sunt ex se formaliter et ex natura rei bona, non accidentaliter et contingenter ex ordinatione divinae volunatis libera. Item, sequitur quod omne bonum est infinite bonum; quia si eo formaliter bonum quo approbatum, cum sit infinite approbatum quia infinita approbatione, igitur...

put God and his commands second.

NINTH, against this conclusion and the preceding one, it follows that all things which are good and just and virtuous are equally good and virtuous.

I prove this as follows [b****]. They are good not of themselves formally nor by their natures, but precisely because they are antecedently and contingently willed and approved freely by the will of God. If they are equally willed and approved on the part of the divine will, they are equally good. So it will be with respect to any virtuous goods whatever. Therefore the major is evident because the reason for being good is the same and equal. The minor is proved as follows. The divine will does not will and approve them unequally on its part because there would be formally a distinction and imperfection in the love of God. For where formally there is inequality, there are unequal things; but where there are unequal things, there are distinct things.

Confirmation: On the assumption that God unequally approves a and b and that a and b are approved unequally, either this inequality is formally and first in the divine will or in a and b. If the first is the case, then they are distinguished in the divine will. If the second alternative is chosen, the following may be said in opposition to it. First, God is not formally approving of them through something created which is outside himself, but through his will. But God is formally approving of a and b and a and b are approved through the same thing. Second, a and b would be unequally approved and good through intrinsic denomination, not externally, and not because God would approve them unequally. For inequality is said primarily of those things in which it is formally present, rather than of the external.

Confirmation: When it is said that God unequally approves a and b and that a and b are unequally good, then either this occurs through the same inequality or through different ones. If the second is the case, then one inequality is prior and causal with respect to the other. And therefore, the other one is in the divine will formally. If the first is the case, that inequality is not formally and first in God. This is evident as before. But if it is in a and b, then a and b are unequal goods formally and intrinsically, not by extrinsic, accidental denomination from free, divine approval. Nor are they unequally good because God may first and so approve them unequally, but rather, the contrary.

Confirmation: A is not precisely so good and of so much goodness because God may precisely so approve, nor is b a greater good because God may approve b more. Therefore they are not simply good because God simply approves them.

Proof of the antecedent: More and less would be formally in the divine will, and therefore they are distinguished.

Suppose it is said that although the divine will does not have inequality in itself formally because it is supremely simple, God is said to approve a and b unequally and this inequality is maintained formally on the part of those goods towards which it is accepted and ordered, namely, the inequality of rewards. In opposition to this the following may be said. As is evident from the first conclusion, a and b are just goods without respect to reward and prior to every relation to reward. Nothing, however, is formally so great a good through that which is naturally posterior to its goodness. Therefore a and b are not formally unequally good through the non-essential goodness of rewards. Again, it can be argued of those rewards which are unequally good just as it was argued of a and b. Either there will be an infinite regress or those rewards are good of themselves formally and by their nature, not accidentally and contingently from the free decree of the divine will. Again,

AD PRIMUM: non est simile quoad contingentiam et necessitatem. Veritas enim convenit propositioni ex conformitate ad significatum; convenit autem quod, sic esse significatur per propositionem formatam de entibus secundis, sit necessarium vel impossibile vel contingens. Bonitas autem iustae actionis humanae ex determinata conformitate ad ordinationem divinae voluntatis praecipientis vel persuadentis.

AD SECUNDUM: minor in sensu divisionis est falsa, scilicet velle conformiter voluntati divinae est necessario bonum et non potest esse non bonum, quia id quod realiter est [c***] velle bene et conformiter divinae voluntati potest esse velle non bene et non conformiter divinae voluntati praecipienti, sicut illud realiter quod est voluntatem diligere *b* meritorie potest esse voluntatem diligere *b* non meritorie. In sensu vero compositionis conceditur; sed tunc non valet discursus ad inferendum, *igitur aliquid aliud a Deo est necessarium bonum et iustum*, sed est figura dictionis sicut *Sortem appetere b cibum virtuose et meritorie non potest esse non bonum, igitur Sortem appetere b cibum mihi non* [d****} *potest esse non bonum*, vel sicut *Actus meritorius non potest esse a solo Deo, igitur aliquod aliud ens a Deo non potest esse a solo Deo*.
  Ad confirmationem negatur consequentia in sensu compositionis sumendo consequens.

AD TERTIUM: minor de virtute verbi est falsa sumptis terminis personaliter. Sit enim *b* aliquod aliud ens a Deo quod dicis esse actum vel virtutem oboedientiae [e****] existentem in Sorte; tunc falsum est quod *b* sit causa propter quam omnis actio hominis bona sit bona, non enim est causa propter quam actiones Platonis sunt bonae. Et cum dicitur quod oboedientia est verissima et sola virtus, videtur falsum sumendo terminos personaliter; sed sumendo terminos simpliciter, potest concedi in hoc sensu: oboedientia dicitur de omni virtute, nec aliquid in viatore esset virtuosum nisi ipsum esset oboedientia aliqualiter. Et potest sermo reduci ad enuntiationem de actu exercito et ex terminis supponentibus personaliter, puta quod omnis virtus est oboedientia et est conformitas voluntatis creatae ad Deum, quod omne virtuosum est virtuosum quatinus oboedienter conforme voluntati divinae. Et sic discursus non valet ad inferendum quod aliquid aliud a Deo bonum creaturae rationali sit necessario bonum et iustum, sed [f****] solum ad inferendum quod de aliquo subiecto praedicatur per se tale praedicatum et quod propositio est necessaria supposita constantia non solum rei pro qua stat subiectum sed quod simul de ea et pro ea verificetur subiectum formaliter.
  Ad confirmationem negatur minor in sensu divisionis.
  Ad probationem: non concludit quod actus vel habitus oboedientiae existens in viatore sit bonus et iustus prius naturaliter omni praecepto divino, sed solum probat quod ante dationem [g****] praecepti actualem a Deo prior est haec veritas, quod creatura rationalis tenetur oboedire Deo si sibi a Deo praeceptum detur. Et hoc per modum legis et dictaminis est rectum et iustum, non iustitia secundum quam formaliter voluntas creata sit iusta, sed iustitia qua legislator est iustus [h****] et rectus in sic dictando.

it follows that every good is infinitely good. For it is formally good because approved, and since it is infinitely approved because with infinite approval, therefore... .

REPLY TO THE FIRST OBJECTION: There is not a parallel with respect to contingency and necessity. For truth is found in a proposition from conformity to the thing signified, but necessity or impossibility or contingency is found in a proposition from this status being signified by a proposition formed about secondary beings. However, the goodness of a just human action is found in it from determined conformity to the decree of the divine will commanding or persuading.

REPLY TO THE SECOND OBJECTION: In the sense of division, the minor is false, namely, that to will conformably to the divine will is necessarily good and cannot fail to be good. For that which really is [c****] willing rightly and conformably to the divine will can be willing not rightly and not conformably to the divine will commanding, just as that which really is a will loving *b* meritoriously can be a will loving *b* non-meritoriously. In the sense of composition, the minor is conceded. But then the argument does not warrant the inference, *therefore something other than God is necessarily good and just*, but it is a figure of speech just as are the following: *That Socrates seeks b, food, virtuously and meritoriously cannot fail to be good, therefore that Socrates seeks b, food, for me cannot* [d****] *fail to be good;* or again, *A meritorious act cannot come from God alone, therefore some being other than God cannot come from God alone.*

Reply to the confirmation: The inference is denied, taking the consequent in the sense of composition.

REPLY TO THE THIRD OBJECTION: By virtue of linguistic considerations, the minor is false, taking the terms personally. For let *b* be some being other than God, which you say to be an act or a virtue of obedience [e****] existing in Socrates. Then it is false that *b* is the cause on account of which every good action of a human being is good, for it is not the cause on account of which the actions of Plato are good. And when it is said that obedience is the truest and sole virtue, this seems to be false in taking the terms personally. But in taking the terms simply, it can be conceded in this sense: obedience is affirmed of every virtue, nor would anything be virtuous in a viator unless it were obedience in some way. And the discourse can be reduced to a statement about an act carried out and from terms suppositing personally, for example, that every virtue is obedience and is the conformity of the created will to God, or that everything virtuous is virtuous in so far as it is obediently conformed to the divine will. And thus the argument does not warrant the inference that something other than God which is a good for a rational creature is necessarily good and just, but [f****] only the inference that such a predicate is predicated per se of some subject and that the proposition is necessary with supposited constancy, not only of the thing for which the subject stands, but also that the subject may be formally shown to be true at the same time of that thing and for that thing.

Reply to the confirmation: The minor is denied in the sense of division.

Reply to the proof: It does not demonstrate that an act or habit of obedience existing in a viator is good and just naturally prior to every divine precept, but proves only that, before the actual giving [g****] of a precept by God, this truth is prior, namely, that a rational creature is bound to

Notandum quod oboedientia potest sumi pro virtute in communi vel pro virtute speciali distincta contra alias; sicut distingui solet de iustitia oboedientia. Ut est virtus particularis, est virtus cuius per se actus sunt velle oboedire divinis mandatis. Oboedientia vero, ut est virtus in communi, est subiectatio voluntatis creatae per conformitatem ad mandata divinae voluntatis, et eius actus [i****] sunt generaliter actus quibus habitis voluntas creata secundum illos conformatur praeceptis vel consiliis Dei.

AD QUARTUM negatur minor.

Ad probationem: est figura dictionis mutando *quid* vel *quasi quid* in *quale* vel *quasi quale* in discursu ex praemissis de possibili explicite vel aequivalenter. Implere enim divina mandata non est praecise facere *b* opus realiter, sed facere *b* ex ratione et libere et conformiter ordinationi divinae ut praeceptivae vel consultivae. Id autem realiter quod nunc est implere mandata Dei poterat esse non implere mandatum Dei quia etiam poterat esse non praeceptum vel non sic praeceptum.

AD QUINTUM: Sortem diligere Deum super omnia potest intellegi dupliciter: uno modo mere formaliter, nudo actu formalis dilectionis; alio modo non pure formaliter per explicatum actum talis dilectionis, sed etiam virtualiter et constanter et efficaciter per exclusionem alterius aeque vel magis dilecti et praepositi, sive formaliter sive habitualiter sive implicite et interpretative.

Primo modo Sortes diligit Deum super omnia si habet formaliter actum dilectionis secundum quem formaliter et explicite voluntas mavult omne aliud perdere quam Deum perdere vel offendere, vel secundum quem formaliter et explicite vult vel vellet mori ad honorem [j****] et beneplacitum Dei. Et sic possibile est infidelem et hereticum vel Iudeum diligere Deum super omnia. Et videtur quod homo possit se experiri diligere Deum super omnia hoc modo.

Secundo modo Sortem diligere Deum super omnia est sic diligere Deum quod nihil aliud magis vel aeque diligit nec formaliter et explicite nec habitualiter nec implicite et interpretative [k****], per exclusionem contrarii formaliter vel interpretative quantum potest et quantum in se est, ita quod nihil committit vel omittit quod implicite et interpretative deroget amori Dei et quod implicite vel interpretative sit aliquid praeponere Deo sed, quantum in se est, vivit conformiter praeceptis Dei et cavet ab omni repugnante praeceptis Dei. Et sic nullus in peccato mortali diligit Deum super omnia, commisit enim vel omisit unde Deus offenditur, nec facit quod potest et quod in se est et quod debet de reconciliando. Hoc etiam modo non est homo certus an diligat Deum super omnia; contingit enim quod habet aliquid vel caret aliquod unde offendatur Deus et non est sufficienter excusatus super ignorantia vel negligentia. Unde Apostolus loquens in persona communis viatoris dicit: *Nihil mihi conscius sum, sed non in hoc iustificatus sum* (I *Corinthiorum* 4) [77].

Iuxta hunc modum dici solet quod peccator, quamvis actu formali vel habitualiter diligat se ipsum super omnia, dicitur tamen interpretative odire se ipsum secundum Augustinum, *Homeliarum* 51 [78], super illud *Ioannis* 12, *Qui odit animam suam in hoc mundo...* [79]; et *Psalmistae*, *Qui diligit iniquitatem, odit animam suam* [80]; et *Tobiae* 12, *Qui faciunt peccatum et iniquitatem,*

obey God if a precept is given him by God. And this is right and just by the mode of a law and a dictate; not the justice according to which the created will formally is just, but the justice by which the legislator is just [h****] and right in so dictating.

It should be noted that obedience can be taken for a virtue in common or for a particular virtue distinct from others, as obedience is customarily distinguished from justice. As it is a particular virtue, it is the virtue whose very acts are to will to obey the divine commands. As it is a virtue in common, obedience is the subjection of the created will through conformity to the commands of the divine will. And its acts [i****] are generally the acts by which the created will is conformed to the precepts or counsels of God, in accordance with them.

REPLY TO THE FOURTH OBJECTION: The minor is denied.

Reply to the proof: It is a figure of speech in changing *what* or *as if what* into *of what kind* or *as if of what kind* in an argument from premises about the possible explicitly or equivalently. For to fulfill divine commands does not consist precisely in really doing a work, *b*, but in doing *b* according to reason and freely and conformably to the divine decree as preceptive or consultative. However, that which now really is fulfilling the commands of God could have been not fulfilling the commands of God because it could also not have been commanded or not have been commanded in this manner.

REPLY TO THE FIFTH OBJECTION: That Socrates loves God above all things can be understood in two ways. In one way, it is taken merely formally, as the bare act of formal love. In another way, it is not taken purely formally for the plain act of such love, but also virtually and constantly and efficaciously by the exclusion of something else which is loved equally or more so and preferred, whether formally or habitually or implicitly and interpretatively.

In the first way, Socrates loves God above all things if he has formally the act of love according to which the will formally and explicitly prefers to lose everything else rather than to lose or offend God, or according to which the will formally and explicitly wills or would will to die for the honor [j****] and good pleasure of God. And in this way it is possible for an infidel and a heretic or a Jew to love God above all things. And it seems that, in this way, a human being could test himself whether he loves God above all things.

In the second way, Socrates loving God above all things is so to love God that nothing else, either formally and explicitly or habitually or implicitly and interpretatively [k****], is loved more or equally through exclusion of the contrary, formally or interpretatively, as much as he can and to the very best of his ability [l****]. Thus he commits or omits nothing which may implicitly and interpretatively detract from the love of God and which may implicitly or interpretatively be putting something before God, but he lives conformably to the precepts of God and guards against everything inconsistent with the precepts of God to the very best of his ability. And, in this way, no one in a state of mortal sin loves God above all things, for he committed or omitted something whereby God is offended, and he does not do what he can nor his very best nor what he ought about becoming reconciled. Furthermore, in this way a human being is not certain whether he loves God above all things. For it happens that he has something or lacks something whereby God may be offended and that he is not adequately excused on grounds of ignorance or negligence. So the Apostle, speaking in the person of the common viator, states: *I am aware of nothing against myself, but I am not*

hostes sunt animae suae [81]; et *Proverbiorum* 1, *Ipsi quoque contra sanguinem suum insidiantur, et moliuntur fraudes contra animas suas* [82]. Dicitur igitur talis odire se ipsum implicite et interpretative quia nocet sibi ipsi et se ipsum corrumpit et perdit, et ita implicite se habet erga se ipsum quoniam erga alterum quem odit formaliter.

Primus modus diligendi Deum super omnia est imperfectus. Secundus autem perfectior, sed tertio modo potest aliquis adeo efficaciter et virtualiter diligere Deum super omnia quod actualis vel habitualis amor ipsius ad Deum est ita sufficiens et efficax et tantae virtutis quod, quocumque aliquo amabili vel odibili, delectabili vel tristabili oblato voluntati, amor Dei vinceret amorem vel timorem illius. Et sic Petrus putabat se diligere Christum super omnia, et non erat ita quia amor illius victus est timore mortis. Sic autem diligebat Paulus Christum dicens *Romanorum* 8, *Certus sum quod neque mors,* etc. [83].

Ad propositum conceditur quod, saltem de potentia Dei absoluta, omnis actus voluntatis creatae in via, secundum suam materialem entitatem sumptus, potest esse non bonus secundum virtuosam et iustam bonitatem; sed an possit esse malus potest dici dupliciter. Uno modo quod non, quia sive eliciatur a furioso sive sit prohibitus pro tempore, tamen ex natura talis actus est quod non potest ab homine produci quin habeat aliquas circumstantias excusantas a mortali vel quin desint aliquae circumstantiae requisitae ad aggravationem mortalem et ad hoc quod Deus imputet pro mortali; Deus enim non imputaret ad mortale talem actum nisi procederet ex conscientia transgressionis habituali. Si autem prohibeatur pro certo tempore vel loco diligere Deum super omnia, impossibile est quod scienter et advertenter agat haec contra praeceptum sciens se in hoc transgredi praeceptum; immo habitualiter et implicite putat in hoc placere Deo et velle conformiter eius voluntati. Eodem modo de velle vivere et se habere conformiter voluntati divinae. Si quis vero alio modo velit concedere quod non absolute est impossibile huiusmodi actum elici vitiose, tunc dicendum quod diligere Deum super omnia secundo modo non potest esse malum quia hoc implicat voluntatem recte et conformiter voluntati divinae se habere et efficaciter et perfecte. Sed ex hoc non probatur propositum, quia nulla res est diligere sic Deum super omnia quin illa res possit esse non diligere sic Deum super omnia; non enim significatur praecise et absolute aliquem actum vel habitum determinatum inesse voluntati, sed taliter vivere et disponi. Sed secundo modo concederetur posse esse malum.

Ad improbationem dicitur quod quando magis diligeret Deum et adhaereret Deo per talem modum formalis dilectionis, tanto plus interpretative recederet a Deo, sicut quanto intellectus Sortis diligit se ipsum formaliter actu inordinato, magis odit se interpretative. Similiter, si Sortes velit facere *a* quia credit hoc esse ad voluntatem et honorem vel commodum domini sui et non est ita sed econtrario, tunc quanto Sortes nititur magis oboedire et placere domino suo in faciendo *a*, tanto interpretative magis facit contra voluntatem domini sui. Eodem modo licet velit oboedire et se conformare voluntati divinae, non tamen vult oboedienter et conformiter voluntati divinae ut praecipienti pro tunc.

Ad confirmationem negatur consequentia accipiendo *uti* ut opponitur ipsi *frui*, et accipiendo *praeponere* et *postponere* ut sunt opposita. Fruitur igitur ipso Deo secundum formalem et explicitam tendentiam in Deum, sed utitur eo et postponit eum implicite et interpretative per commissionem vel omissionem contra praeceptum, et ita per alterius a Deo implicitam praeponem. Hunc autem secundum modum respondendi non affirmo nec pono.

thereby justified (I *Corinthians* 4) [77].

According to this mode it is customary to say that, although a sinner loves himself above all things by a formal act or habitually, yet interpretatively, he hates himself. This is according to Augustine in the *Sermons* 51 [78], commenting on that verse of *John* 12, *He who hates his life in this world...* [79]. Further, there is the verse of the Psalmist, *He who loves iniquity hates his own soul...* [80]; and the verse of *Tobit* 12, *They who commit sin and iniquity are enemies of their own soul* [81]; and the verse of *Proverbs* 1, *They too lie in wait for their own blood, and bring about deceptions for their own soul* [82]. Therefore it is said that such a person hates himself implicitly and interpretatively because he does harm to his very self and destroys and loses himself, and so he implicitly works against himself since he works against the other whom he formally hates.

The first way of loving God above all things is imperfect. The second, however, is more perfect. But in a third way someone can so efficaciously and virtually love God above all things that his actual or habitual love for God is so sufficient and efficacious and of such great strength that, when anything whatever which is lovable or hateful, pleasurable or painful was offered to his will, the love of God would overcome the love or fear of that thing. And in this way Peter thought himself to love Christ above all things, but it was not so because his love for Christ was overcome by the fear of death. Paul, however, loved Christ in this way, saying in *Romans* 8, *I am certain that neither death*, etc. [83].

Reply to what was to be proved: It is conceded that every act of the created will in this earthly life, taken according to its material entity, can fail to be good according to virtuous and just goodness, at least with respect to the absolute power of God. But whether it can be evil can be answered in two ways. In one way, the answer is no. For whether it be elicited by a madman or prohibited for a time, yet the act by nature is such that it cannot be produced by a human being without having some circumstances excusing from mortal sin or without some circumstances being absent which are required for its being worsened to a mortal degree and for the purpose of God imputing it as mortal. For God would not impute such an act as mortal unless it proceeded from a conscience which transgresses habitually. If, however, loving God above all things is prohibited for a certain time or place, then it is impossible that a human being knowingly and intentionally do these things contrary to a precept while knowing himself to transgress a precept in doing this. On the contrary, he habitually and implicitly thinks that he pleases God and wills conformably to his will in doing this. The same may be said about willing to live and conduct oneself conformably to the divine will. But if in fact someone wishes to concede that, in another way, it is not absolutely impossible that such an act be elicited viciously, then one can say that loving God above all things in the aforementioned second way cannot be evil because this implies that the will conducts itself rightly and conformably to the divine will and efficaciously and perfectly. But this does not demonstrate what is to be proven, because no thing is so loving God above all things without being able to fail to be that. For what is precisely and absolutely signified is not that some determined act or habit is present in the will, but rather, living and being disposed in such a manner. But in a second way, it would be conceded that it can be evil.

Reply to the disproof: How much the more he would love God and would adhere to God through such a mode of formal love, so much the more would he withdraw from God interpretatively, just as it is the case that, as much as the intellect of Socrates loves itself formally with a disordered act, the more it hates itself interpretatively. Similarly, if Socrates wills to do *a* because he believes

AD SEXTUM principale: sumendo iustitiam in communi pro actuali rectitudine voluntatis secundum bonum iusti, virtuosi et honesti, sic impossibile est iustitiam convenire voluntati quin sit iusta; sed nulla inexistens animae est hoc modo iustitia necessario et essentialiter. Sumendo vero iustitiam pro determinato habitu voluntatis supernaturaliter tantum causabili, qui dicitur caritas infusa, sic impossibile est illum inesse voluntati et voluntatem secundum illum esse iniustam quia ille est a solo Deo. Impossibile est autem talem habitum inesse voluntati quin secundum illum voluntas sit iusta et recta aptitudinaliter et secundum quid quia ille habitus inclinat in generali voluntatem ad conformandum se voluntati divinae, sive in agendo sive in cessando, sive in agendo sic si Deus praecipiat sic agere sive in agendo contrarie si Deus praecipiat agere contrarie. Dicitur tamen quod, de potentia Dei absoluta, non est impossibile talem habitum inesse voluntati secundum id quod est realiter et physice et voluntatem non esse iustam simpliciter, ut si manuteneretur a Deo in anima quae omittit vel committit contra praeceptum vel si infunderetur a Deo voluntati quae peccavit et nedum paenituit. Et cum dicitur quod talis voluntas erit cara et grata Deo, negatur quia iste non est formalis et per se effectus illius qualitatis, sed esse habitualiter diligentem Deum gratis et habere carum super omnia; de hoc dictum est supra dist. 14 [84].

Ad confirmationem: voluntas Sortis nunc habens caritatem ideo est bona et iusta quia secundum leges statutas Deus illum habitum instituit et approbat [m****] ut rectitudinem voluntatis, et quia voluntas habens illum se habet ut debet et ut Deus vult, nec stat cum deformitate voluntatis ad Dei praecepta, et consequenter Deus huiusmodi voluntatem acceptat ad beatitudinem. Possibile est autem ista non verificari de Platone licet habeat qualitatem illam.

AD SEPTIMUM potest dici quod conclusio est posita de eo quod est bonum viatoris, non de bono finali beatificante et praemiante. Talis enim actus est implicite et interpretative et virtualiter expulsio omnis peccati et remissio, si praefuerit peccatum, nec potest haberi nisi supernaturaliter a Deo. Nec videtur simile de huiusmodi actibus et de habitu caritatis quia probabilius est quod tali habitui viae non absolute et simpliciter repugnat actus transgressivus praecepti secundum id quod est realiter et physice, quia similis actus potest esse concessus vel consultus habenti caritatem; et quia habitus naturaliter acquisitus ex determinatis actibus et inclinans naturaliter et perceptibiliter ad similes

this to be for the will and the honor or benefit of his lord and this is not so, but the contrary, then how much the more Socrates strives to obey and please his lord in doing *a*, so much the more he acts contrary to the will of his lord interpretatively. In the same way, although someone wills to obey and to conform himself to the divine will, yet he does not will obediently and conformably to the divine will as it commands for that time.

Reply to the confirmation: The inference is denied in taking *use* as it is opposed to *enjoy*, and in taking *put before* and *put after* as they are opposites. Therefore he enjoys God himself according to a formal and explicit tendency to God, but uses him and puts him second implicitly and interpretatively by a commission or omission contrary to a precept, and so by an implicit putting of another before God. However, I neither affirm nor propose this second way of responding.

REPLY TO THE SIXTH OBJECTION: In taking justice in common for the actual rectitude of the will according to just, virtuous, and noble good, it is impossible that justice be found in the will without being just. But no justice existing in the soul is necessarily and essentially justice in this sense. In taking justice for a determined habit of the will able to be caused only supernaturally, which is called infused charity, it is impossible that it be present in the will and that the will be unjust in accordance with it because it comes from God alone. But it is impossible that such a habit be present in the will without the will being just and right in accordance with it by way of aptitude and in a certain respect because that habit inclines the will in general to conform itself to the divine will, whether in acting or in ceasing action, whether in acting in this manner if God commands that one so act or in acting in the contrary manner if God commands that one act that way. Nevertheless, it is said that, with respect to the absolute power of God, it is not impossible that such a habit be present in the will according to that which it is really and physically and that the will fail to be simply just. Such would be the case, for example, if it were maintained by God in a soul which omits or commits something contrary to a precept, or if it were to be infused by God into a will which sinned and by no means repented. And when it is said that such a will will be dear to and beloved by God, this is denied because that is not the formal and direct effect of that quality, but rather, to be in a state of habitually loving God gratuitously and to hold God dear above all things. This has been discussed above in dist. 14 [84].

Reply to the confirmation: The will of Socrates which now has charity is good and just because, according to the laws which have been established, God establishes and approves [m****] that habit as rectitude of the will. And second, a will which has that habit conducts itself as it ought and as God wills, nor does that habit remain with deviation of the will from the precepts of God. And consequently, God accepts such a will for beatitude. It is possible, however, that those things not be proven true of Plato although he has that quality.

REPLY TO THE SEVENTH OBJECTION: The conclusion is asserted of that which is the good of a viator, not of the final good which beatifies and rewards. For such an act is implicitly and interpretatively and virtually the expulsion and remission of every sin, if sin shall have been present, and it can only be had supernaturally from God. Nor does there seem to be a parallel between acts of this kind and the habit of charity because it is more probably the case that an act transgressive of a precept according to that which it is really and physically is not inconsistent with such a habit of life absolutely and simply. First, a similar act can be allowed or counseled to someone having charity.

et natus corrumpi naturaliter ex contrariis potest in aliquo gradu stare naturaliter cum actibus generativis habitus vitiosi, igitur multo magis erit Deo possibile conservare habitum caritatis in anima licet ponatur omissio vel actus prohibitus.

AD OCTAVAM negatur minor loquendo de praecepto quocumque quo absolute et determinate praeciperetur talem actionem realem fieri ab homine, non loquendo de praecepto quo in generali praecipitur creaturam rationalem vivere et se habere recte et conformiter divinis mandatis.

Ad Bernardum [n****]: ... [o****] de potentia ordinata vel de praeceptis in quibus praecipitur absolute determinata actio fieri, sed quibus in generali praecipitur vivere et se habere conformiter divinae ordinationi et non transgressione sed prout ratio recta dictat, etc. Videtur autem quod Bernardus [p****] loquitur de potentia Dei ordinata, quia secundum ipsum ibidem sub illo genere immutabilis necessitatis dispensationem non recipientis continetur omnis illa traditio dominici sermonis in monte [q****] et quicquid de dilectione, humilitate, mansuetudine, ceterisque virtutibus tam in Novo quam in Veteri Testamento specialiter traditur observandum [85].

AD NONUM negatur consequentia.

Ad probationem potest negari minor. Ad probationem potest dici quod per volitionem immo omnino eandem Deus inaequaliter approbat *a* et *b*, sicut per eundem actum quo diligo finem et ens ad finem diligo inaequaliter utrumque, ut dictum est supra dist. 1 [86]. Similiter, *a* album per eandem omnino realiter similitudinem est inaequaliter simile ipsi *b* et ipsi *c* quia similitudo secundum quam formaliter est simile est sua albedo. Et cum dicitur, *Ubi inaequalitas, ibi inaequalia*, illud probat quod Deus aequaliter diligat iustos omnes et odit peccatores omnes. Potest igitur dici quod nullibi est formaliter et actualiter ista inaequalitas quia ista denominatio qua dicimus Deum inaequaliter approbare *a* et *b* non sumitur ab aliqua inaequalitate rerum secundum propriam et realem maioritatem et minoritatem entitatis, sed sumitur ab actu divinae voluntatis infinito et illimitato et aequivalente infinitis actibus quorum unus esset maior alio et alter minor. Non enim omni omissioni vere secundum magis et minus oportet correspondere veram et propriam maioritatem et minoritatem in rebus significatis pro quibus verificatur, ut de actibus inaequaliter malis, cum interdum magis malus sit minoris entitatis. Potest igitur dici quod haec inaequalitas non est in aliquo formaliter, sed aequivalenter et virtualiter est in actu divinae voluntatis.

Aliter potest dici quod Deus dicitur inaequaliter approbare quia ad inaequalis gradus bonitatis determinare, sicut enim Deus unicuique rei dat determinatum gradum entitatis et bonitatis naturalis, ita Deus per determinationem voluntatis et dictamen intellectus statuit hoc esse tanti gradus bonitatis iusti et honesti. Haec igitur denominatio qua dicitur Deus approbare inaequaliter *a* et *b* partim est ab extrinseco quoad *inaequaliter*, partim ab intrinseco quoad *approbare*, sicut denominative dicitur Deus esse temporaliter a tempore. Vel potest etiam dici approbare aequaliter quoad actum approbationis est approbare inaequaliter quoad gradus bonitatis quos determinat circa *a* et *b*. Sumendo igitur *approbare aequaliter* quoad actum intrinsece approbationis, negatur maior.

Ad confirmationem patet ex dictis.

Second, a habit naturally acquired from determined acts and inclining naturally and perceptibly to similar ones and designed to be naturally destroyed by contraries can, to some degree, naturally remain with acts productive of a vicious habit. Therefore, so much the more will it be possible for God to preserve a habit of charity in the soul although an omission or prohibited act is placed in it.

REPLY TO THE EIGHTH OBJECTION: The minor is denied in speaking of any precept whatever by which it would be absolutely and determinately commanded that such a real action be done by a human being, not in speaking of a precept by which it is commanded in general that a rational creature live and conduct himself rightly and conformably to divine commands.

Reply to Bernard [n****]: ...[o****] with respect to ordained power or with respect to the precepts in which a determined action is absolutely commanded to be done, but in which it is commanded in general to live and conduct oneself conformably to the divine decree, and not with transgression, but as right reason dictates, etc.. It seems, however, that Bernard [p****] is speaking with respect to the ordained power of God, because in the same place he expresses the view that under that genus of immutable necessity not receiving a dispensation is included all the teaching of the Lord's Sermon on the Mount [q****] and whatever about love, humility, meekness, and the other virtues is specifically taught to be observed, as much in the New as in the Old Testament [85].

REPLY TO THE NINTH OBJECTION: The inference is denied.

Reply to the proof: The minor can be denied. In response to the proof it can be said that God unequally approves a and b by a volition which is entirely the same, just as by the same act by which I love the end and the means to the end I love each one unequally, as stated above in dist.1 [86]. Similarly, something white, a, is unequally similar to b and to c through what is really entirely the same similarity, because the similarity according to which it is formally similar is its whiteness. And when it is said, *Where there is inequality, there are unequal things*, that proves that God loves equally all who are just and hates equally all who are sinners. Therefore it can be stated that that inequality does not exist formally and actually anywhere because the denomination by which we say that God unequally approves a and b is not taken from some inequality of things according to a proper and real superiority and inferiority of entity, but is taken from an act of the divine will which is infinite and unlimited and equivalent to infinitely many acts of which the one would be greater than the other, and the other lesser. For it is not necessary that to every omission truly according to more and less there correspond a true and proper superiority and inferiority in the things signified for which it is shown to be true, as, for example, with respect to acts unequally evil, since a greater evil sometimes belongs to a lesser entity. Therefore it can be said that this inequality does not exist in anything formally, but exists equivalently and virtually in an act of the divine will.

In another manner, God is said to approve things unequally because he is said to determine them to unequal degrees of goodness. For just as God gives to one thing a determined degree of entity and of natural goodness, so God establishes that this has so great a degree of just and noble goodness by a determination of his will and a dictate of his intellect. Therefore this denomination, by which God is said to approve a and b unequally, is partly extrinsic (with respect to *unequally*) and partly intrinsic (with respect to *to approve*), just as denominatively God is said to exist temporally in relation to time. Or it can also be said that God approves equally with respect to the act of approval and approves unequally with respect to the degrees of goodness which he determines concerning a

Ad rationem in principio quaestionis patebit in quaestione sequenti.

and *b*. Therefore, taking *to approve equally* with respect to the intrinsic act of approval, the major is denied.

Reply to the confirmation: This is evident from what has been said.

The reply to the argument given at the beginning of the question will be evident in the following question.

Quaero secundo circa eadam distinctionem:

Utrum omne quod est creaturae rationali malum culpae ideo sit malum quia a deo libere et contingenter prohibitum.

Quod non: quia odium Dei posset esse non prohibitum, et per consequens licitum et concessum.

Contra: quia si omne bonum iusti ideo est taliter bonum quia a Deo libere sic ordinatum et dictatum [1], igitur pari ratione econtra de malo opposito, quia idem est regula et iudex recti et obliqui.

Primo, de malo poenae; secundo, de malo culpae quoad primum.

DE PRIMO ARTICULO

PRIMA CONCLUSIO: Id quod est creaturae malum poenae sensus non potest ei inesse quin sit ei malum.

Probatur, quia ex natura sua est creaturae rationali disconveniens et indispositio; sicut enim quaedam entia sunt naturales dispositiones convenientes creaturae rationali et eius perfectiones secundariae spectantes ad eius bene esse [b], ita econtrario de quibusdam.

Confirmatur, quia id quod est formaliter bonum delectabile creaturae rationali non potest ei inesse quin sit ei formaliter delectatio; igitur similiter de aliquo malo poenali.

SECUNDA CONCLUSIO: Id quod est alicui creaturae rationali malum poenae sensus potest eidem vel alteri esse magis vel minus malum.

Probatur, quia circumstantiae aggravantes possunt variari secundum magis et minus. Patet, quia *a* malum poenae sensus potest inferri alicui in punitionem culpae et ad sui confusionem, et haec est circumstantia faciens ad aggravationem mali poenae secundum Boethium, libro 1, *Consolatio: Haec est* inquit *maxima fortunae adversae sarcina, quia miseri, quae perferunt, meruisse creduntur* [2]; et super illud Psalmi 141, *Educ de custodia animam meam* [3], Augustinus: *Merita carcerem faciunt. Nam in uno habitaculo alteri domus est, alteri carcer est. Alteri facit domum libertas,*

QUESTION 2

Is everything which is an evil of fault for a rational creature evil because it is freely and contingently prohibited by God?

The answer seems to be no, for <otherwise> the hatred of God could fail to be prohibited, and consequently be licit and permitted.

On the other hand, if all just good is this kind of good because it is freely decreed and prescribed by God [1], then, in like manner, the contrary holds with respect to the opposite evil because the same thing is the rule and judge of rightness and obliquity.

First, the evil of penalty [a] will be discussed. Second, the evil of fault will be considered with respect to the first topic of inquiry.

ARTICLE 1

FIRST CONCLUSION: That which is an evil of penalty for the senses for a <rational> creature cannot be present in him without being evil for him.

Proof: It is unsuitable to and unbefitting a rational creature by its nature. For just as certain beings are natural dispositions suitable to a rational creature and are its secondary perfections pertaining to its well-being [b], so the contrary is true of certain others.

Confirmation: That which is formally a pleasant good for a rational creature cannot be present in him without being formally a pleasure for him. Therefore, in like manner with regard to any evil of penalty.

SECOND CONCLUSION: That which is an evil of penalty for the senses for some rational creature can be a greater or a lesser evil for himself or for someone else.

Proof: Circumstances which make a situation worse can be varied according to greater and lesser. This is evident because an evil of penalty for the senses, *a*, can be inflicted on someone as punishment for a fault and to his shame, and this is a circumstance contributing to the worsening of the evil of penalty according to Boethius in *The Consolation of Philosophy*, bk. I. *This is*, he says, *the greatest burden of adverse fortune, that it is believed that the unfortunate ones have merited what they suffer* [2]. And on the verse of Psalm 141, *Bring my soul out of prison* [3], Augustine comments: *Deserts make a prison. For in one dwelling-place one person has a home, another has*

alteri facit carcerem servitus [4].

Item, idem vel consimile malum poenae magis nocet uni quam alteri et magis expedit uni quam alteri quia illum praeservat a peccatis, illum autem impedit a bonis laboribus.

CONTRA:

HAEC CONCLUSIO videtur repugnare priori, quia illud quod potest creaturae esse nunc tantum malum et postea esse maius malum et iterum esse minus malum potest tandem ei esse non malum, saltem de potentia Dei absoluta, quia non ex se essentialiter est ei malum, et quia finitum per ablationem finiti tandem consummitur.

SECUNDO, non videtur verum quod poenam inesse per modum punitionis pro culpa sit circumstantia reddens illum esse magis malum. Patet per illud dictum poetae: *Leviter ex merito, quicquid patiare, serendum est; quae venit indigne, poena dolenda venit* [5].

AD PRIMUM negatur minor. Licet possit tolli tota aggravatio mali quae erat ratione talis circumstantiae si talis circumstantia totaliter tollitur, sicut peccatum: aliquid potest aggravari ex circumstantia loci, et minus aggravari per diminutionem circumstantiae eius, et tandem post totalem ablationem illius circumstantiae manebit aliqua culpa, licet tollatur gradus malitiae proveniens ex illa circumstantia.

AD SECUNDUM: Si Sorti infertur *a* poena per modum punitionis pro culpa et aequalis poena materialiter quae est Platoni innocenti circumscribendo has circumstantias, scilicet quod huiusmodi poena sit meriti acquisitiva vel debiti quittativa et ita beatitudinis accelerativa; stando praecise in istis circumstantiis, scilicet quod Sorti sit vera punitio, Platoni autem non sit, huiusmodi poena quantum est ex ista circumstantia est Sorti magis mala, et sic supra adducuntur. Poeta [c] vero intendit quod homines ut communius de facto assumunt maiorem patientiam et minorem tristitiam et displicentiam cum eis infertur malum poenae quam iuste meruerunt reflectendo et convertendo se super suam poenam, sive illa sit magis mala ex circumstantia demeriti [d] sive non.

TERTIA CONCLUSIO: Aliquid vel aliqua privatio est creaturae rationali malum damni quam impossibile est ei convenire quin sit ei malum damni.

Probatur, quia impossibile est quin sit ei privatio perfectionis et integritatis substantialis et defectus membri convenientis et deformitas naturalis, ut privatio oculorum.

a prison. Liberty makes it a home for the one, slavery makes it a prison for the other [4].

Again, the same or an entirely similar evil of penalty does more harm to one person than to another and is more advantageous to one than to another because it keeps the person away from sins but hinders him from doing good works.

OBJECTIONS:

THIS CONCLUSION seems to be inconsistent with the first. For that which can presently be evil for a <rational> creature to a certain degree and can afterwards be a greater evil and can in turn be a lesser evil can finally fail to be evil for him, at least with respect to the absolute power of God. For it is not essentially evil of itself for him, and further, the finite, through the removal of what is finite, is finally perfected.

SECOND, it does not seem to be true that a penalty present in someone as a means of punishment for a fault is a circumstance rendering it a greater evil. This is evident from that saying of the poet, *Easily from merit, whatever you may suffer, it is necessary to make yourself serene; punishment which comes undeservedly, comes deserving of grief* [5].

REPLY TO THE FIRST OBJECTION: The major is denied. Although all the worsening of the evil which occurred by reason of a particular circumstance can be eliminated if such a circumstance is completely eliminated, the same holds true here as in the case of sin. Something can be made worse by the circumstance of place and be made less bad through a diminution of that circumstance, yet finally, after the total removal of that circumstance, some fault will remain, although the degree of evilness resulting from the circumstance in question has been eliminated.

REPLY TO THE SECOND OBJECTION: Suppose there is a penalty, *a*, which is inflicted on Socrates as a means of punishment for a fault and a penalty equal materially which belongs to an innocent Plato, and further suppose that certain circumstances are excluded, namely, that the penalty in question acquires merit or is the discharge of a debt and so hastens beatitude. Under precisely these circumstances, namely, that the real punishment belongs to Socrates but not to Plato, the penalty in question is a greater evil for Socrates as far as that circumstance is concerned. And so it is in the above citation. The poet [c] in fact has in mind that human beings for the most part actually assume greater patience and feel less sadness and displeasure when an evil of penalty is inflicted on them as much as they have justly merited it by turning themselves away from and raising themselves above their punishment, whether it is a greater evil from the circumstance of demerit [d] or not.

THIRD CONCLUSION: Something or some privation is an injurious evil for a rational creature such that it is impossible that it be found in him without being an injurious evil for him.

Proof: It is impossible that it fail to be a privation of perfection and of the integrity of his substance and the lack of a suitable part and a natural deformity, as is blindness.

QUARTA CONCLUSIO: Aliquid seu aliqua privatio est creaturae rationali malum damni quam possibile est ei convenire et non esse ei malum damni.

Probatur, quia privationem quae est boni debiti inesse convenit postea esse privationem boni non debiti inesse; igitur...

DE SECUNDO ARTICULO

PRIMA CONCLUSIO: Quicquid est creaturae rationali malum culpae eo est illi malum culpae quo est deforme legi vel ordinationi divinae et quia antecedenter a divine voluntate prohibitum vel dissuasum vel aliqualiter reprobatum.

Probatur, quia quicquid est creaturae rationali bonum iusti eo est illi sic bonum quia divinae ordinationi conforme; patet praecedenti quaestione [6]; igitur proportionabiliter econtra de malo, ab eodem enim ut regula. Prima accipitur rectitudo et tortitudo, *idem enim est iudex recti et obliqui*, primo *De Anima* [7]. Si igitur rectitudo bene vivendi sumitur primo ex conformitate ad divinam voluntatem, sequitur quod tortitudo et obliquitas male vivendi sumitur primo ex deformitate ab eadem regula.

Confirmatur: nullum agens subiectum et regulabile peccat et errat seu deficit in agendo nisi quatenus deviat a sua regula cui maxime debeat conformari.

Praeterea, malum culpae actualis non est nisi ex commissione vel omissione contra statuta Dei.

Confirmatur: eo quis peccat quo est inoboediens; sed eo est inoboediens quo devians a mandato et ordinatione Dei.

Praeterea, patet per definitiones peccati datas per Augustinum et Ambrosium, quae allegantur secundo *Sententiae* dist. 35 [8].

Praeterea, voluntas est iniusta [e] per deformitatem ab illa regula per conformitatem ad quam habet rectificari et ad rectitudinem reduci, sic est in proposito, secundum glossam super illud Psalmistae 35, *Et iusitiam tuam his qui recto sunt corde* [9]; dicit Augustinus: *Recti corde sunt qui sequuntur in hac vita voluntatem Dei. Non es rectus corde si non vis voluntatem tuam dirigere ad voluntatem Dei sed Dei vis curvare ad tuam. Voluntas tua corrigenda est ad illam, non illa curvanda ad tuam* [10].

Item, Augustinus, libro 2 *De Baptismo Parvulorum: quomodo non erit peccatum si non divinitus iubetur ut non sit;* et infra, *quomodo non vetatur* [f] *per Dei iustitiam si peccatum est?* [11].

Respondetur quod quicquid est peccatum est prohibitum prohibitione et lege indicativa quae scilicet iudicat inesse iniustum [g], sed non imperativa [12]. Contra: aut divina determinatio et ordinatio circa hoc obligat creaturam rationalem, et ita est imperativa quia obligativa; aut non obligat, igitur homo nullo iure tenetur illud cavere. Item, oratio indicativa de agibili, si non obligat, non est

FOURTH CONCLUSION: Something or some privation is an injurious evil for a rational creature such that it is possible that it be found in him without being an injurious evil for him.

Proof: A privation which is of a good which ought to be present in him is afterwards found in him to be the privation of a good which ought not to be present. Therefore...

ARTICLE 2

FIRST CONCLUSION: Whatever is an evil of fault for a rational creature is this kind of evil because it deviates from a divine law or decree and because it is antecedently prohibited or discouraged or in some way reprobated by the divine will.

Proof: Whatever is a just good for a rational creature in this kind of good because it is conformed to the divine decree, as is evident from the preceding question [6]. Therefore, correspondingly the contrary holds true in the case of evil, for it takes the same thing as its rule. First is taken rectitude and then wrongness, *for the same thing is the judge of rightness and obliquity, De Anima* I [7]. Therefore, if the rectitude of living rightly is taken first from conformity to the divine will, it follows that the wrongness and obliquity of living badly is taken first from deviation from the same rule.

Confirmation: No agent who is subject to and regulated by something sins and errs or fails in action except in so far as he deviates from his rule, to which he ought to conform himself to the highest degree.

Moreover, there is no actual evil of fault except by a commission or omission contrary to the statutes of God.

Confirmation: Someone sins because he is disobedient; but he is disobedient because he deviates from the command and decree of God.

Morever, this conclusion is evident from the definitions of sin given by Augustine and Ambrose, which are cited in the *Sentences* II, dist. 35 [8].

Moreover, the will is unjust [e] on account of deviation from that rule through conformity to which it is able to be set right and brought to a state of rectitude (as in what we propose to prove) according to a gloss on the verse of the Psalmist, 35, *And your justice to those who are upright in heart* [9]. For Augustine states: *Upright in heart are those who follow in this life the will of God. You are not upright in heart if you do not wish to direct your will to the will of God but wish the will of God to bend to yours. Your will must be adjusted to that, not that bended to yours* [10].

Again, in *On the Baptism of Infants*, bk. II, Augustine comments *how sin will not exist if it is not divinely commanded that it not be;* and later, *how is it not prohibited* [f] *by the justice of God if there is sin?* [11].

It might be replied that whatever is a sin is prohibited by an *indicative* prohibition and law

praeceptum. Patet, quia indicare quod agere *b* est bonum non est praeceptum si non sit obligatio.

CONTRA:

PRIMO, per Augustinum, I *De Libero Arbitrio* cap. 3: *Adulterium non ideo malum est quia vetatur lege, sed ideo vetatur lege quia malum est.* Idem ponit de homicidio et sacrilegio et huiusmodi [13].

Item, super illud *Levitici* 19, *Non facietis furtum, non mentiemini* [14], glossa Augustini: *Quia iniustum erat mendacium, ideo est prohibitum; non quia prohibitum, ideo iniustum* [15].

Confirmatur: in articulis Parisiensibus posterioribus dicitur sic: *Quod odium proximi non est demeritorium nisi quia prohibitum a Deo--Error* [16].

SECUNDO principaliter, illa sunt formaliter et essentialiter ex se mala non ideo quia lege prohibita, quia circumscripto omni praecepto et omni lege apparenti, secundum dictamen rectae rationis mala et fugibilia ex rationibus terminorum; quaedam sunt huiusmodi, ut blasphemare Deum, nocere innocenti sine culpa et sine causa, etc.

TERTIO, illi convenit malitia ex se formaliter non tantum ex institutione divinae voluntatis quod est ex se dignum aliqua poena secundum rigorem iustitiae, non tantum ex institutione nec quia Deus deputavit illud ad huiusmodi poenam--patet quia esse dignum poena praesupponit malitiam; sed aliqua actio hominis est huiusmodi.

Probo, quia Deus punit citra [h] condignum; igitur illud peccatum meruit maiorem poenam quam erit illa quam Deus infliget, et est dignum maiore. Et tamen Deus non ordinavit punire nec deputavit illud peccatum ad illam maiorem, quia non ordinavit inferre pro illo nisi illam quam inferet et punire nisi illa qua puniet.

Confirmatur: sit *b* poena qua punit hunc damnatum, tunc sic: Deus punit vel puniet hunc damnatum pro peccato praeterito maiori poena quam sit *b*; igitur huiusmodi damnatus per peccatum praeteritum demeruit *b*. Consequentia est necessaria; aliter Deus esset iniustus vel crudelis vel non puniret de facto ad condignum. Et antecedens est possibile, igitur consequens; igitur est verum et necessarium quia est de praeterito simpliciter.

QUARTO, aliquid est magis malum non quia magis prohibitum, et aliquis peccat gravius altero non ex circumstantia maioris prohibitionis, sed praecise ex hac circumstantia, quia consenserit

which judges the unjust [g] to be present, but not by an *imperative* prohibition and law [12]. In opposition to this the following may be said. Either the divine determination and decree about that obliges a rational creature, and so it is imperative because it is obligatory; or it does not oblige, and therefore a human being is bound by no law to avoid that. Again, an indicative discourse concerning action, if it does not oblige, is not a precept. This is evident because to indicate that doing *b* is good is not a precept if it is not an obligation.

OBJECTIONS:

FIRST, from Augustine in *The Free Choice of the Will* I, chap. 3: *Adultery is not evil because it is prohibited by the law, but it is prohibited by the law because it is evil.* He asserts the same thing regarding homicide and sacrilege and similar actions [13].

Again, on the verse of *Leviticus* 19, *You shall not steal, You shall not lie* [14], the gloss of Augustine states: *Because lying was unjust, therefore it is prohibited; it is not the case that because it is prohibited, it is therefore unjust* [15].

Confirmation: It is stated in the later articles of Paris, *that the hatred of one's neighbor is not demeritorious except because it is prohibited by God--Error* [16].

SECOND, those things which are formally and essentially evil of themselves are not such because they are prohibited by the law because, with every precept and every apparent law excluded, they are evil according to the dictate of right reason and to be avoided by the definitions of their terms. Certain actions are of this type, such as blaspheming God, doing harm to an innocent person without fault and without cause, etc. .

THIRD, evilness of itself formally is found in that which is of itself deserving of some punishment according to the rigor of justice not only by the establishment of the divine will nor because God assigned it to such punishment. This is evident because to be deserving of punishment presupposes evilness. But some human action is of this type.

I prove this as follows. God punishes apart from [h] desert. Therefore, that sin merits a greater punishment than will be that which God inflicts, and it is deserving of greater. And yet God neither decreed to punish that sin with that greater punishment nor assigned it to that greater punishment, for he did not decree to inflict any punishment for that sin except what he shall inflict and to punish in any way except that by which he shall punish.

Confirmation: Let *b* be a punishment by which God punishes a particular person who is damned. Then this follows: God punishes or will punish this damned person for a past sin with a greater punishment than is *b*; therefore this damned person deserved *b* on account of his past sin. The inference is necessary; otherwise God would be unjust or cruel or would not in fact punish in relation to desert. And the antecedent is possible, therefore also the consequent. And therefore it is true and necessary because it has to do with the past absolutely.

FOURTH, something is a greater evil not because it is prohibited more, and somone sins more gravely than another not on account of the circumstance of a greater prohibition, but precisely on

in id quod est magis malum; igitur aliquid est ex se malum, non quia prohibitum.

Antecedens probatur, quia ceteris paribus gravius peccat volens occidere Sortem quam volens furari res eius, et tamen non est differentia in forma prohibitionis, *Exodi* 20, *Non occides, Non furtum facies* [17]. Unde ex nulla via arguimus hunc gravius peccare nisi quia consenserit [i] in rem magis malum.

Confirmatur: nullum malum erit gravius altero, ut deductur quaestione praecedenti [18], erit enim tantum malum quantum est a Deo reprobatum; sed non magis reprobatum est hoc quam illud quia omnino eadem est reprobatio utriusque, scilicet divina volitio. Ex quo etiam sequitur quod utrumque est infinite malum quia infinite reprobatum. Nec valet dicere quod ad poenam finitam reprobatur, quia prius naturaliter est esse malum et iniustum quam deputari ad poenam; ideo enim ad tantam vel maiorem poenam deputatur quia est tantum vel maius malum.

QUINTO, si [j] quicquid est malum et iniustum ideo est malum quia a divina voluntate prohibitum, sequitur quod a Deo est malum et habet a Deo causaliter esse malum; et consequenter Deus faceret hominem et actum esse malum.

Probatio consequentiae: quia eo est malum quo prohibitum secundum te; sed a Deo habet antecedenter et causaliter esse prohibitum.

SEXTO, sequitur quod non ideo Deus reprobat hominem vel actum quia malus sit, sed ideo homo et actus esset malus quia prius natura vel naturali intelligentia Deus reprobaret et odiret et detestaretur illum.

Consequentia probatur, quia prius natura vel naturali intelligentia et causaliter erit Deum prohibere *a*, et posterius causaliter et naturaliter erit *a* esse malum; sed Deum prohibere *a* est Deum reprobare et detestari *a*.

Falsitas consequentis probatur, quia Deus gratis reprobaret et odiret hominem, non propter demerita; et Deus prius esset ultor quam homo peccator.

Confirmatur: cum intellectus divinus offert divinae voluntati *a* actionem ante omnem determinationem liberam, aut offert *a* ut malum, et propositum; aut ut bonum, igitur id quod est ex se formaliter bonum, Deus gratis ordinat esse malum et reprobat; aut ut neutrum et indifferens. Contra: tum quia divina voluntas reprobaret et odiret *a* gratis, non ex ratione malitiae visae in *a*; tum quia omnia essent ex se indifferentia equaliter, nec unum esset ex se magis bonum vel malum quam aliud, et ita levare festucam non est ex se et ex natura rei et obiecti magis actus indifferens quam actus blasphemandi Deum vel nocendi innocenti.

SEPTIMO, sequitur quod nullum malum eveniret in entibus.

Probo: sit illud *a* fieri; aut igitur *a* fieri est simpliciter et absolute a Deo volitum formaliter,

account of the circumstance that he has consented to that which is a greater evil. Therefore something is evil of itself, and not because it is prohibited.

Proof of the antecedent: Other things being equal, someone sins more gravely in willing to kill Socrates than in willing to steal one of his possessions, and yet there is no difference in the form of the prohibition in *Exodus* 20, *You shall not kill; You shall not steal* [17]. So in no way do we prove that this person sins more gravely except on the grounds that he has consented [i] to a thing which is a greater evil.

Confirmation: No one evil will be more gravely committed than another, as is deduced from the preceding question [18]. For the degree of evil something has will be a function of the extent to which it is reprobated by God. But this one is no more reprobated than that one because the reprobation of each one is entirely the same, namely, the divine volition. From this it also follows that each one is infinitely evil because infinitely reprobated. Nor can it be said that it is reprobated to a finite punishment because being evil and unjust is naturally prior to being assigned to punishment, for it is assigned so much punishment or greater punishment because it is evil to such a degree or more so.

FIFTH, if [j] whatever is evil and unjust is evil because it is prohibited by the divine will, it follows that evil comes from God and receives causally its evil status from God. And consequently, God would make a human being and an act to be evil.

Proof of the inference: According to you, it is evil because it is prohibited; but it receives its prohibited status antecedently and causally from God.

SIXTH, it follows that God does not reprobate a human being or an act because he or it is evil, but a human being and an act would be evil because, prior to its nature or natural understanding, God would reprobate and hate and detest that human being or act.

Proof of the inference: It will be the case that, prior to its nature or natural understanding and causally, God prohibits *a*, and afterwards it will be the case that, causally and naturally, *a* is evil. But for God to prohibit *a* is for God to reprobate and detest *a*.

Proof of the falsity of the consequent: God would reprobate and hate a human being gratuitously, not on account of demerits. And God punishing would come before a human being sinning.

Confirmation: When the divine intellect presents an action, *a*, to the divine will before any free determination has been made, either it presents *a* as evil, and we have what is to be proven; or it presents *a* as good, and then God gratuitously decrees to be evil and reprobates that which is formally good of itself; or it presents *a* as neither the one nor the other and as indifferent. In opposition to this the following may be said. First, the divine will would reprobate and hate *a* gratuitously, not by reason of evilness seen in *a*. Second, everything would of itself be equally indifferent, and one thing would not of itself be a greater good or a greater evil than another. And so to pick up a straw is no more an indifferent act of itself by its nature and the nature of the object than the act of blaspheming God or of doing harm to an innocent person.

SEVENTH, it follows that beings would not have evil befall them.

I prove this as follows. Suppose that *a* is done. Then it is the case either that God formally

aut formaliter et absolute nolitum, aut absolute et formaliter nec volitum nec nolitum. Si primum, igitur *a* fieri est simpliciter et formaliter divinae voluntati placitum; igitur non reprobatum sed approbatum et acceptum. Si secundum, igitur non eveniet; alioquin Deus esset impotens ut patet I *Sententiae* dist. 46 [19]. Si tertium, igitur *a* fieri simpliciter et absolute non est neque bonum neque malum quia neque simpliciter placitum neque displicens.

Dices, non est volitum neque nolitum secundum voluntatem effectivam, sed secundum voluntatem praeceptivam vel prohibitivam. Contra: vel praeceptum divinum est aliquid creatum aut aliquid increatum. Si primum, igitur non est prima regula bonitatis et malitiae actuum nostrorum, nec actus nostri sunt boni vel mali [k] per se et principaliter et ultimate per conformitatem vel deformitatem ad illud. Si secundum, illud non est nisi volitio vel nolitio divina seu approbatio vel reprobatio seu dilectio vel odium, et stat ratio principalis; vel est ratio et dictamen divini intellectus prius omni ordinatione voluntatis, et propositum, quia erat malum ex se, non ex divinae voluntatis prohibitiva ordinatione.

Confirmatur: aut divina voluntas praecipit vel prohibet [l] formaliter volendo et approbando et complacendo et diligendo, aut nolendo et reprobando et odiendo, aut nec sic nec sic. Si primum vel secundum, stat ratio principalis. Si tertium, igitur non eo malum quo divinae voluntati deformatur quia actus divinae voluntatis circa illud non erit nisi aliquo modorum praedictorum.

Item: sit *b* aliquod possibile fieri ab homine quod tamen non fiet, nec est praeceptum nec prohibitum fieri; tunc aut *b* fieri est magis volitum et minus nolitum a Deo [m] quam *a* fieri, aut non. Si primum, igitur eveniet non minus quam *a*. Si secundum, igitur erit non minus malum quam *a* fieri quia non minus simpliciter nolitum et displicens.

OCTAVO, stat voluntatem in agendo esse deformem divinae voluntati et eius actionem esse a Deo reprobatum et oditam, et non esse vitiosam et culpabilem; igitur non eo fore vitiosam quo deformem et reprobatam.

Antecedens probatur: pone quod Deus reprobet et odiat et detestetur formaliter secundum actum intrinsecum voluntatis *a* fieri et quod dictet *a* non esse faciendum, et tamen hoc non revelaverit nec insinuaverit hominibus; tunc stat voluntatem agere *a* quia etiam si prohiberetur expresse, staret voluntatem agere *a*; tunc *a* non est peccatum illi voluntati. Probo, quia ignorantia invincibilis nec culpabiliter contracta nec sequela peccati per modum poenae totaliter excusat; alioquin dementes et parvi possent peccare, immo bestiae.

Dices, non stat creaturam rationalem debere non [n] facere *a* et Deum nullo modo insinuasse, et per consequens Deum reprobare *a*. Contra: divina reprobatio vel prohibitio et odium alicuis actionis possibilis non necessitat Deum ad producendum aliquid extra se, sed est indifferens ad fore vel non fore illius actionis. Illa etiam divina determinatio fuit ab aeterno sine huiusmodi insinuatione; ab aeterno enim Jacob dilexit et Esau odio habuit [20]. Igitur Deum odire et reprobare *a* non necessitat ad revelationem. Item, stat hominem obligari ad id quod ignorat ignorantia invincibili et

wills simply and absolutely that *a* be done, or that God is formally and absolutely unwilling that *a* be done, or that God is absolutely and formally neither willing nor unwilling that *a* be done. If the first is the case, then *a* being done is simply and formally pleasing to the divine will; and therefore, it is not reprobated but approved and accepted. If the second is the case, then it will not happen; otherwise, God would be powerless, as is evident in the *Sentences* I, dist. 46 [19]. If the third is the case, then *a* being done is neither good nor evil simply and absolutely because it is neither simply pleasing nor displeasing.

But you will say that God's willingness or unwillingness are not in accordance with his effective will, but with his preceptive or prohibitive will. In opposition to this the following may be said. Either the divine precept is something created or something uncreated. If the first is the case, then it is not the first rule of the goodness and evilness of our acts, and our acts are not good or evil [k] principally and ultimately by conformity to or deviation from that precept. If the second is the case, that precept is nothing but the divine volition or unwillingness, or approval or reprobation, or love or hate, and the principal reason stands; or it is the reason and dictate of the divine intellect prior to any decree of the will, and we have what was to be proved, because it was evil of itself and not from the prohibitive decree of the divine will.

Confirmation: Either the divine will formally commands or prohibits [l] by willing and approving and being pleased and loving, or by being unwilling and reprobating and hating, or neither the former nor the latter. If the first or the second is the case, the principal reason stands. If the third, then it is not the case that something is evil because it deviates from the divine will, because an act of the divine will concerning it would only take place by some one of the previously mentioned modes.

Again, let *b* be something possible to be done by a human being but which will not be done and which is neither commanded nor prohibited to be done. Then either God wills more and is less unwilling that *b* be done [m] than that *a* be done, or this is not so. If the first is the case, then *b* will happen no less than *a* does. If the second is the case, then *b* being done will be no less evil than *a* being done because no less is it simply unwilled and displeasing.

EIGHTH, it holds true that the will in acting deviate from the divine will and that its action be reprobated and hated by God but that it not be vicious and culpable. Therefore, it will not be vicious because it is deviant and reprobated.

Proof of the antecedent: Assume that God formally reprobates and hates and detests *a* being done according to an intrinsic act of his will and that God prescribes that *a* ought not to be done, but that God shall not reveal this nor give notification of it to human beings. Then it holds that the will does *a*, because even if it should be explicitly prohibited, it would hold that the will does *a*; and then *a* is not a sin for that will. I prove this last point as follows. Invincible ignorance which is neither culpably incurred nor the result of sin as a way of punishment excuses totally. Otherwise, the insane and little children would be able to sin, indeed even beasts.

But you will say that it does not hold true that a rational creature ought not [n] to do *a* while God has in no way given notification of this, and consequently, that God reprobate *a*. In opposition to this the following may be said. The divine reprobation or prohibition and hatred of some possible action does not necessitate God to produce anything outside himself, but is indifferent to the future existence or nonexistence of that action. That divine determination also existed from eternity without

inculpabili, quia obligatur pure ad esse sine peccato originali et ad habere iustitiam originalem.

AD PRIMUM: Augustinus intendit quod aliqua sunt mala non quia prohibita legibus humanis, nec quia a voluntate legis humanae propter illa condemnantur et puniuntur homines, nec ideo praecise sunt mala quia prohibita lege divina scripta et extrinsecus expressa et promulgata hominibus, ita quod per prohibitionem intellegit aliquod signum extrinsecum datum ipsius divinae ordinationis; sed omnia quae possibilia agi ab homine sunt mala ideo sunt mala quia lege aeterna divina sunt prohibita, quae etiam quoad multa est quasi radicaliter scripta in mente creaturae rationalis. Esto enim quod *a* fieri esset ex se essentialiter et necessario malum; adhuc ideo est malum quia sic dictatum a ratione divini intellectus cui conformatur divinae voluntatis determinatio; et per consequens, ideo esset malum quia a Deo sic prohibitum et reprobatum.

Ad confirmationem per idem.

AD SECUNDUM: si intelligitur de circumscriptione reali, negatur maior, quid ad nullam ordinationem et determinationem divinae voluntatis fore sequitur nihil esse malum; si vero intellegatur de circumscriptione secundum nostrum intelligere, negatur maior, ratio enim et dictamen iuris naturalis in intellectu nostro potest esse regula dirigens intellectum nostrum non aspiciendo actualiter ad ordinationem divinae voluntatis, licet secundum Dei [o] voluntatem. Rectitudo actionis humanae et rationis et dictaminis et iuris naturalis reducantur in rectitudinem divinae voluntatis et ab illa causaliter procedant, haec enim regula subordinatur illi.

AD TERTIUM negatur minor accipiendo *esse dignum poena* actualiter et formaliter.

Ad probationem: cum Deus dicitur punire citra condignum, non intellegitur quod praecise meruit formaliter et actualiter determinantam poenam et Deus puniat minori, sed intellegitur quod si Deus vellet pro tali peccato maiorem infligere, posset iuste infligere. Et hoc est ex quadam lege Dei generali dicente quod omnem transgressionem divini praecepti posset Deus punire iuste quantacumque poena vellet.

Ad confirmationem: semper est contingens quod iste meruit formaliter et actualiter tantam poenam praecise quia implicite includit aliquid futurum, scilicet quod Deus ordinaverit eum pro futuro punire tanta poena.

AD QUARTUM negatur antecedens.

Ad probationem: Licet in forma verborum et figura loquendi non sit differentia in illis

such notification, for from eternity he loved Jacob and regarded Esau with hatred [20]. Therefore that God hate and reprobate *a* does not necessitate him to make a revelation. Again, it holds true that a human being is obligated to that of which he is ignorant on account of invincible and inculpable ignorance because he is obligated to exist purely without original sin and to possess that original justice.

REPLY TO THE FIRST OBJECTION: Augustine has in mind that some things are evil not because they are prohibited by human laws, nor because human beings are condemned and punished for those things by the will of a human law, nor because they are prohibited by divine law which is written down and outwardly expressed and promulgated to human beings, so that by *prohibition* he understands some outward sign given of the divine decree itself. Rather, all those things which are possible to be done by a human being which are evil therefore are evil because they are prohibited by the divine eternal law, which also, with respect to many things, is, as it were, radically written in the mind of a rational creature. For suppose it were to be the case that doing *a* is of itself essentially and necesssarily evil. Thus far, it is evil because so prescribed by the divine intellect's reason to which the determination of the divine will is conformed. And consequently, it would therefore be evil because it is so prohibited and reprobated by God.

Reply to the confirmation: Through the same considerations.

REPLY TO THE SECOND OBJECTION: If it is understood of a real exclusion, the major is denied. For from the fact that there will be no decree and determination of the divine will, it follows that nothing is evil. If in fact it may be understood of an exclusion according to our understanding, the major is denied. For reason and the dictate of natural law in our intellect can be a rule directing our intellect without actually looking to the decree of the divine will, although it is in accordance with the will of God [o]. The rectitude of human action and reason and of the dictate and law of nature are reduced to the rectitude of the divine will and proceed from it causally, for the former rule is subordinated to the latter one.

REPLY TO THE THIRD OBJECTION: The minor is denied by taking *to be deserving of punishment* actually and formally.

Reply to the proof: When God is said to punish apart from desert, this is not understood to mean that the sin deserved precisely a determined punishment formally and actually and that God may punish with a lesser one, but rather, that if God would wish to inflict a greater punishment for such a sin, he could justly inflict it. And this comes from a certain general law of God stating that God could justly punish any transgression of a divine precept with however great a punishment he should wish.

Reply to the confirmation: It is always contingent that he deserved formally and actually so great a punishment precisely because something future is implicitly involved, namely, that God will have decreed to punish him in the future with so great a punishment.

REPLY TO THE FOURTH OBJECTION: The antecedent is denied.

Reply to the proof: There is no difference in those prohibitions in the form of the words and

prohibitionibus quia simplici et absoluto sermone sine modificationibus prohibetur hoc et illud, tamen ideo hoc est magis malum quam illud quia a Deo magis prohibitum, et determinatum et dictatum esse magis malum et sub maioris poenae commutatione prohibitum, quod nobis innotescit ex legibus iuris naturalis scripti a Deo in mente nostra et ex legibus Dei scriptis. Si enim prohibetur tanquam malum nocere proximo, intellegimus esse magis malum et prohibitum et determinari esse magis malum magis nocere proximo; sed nocere in propria substantia est magis nocere.

Ad confirmationem patet quaestione praecedenti [21].

AD QUINTUM negatur consequentia. Princeps enim qui prohibet homicidium non est causa homicidii, nec ab eo causaliter sunt homines homicidae.

Ad probationem: non est intellegendum quod esse prohibitum sit per se et formaliter ratio huius quod dico esse malum. Si enim non fiat nec sit, nor erit malum licet sit prohibitum; nec prohibitio vel prohibens est causa mali demeritorie et cui imputanda sit malitia. Sed cum dicitur quod eo malum quo prohibitum, intellegitur quod prohibitio est lex antecedens et per deformitatem ad illam est commissio vel omissio mala. Non igitur est causa demeritorie et culpabiliter vel imputabiliter sed causa cognoscendi et arguendi malitiam a priori, quia per recessum ab illa regula recta est actio vel omissio mala.

AD SEXTUM negatur consequentia.

Ad probationem: reprobatio divina potest accipi quadrupliciter; licet enim actus divinae voluntatis sit simplex, tamen aequivalet infinitis distinctis quibus diversimode volumus.

Uno modo, ut est formaliter prohibitio, id est, ordinatio et determinatio et dictamen quod *a* non est agendum a creatura rationali et quod creatura rationalis debet non agere *a*. Et sic creatura rationalis non est proprie reprobata sed actus, quia creatura rationalis non est prohibita sed ei actio est prohibita.

Secundo modo, ut est displicentia et detestatio et odium actionis vel omissionis actualis utpote deformiter praeordinationi prohibitive, vel etiam displicentia et odium creaturae rationalis simpliciter et actualiter committentis vel omittentis deformiter antecedenti prohibitioni prohibitive et secundum dispositionem in qua est actualiter creatura rationalis. Et sic Deus reprobat illum hominem vel actum quia malum potius quam econtra; eo enim est malus quia priori ordinationi deformis. Hoc modo reprobus existens in gratia non actu reprobatur a Deo sed electus existens in mortali.

Differentia autem huius secundi membri a primo patet in creaturis. Si enim rex prohibet *a* fieri et ordinat [p] *a* non esse agendum, non ex hoc rex odit aliquem subditum. Posito autem quod Sortes, ignorante rege, committit *a*; sequitur Sortem esse malum quia agit deformiter ordinationi. Postea vero rex cognoscens Sortem egisse *a* habet noviter odium, displicentiam et detestationem respectu Sortis, quae potest dici *reprobatio*. Nec ideo Sortes est malus quia sic reprobatus, sed econtra; contingit etiam quod sciens alterum esse malum, non odit illum aut minus odit propter effectum amoris ad illum.

Tertio modo, ut est deputatio ad poenam consequentem. Sic autem non est homo vel actus malus quia a Deo reprobatus, sed potius econtra.

in the figure of speech since the former is prohibited as well as the latter by simple and absolute language without qualifications. Nevertheless, the former is a greater evil than the latter because it is prohibited more by God and determined and prescribed to be a greater evil and prohibited under commutation of a greater punishment, which is made known to us by the laws of the natural law written by God in our mind and by the written laws of God. For if it is prohibited as evil to do harm to a neighbor, we understand it to be a greater evil and prohibited more and determined to be a greater evil to do greater harm to a neighbor; but to bring harm to him in his own substance is to do greater harm.

Reply to the confirmation: The response is evident in the preceding question [21].

REPLY TO THE FIFTH OBJECTION: The inference is denied. For a ruler who prohibits homicide is not the cause of homicide, nor are human beings murderers causally from him.

Reply to the proof: It is not to be understood that being prohibited is through itself and formally the reason for that which I say to be evil. For if something is not done and does not exist, it will not be evil although it is prohibited. Neither the prohibition nor the prohibiting is the cause of the evil with respect to demerit and that to which evilness should be imputed. But when we say that something is evil because prohibited, this is understood to mean that the prohibition is the antecedent law and that a commission or omission is evil by deviating from it. Therefore, it is not the cause with respect to demerit and culpability and imputation, but is the cause of knowing and demonstrating evilness a priori, because an action or omission is evil by virtue of withdrawal from that right rule.

REPLY TO THE SIXTH OBJECTION: The inference is denied.

Reply to the proof: Divine reprobation can be taken in four senses. For although an act of the divine will is simple, it is equivalent to infinitely many distinct acts which we will in various ways.

In one sense, it is taken as formally a prohibition, that is, a decree and determination and dictate that *a* ought not to be done by a rational creature and that a rational creature ought not to do *a*. And in this sense a rational creature is not, properly speaking, reprobated, but rather, an act is, because a rational creature is not prohibited, but rather, an action is prohibited to him.

In the second sense, it is taken as displeasure at and detestation and hatred of an action or actual omission as deviating from what has been previously decreed by way of prohibition. Or even it is displeasure at and hatred of a rational creature simply and actually committing or omitting something in a way deviating from an antecedent prohibition and according to the disposition in which a rational creature actually is. And in this sense God reprobates the human being or the act because it is evil, rather than the contrary. For he or it is evil because he or it deviates from a prior decree. In this sense, the reprobate living in a state of grace is not in reality reprobated by God, but rather, the elect living in a state of mortal sin.

The difference, however, between the second part and the first is evident in the case of creatures. For if a king prohibits *a* being done and decrees [p] that *a* ought not to be done, it is not on account of this that the king hates some subject. Assume, however, that Socrates, ignoring the king, commits *a*. It follows that Socrates is evil because his action deviates from the decree. Afterwards in fact the king, knowing that Socrates has done *a*, now begins to experience hatred, displeasure, and detestation with respect to Socrates, which can be called *reprobation*. And it is not the case that Socrates is evil because so reprobated, but rather, the contrary is the case. It even

Quarto, ut est odium et displicentia creaturae, vel etiam deputatio eius ad poenam aeternam secundum dispositionem quam est finaliter habitura. Et sic ab aeterno reprobavit et odio habuit Esau, et approbavit et dilexit Jacob. Sic etiam nullus electus umquam reprobatur, et quilibet praescitus semper reprobatur.

Accipiendo igitur *reprobationem* tribus ultimis modis, patet quod probatio consequentiae non valet. Accipiendo autem primo modo, conceditur quod ideo homo vel eius actus est malus quia reprobatur, ut non notetur causalitas formalis quia non eo formaliter malus quo prohibitus sed quo actualiter prohibitioni, id est, legi prohibitive, deformis et contra eam [q] elicitus; nec ut notetur causalitas effectiva ut malum potest habere causalitatem effectivam; sed ut notetur causalitas regulativa, a qua derivatur et cui conformiter debuit creatura rationalis moveri et agere.

Notandum igitur quod secundum ordinem rationis et intelligentiae naturalis circa Deum: primo, voluntas vult et ordinat creaturam debere non agere *a* et intellectus divinus conformiter dictat et iudicat, et hoc est *a* prohibere; secundo, sequitur Sortem agere *a*; tertio, sequitur *a* actionem esse malam et Sortem esse malum quatenus agentem *a* et deformiter se habentum praeordinationi divinae; quarto, Deum sequitur odire et displicere in Sorte, et quasi inimicari contrarie ad animam; quinto, deputatio ad poenam futuram.

Ad confirmationem patet ex dictis.

AD SEPTIMUM negatur consequentia.
Ad probationem dictum est supra dist. 22, quaest. tertia [22].

AD OCTAVUM negatur antecedens.
Ad probationem: repugnantia est quod Deus velit et ordinaverit simpliciter et ultimate Sortem debere facere *a* et quod Deus hoc nullo modo insinuaverit, nec lege naturali scripta radicaliter et seminaliter in mente rationali, nec alia lege speciali, nec revelatione, nec inspiratione; sequitur enim Sortem iuste et rationabiliter obligari et non obligari ad faciendum *a*. Prima pars patet, quia per te Deus determinat Sortem debere facere *a*. Secunda probatur, quia per se notum. Videtur quod nullus subditus obligatur rationabiliter ad agendum id quod nulla via ei est insinuatum; immo nec est praeceptum nec mandaum ex quo nulla via insinuatum; immo subditus se habet in hoc quasi non rationalis.

Conceditur igitur responsio ad probationem [r]. Licet Deus nihil agat simpliciter, necessario ex se, tamen ordinans antecedens necessitat; si ad consequens, ex hypothesi antecedenti. Ideo si Deus determinavit deputare *a* Sorti ad peccatum et punire Sortem propter *a* peccatum, consequens est ut Sortem obligaverit per praeceptum ad non faciendum *a*. Hoc autem infert et exigit aliqualem insinuationem.

happens that the king, knowing another to be evil, does not hate him or hates him to a lesser degree as an effect of loving him.

In the third sense, it is taken as the assignment to subsequent punishment. In this sense, however, it is not the case that a human being or an act is evil because it is reprobated by God, but rather, the contrary is the case.

In the fourth sense, it is taken as hatred of and displeasure at a <rational> creature, or even as the assignment of him to eternal punishment according to the disposition which he is finally going to have. And in this sense God, from eternity, reprobated Esau and regarded him with hatred and approved of and loved Jacob. Likewise in this sense no one who is elect is ever reprobated, and anyone predestined to damnation is always reprobated.

Therefore, taking *reprobation* in the last three senses, it is evident that the proof of the inference is not valid. Taking it in the first sense, however, it is conceded that a human being or his act is evil because he or it is reprobated. But this does not signify formal causality, since that in question is not formally evil because it is prohibited but because it actually deviates from and is elicited contrary to a prohibition [q], that is, a law by way of prohibition. Nor is effective causality signified as evil can have effective causality. But regulative causality is signified, from which it is derived and conformably to which a rational creature ought to be moved and to act.

Therefore it should be noted that, according to the order of reason and of natural understanding, the following is the case concerning God. First, the divine will wills and decrees that a <rational> creature ought not to do *a* and the divine intellect prescribes and judges conformably; and this is prohibiting *a*. Second, it follows that Socrates does *a*. Third, it follows that action *a* is evil and that Socrates is evil in so far as he does *a* and conducts himself in a way deviating from the antecedent divine decree. Fourth, it follows that God hates and is displeased with Socrates and, as it were, is made an enemy of his soul. Fifth, there is the assigment to future punishment.

Reply to the confirmation: The response is evident from what has been said.

REPLY TO THE SEVENTH OBJECTION: The inference is denied.
Reply to the proof: This is stated above in dist. 22, q. 3 [22].

REPLY TO THE EIGHTH OBJECTION: The antecedent is denied.
Reply to the proof: The inconsistency is that God should will and shall have decreed simply and finally that Socrates ought to do *a* but that God shall not have given notification of this in any way, neither by a natural law written radically and seminally in the rational mind, nor by another special law, nor by revelation, nor by inspiration. For it follows that Socrates is justly and reasonably both obligated and not obligated to do *a*. The first part is evident because, according to you, God determines that Socrates ought to do *a*. The second part is proved because it is known per se. It seems that no subject is reasonably obligated to do that for which he has not received notification in any way. Indeed, it is neither a precept nor a command since notification has not been given of it in some way. Indeed, the subject here behaves as if it were not rational.

Therefore the response to the proof [r] is conceded. Although God does nothing simply, necessarily, of itself, nevertheless, decreeing the antecedent, he does necessitate; if to the consequent, from the antecedent supposition. Therefore, if God determined to designate *a* as a sin for Socrates and to punish Socrates on account of sin *a*, the consequent is that he will have obligated Socrates by

Ad aliud negatur de obligatione ad agendum et quae obligat ad peccatum actuale, quicquid sit de obligatione habendi aliquid ratione alterius personae a qua origo trahitur.

SECUNDA CONCLUSIO, quam pono sine assertione sed per modum praedicabilis collocutionis disputative, est quod nullus actus vel habitus aut privatio est creaturae rationali malum culpae quin de omnipotentia Dei absolute possit creaturae rationali convenire et ei esse non malum culpae.

Probatur primo de privatione, quia sit *a* privatio alicuius boni, puta *b*; tunc *b* existente in creatura rationali, Deus potest ipsum auferre et annihilare sine culpa praecedente in illa creatura rationali. Deus etiam posset creaturam rationalem creare in puris naturalibus sine omni accidente, igitur sine *b*; et ita privatio ipsius *b* non esset illi naturae peccatum.

Item, de habitu patet, quia tali habitu existente possibile est peccatum remitti, cum etiam habitus prius vitiosus maneat secundum aliquem gradum in converso noviter.

De actu etiam. Probatur primo, quia talis actus potest elici in furia quam quis incurrit naturaliter vel inculpabiliter, et ita talis actus non solum non erit peccatum, immo potest etiam stare cum gratia, ut si post baptismum ante annos discretionis incurrit furiam.

Item, potest elici a somniante.

Item, posset a solo Deo totaliter causari in anima rationali; igitur non esset tunc anima iniusta per illud.

Consequentia patet per Anselmum, *De Casu Diaboli* cap. 14 [23]; et quia illud peccatum esset a Deo et esset Deo imputandum.

Antecedens probatur, quia est omnipotens, et quia quemcumque effectum potest Deus mediante causa secunda potest se solo immediate secundum articulum Parisiensem [24].

Praeterea, Deus non necessitatur prohibere *a* actum vel reprobare et detestari *b* ens positivum tanquam iniustum cum *b* non sit essentialiter ex natura sua necessario iniustum [s]; patet per media prius posita.

Praeterea, in libera potestate Dei est quod *b* sit magis vel minus malum; igitur et quod sit simpliciter malum.

Consequentia patet, quia si esset essentialiter et necessario malum, esset certe malitiae alicuius.

Antecedens probatur, quia potest reprobare et detestari et odire *b* magis vel minus sicut et approbare magis vel minus *d* bonum contrarium actum, quia potest prohibere pro certo loco specialiter.

Praeterea, sit *b* huiusmodi actus, tunc sic: nullus est actus ita indifferens quin possit fieri peior quam sit *b*; igitur *b* potest esse non malus.

Antecedens patet, quia potest noviter prohiberi et post prohibitionem elici cum eat et talibus circumstantiis aggravantibus quod excedet *b* elicitum a Sorte.

Consequentia patet, quia malitia non est magis essentialis ipsi *b* quam indifferentia ipsi *c*, non minus essentialiter ex se est *c* indifferens quam *b* malum et iniustum.

Praeterea, hoc maxime videretur de actionibus quae, iure naturae et dictamine rationis

a precept to not doing *a*. This, however, brings in and requires notification of some kind.

Reply to the other argument: This is denied with respect to the obligation to action and to what obliges in relation to actual sin, whatever may be the case with respect to the obligation to have something by reason of another person from whom one's origin is derived.

The SECOND CONCLUSION, which I set out without assertion and disputatively after the manner of a laudable discussion, is that no act or habit or privation is an evil of fault for a rational creature such that, with respect to the omnipotence of God absolutely, it is not possible that it be found in a rational creature and fail to be an evil of fault for him.

This conclusion is proved first of a privation. For let *a* be the privation of some good, for example, *b*. Then, with *b* existing in a rational creature, God can take it away and annihilate it without a preceding fault in that rational creature. God could also create a rational creature in a state of purely natural capacities without any accident, and therefore, without *b*; and so the privation of *b* would not be a sin for that nature.

Again, this conclusion is evident with respect to a habit. For it is possible that sin be remitted with such a habit existing, since even a previously vicious habit remains to some degree in someone who is newly converted.

This conclusion is likewise evident with respect to an act. This is proved first, because such an act can be elicited in a state of madness which someone incurs naturally or inculpably. And so such an act not only will not be a sin, indeed it can even coexist with grace, as is the case if someone incurs madness after baptism and before the years of discretion.

Again, an act can be elicited by someone dreaming.

Again, an act could be totally caused in the rational soul by God alone; therefore, the soul would not then be unjust on account of it.

The inference is evident from Anselm in *On The Fall of the Devil*, chap. 14 [23], and because that sin would come from God and be imputable to God.

The antecedent is proved because God is omnipotent, and because, according to the article of Paris, whatever effect God can bring about through the medium of a secondary cause, he can bring about immediately by himself [24].

Moreover, God is not necessitated to prohibit an act, *a*, or to reprobate and detest a real being, *b*, as unjust since *b* is not necessarily unjust [s] essentially by its nature.

This is evident from the means of proof previously set out.

Moreover, it is within the free power of God that *b* is a greater or a lesser evil; therefore also that it is simply evil.

The inference is evident because if it were essentially and necessarily evil, it would certainly have some evilness.

Proof of the antecedent: God can reprobate and detest and hate *b* to a greater or lesser degree just as God can approve of an opposite good act, *d*, to a greater or lesser degree, because God can prohibit it specifically for a certain place.

Moreover, let *b* be such an act. Then there is no act which is so indifferent that it could not be made worse than *b* is; therefore *b* can fail to be evil.

The antecedent is evident because an act can be newly prohibited and, as it turns out, be

naturalis per se notae, apparent prohibitae, ut actiones quae sunt homicidia, furta, adulteria, etc.; sed huiusmodi actiones possibile est de potentia Dei absoluta esse non peccata.

Patet per Bernardum, *De Praecepto et Dispensatione* [t] cap. 4: *Non occides, Non furtum facies, Non moechaberis, et reliqua illius tabulae praecepta, etsi nullam prorsus dispensationem admittunt, Deus tamen eorum quod voluerit quando voluerit solvit; sicut cum ab Hebraeis Aegyptios spoliari sive cum prophetam cum muliere fornicaria misceri praecepit. Quorum alterum grave furti facinus, aliud flagitii turpitudo reputaretur si non excusasset utrumque factum auctoritas imperatoris* [25]. Habet et addit etiam exemplum de Samsone *qui se ipsum cum hominibus opprimens interfecit; quod indubitanter* inquit *credendum est habuisse Dei privatum consilium si non fuit peccatum* [26]. Idem de Samsone patet per Augustinum, I *Civitate* 21 [27].

Et confirmatur, quia Abraham voluit interficere filium suum ut oboediret Deo praecipienti, nec in hoc peccasset si Deus mandatum non revocasset [28]. Idem habetur extra de divortiis [29]. Gaudemus [u] ubi dicitur quod Jacob a mendacio [30], Israelitae a furto [31], Samson ab homicidio [32], antiqui patres plures uxores habentes ab adulterio [33] excusantur quia per revelationem divinam haec eis concessa sunt, haec ibi.

CONTRA:

QUOD ex sua ratione formali includit malitiam non potest esse non malum; quaedam actiones humanae sunt huiusmodi.

Probatur per Aristotelem, secundo *Ethicorum* cap. 7: *Non omnis operatio neque omnis animae passio suscipit medietatem. Quaedam enim confestim nominata convoluta sunt cum malitia, puta gaudium de malo et inverecundia et invidia, et in operationibus adulterium, furtum, homicidium; haec enim omnia dicuntur secundum se ipsa mala esse. Non igitur est umquam circa hoc dirigere, sed semper peccare; neque est bene vel non bene circa talia in eo quod, ut oportet, et quando et quomodo, sed simpliciter facere quodcumque horum peccatum est* [34].

SECUNDO, quod non potest bene fieri nec excusari sufficienter quacumque intentione et quocumque animo vel fine fiat non potest esse non malum; aliquae actiones humanae sunt huiusmodi.

Probatur per Augustinum, libro 2 *De Sermone Domini in Monte*, super illud *Matthaei* septimo *Nolite iudicare et non iudicabimini* [35], dicentem sic: *Hic praecipimur ut ea facta quae dubium est quo animo fiant, in meliorem partem interpretamur; temerarium enim est de talibus iudicare quia*

elicited after the prohibition and with such circumstances making it worse that it will surpass *b* elicited by Socrates.

The inference is evident because evilness is no more essential to *b* than is indifference to *c*, and no less is *c* essentially indifferent of itself than is *b* evil and unjust.

Moreover, this should be seen most of all in the case of those actions which, known per se by the law of nature and by the dictate of natural reason, appear to be prohibited, actions such as homicides, thefts, adulteries, etc.. But it is possible that such actions not be sins with respect to the absolute power of God.

This is evident from Bernard in *On Precept and Dispensation* [t], chap. 4: *You shall not kill, You shall not steal, You shall not commit adultery, and the remaining precepts of that table, although they admit no dispensation absolutely, yet God has given release from those which he wished when he wished, as when he ordered that the Egyptians be plundered by the Hebrews or when he ordered the prophet to have intercourse with a woman who was a fornicator. A grievous crime of theft would be ascribed to the one, and the turpitude of a shameful act, to the other if the authority of the commander should not have excused each act* [25]. Bernard likewise has and adds the example of Samson *who, bearing down, killed himself along with other men; which,* he says, *must without doubt be believed to have had the private counsel of God if it was not a sin* [26]. The same point regarding Samson is evident from Augustine's *The City of God* I, 21 [27].

Confirmation: Abraham wished to kill his son so that he would be obedient to God commanding this, and he would not have sinned in doing this if God should not have withdrawn his command [28]. Besides, the same is held regarding divorces [29]. We rejoice [u] where it is said that Jacob was excused from lying [30], the Israelites, from theft [31], Samson, from homicide [32], and the polygamous ancient fathers, from adultery [33] because they were then permitted to perform these actions by a divine revelation.

OBJECTIONS:

THAT WHICH includes evilness from its formal definition cannot fail to be evil. Certain human actions are of this type.

This is proved by Aristotle in the *Ethics* II, chap. 7: *Not every operation nor every passion of the soul admits a middle course. For certain ones, as soon as named, are involved with evilness, for example, spite and shamelessness and envy, and in operations, adultery, theft, homicide; for all these are said to be evil in themselves. Therefore it is not possible ever to be set right with regard to them, but one always sins. Nor does acting rightly or wrongly with regard to such things lie in the conditions of because, as it ought, and when and how, but simply to do any of these whatever is a sin* [34].

SECOND, that which cannot be done rightly nor be sufficiently excused by whatever purpose for which and intention with which it may be done or by whatever end for which it may be done cannot fail to be evil. Some human actions are of this type.

This is proved by Augustine in *The Lord's Sermon on the Mount*, bk. II, commenting on the verse in the seventh chapter of *Matthew, Do not judge and you shall not be judged* [35]: *Herein we*

et bono et malo animo fieri possunt. Quaedam autem sunt quae non possunt bono animo fieri, ut
scripta blasphemiae, furta [36].

Item, Augustinus diffuse haec determinat primo *Contra Mendacium* [37], et ponitur secundo
Sententiarum dist. 40, cap. 3, ubi dicitur quod *quaedam nullo bonae causae obtentu, nullo quasi*
bono fine, nulla velut bona intentione facienda sunt etc. [38], et ponit exemplum in multis specialiter
de mendacio.

Item, Anselmus, I *Cur Deus Homo* cap. 12, *Nequaquam velle mentiri potest voluntas nisi in*
qua corrupta est veritas [39]; et libro *De Conceptu Virginali* cap. 4: *Periurium et quaedam alia*
nunquam nisi iniuste possunt esse [40].

TERTIO, si nihil sit ab homine quin possit bene vel non male fieri, perit iudicium et iustitiae
exercitium et malefactorum condemnatio quia incertum et ignotum erit an bene vel non male facta
sint, nec poterit certitudinaliter constare de opposito.

QUARTO, illa actio non potest esse non mala quae necessario est deformis rectae rationi;
aliqua actio hominis est huiusmodi.

Probo de actu formalis et actualis et expressae inoboedientiae et rebellionis ad divinam
voluntatem: si enim potest conformari rectae rationi, igitur secundum rectam rationem inoboediendum
est Deo; igitur voluntas Dei non est recta, sed actio illi contraria et deformis. Unde potest sic argui:
aliuqod dictamen de agibili vel fugibili est necessario verum, nec potest esse falsum; igitur actio illi
deformis est necessario mala. Antecedens probatur, quia hoc dictamen est necessario verum, *Non*
est Deo inoboediendum nec rebellandum sed suae voluntati conformiter vivendum, nec est male sed
bene vivendum et agendum.

Confirmatur: si actus inoboedientiae et rebellionis formalis potest esse non deformis rationi
rectae et non esse malus, igitur per actum inoboedientiae non est inoboediens nec rebellis divinae
ordinationi.

QUINTO, actus contemnendi, blasphemandi, et odiendi Deum vel formaliter et actualiter
praeponendi creaturam et postponendi Deum creaturae non potest non esse malus et vitiosus.

Probo:

Primo, si Sortes secundum talem actum non peccat, igitur non transgreditur Dei mandatum;
igitur non est inoboediens; igitur nec contemnit nec blasphemat nec inhonorat nec praeponit
creaturam Deo.

Secundo, si *a* actus quo voluntas formaliter et expresse contemnit Deum et postponit
creaturae et vult esse inoboediens et transgredi praecepta et deformari divinae voluntati, tunc sic: si
voluntas in habendo *a* non peccat et licite hoc facit et sic se habet, igitur licitum et non irrationabile
est praeceptum Dei relinquere et contemnere propter creaturam; igitur voluntas Dei et eius ordinatio
non est summe recta nec prima regula rectitudinis quia aliquid est ei deforme et discors non est
iniustum, et ultra; igitur licitum est creaturam non subiici sed praeponi creatori; igitur licitum et non

are commanded so that we may interpret in the better sense those deeds for which it is doubtful with what intention they are done; for it is rash to make a judgment about such deeds because they can be done with a good or with a bad intention. There are certain ones, however, which cannot be done with a good intention, as blasphemous writings and thefts [36].

Again, Augustine copiously determines these things in *Against Lying* I [37]. And it is asserted in the *Sentences* II, dist. 40, sect. 3, where it is said that *certain things must be done with no pretense of a good motive, with no seemingly good end, with no apparently good intention*, etc. [38]. And he often offers the example of lying specifically.

Again, Anselm states in *Why God Became Man* I, chap. 12: *By no means can the will choose to lie unless the truth is corrupted in it* [39]. And in the book *The Virgin Conception*, chap. 4, he states: *Perjury and certain other actions can never be done except unjustly* [40].

THIRD, if there is nothing that cannot be done by a human being rightly or not wrongly, then judgment is lost as well as the exercise of justice and the condemnation of evildoers. For it will be uncertain and unknown whether the acts have been done rightly or not wrongly, nor will it be possible to establish the opposite with certainty.

FOURTH, that action cannot fail to be evil which necessarily deviates from right reason. Some human action is of this type.

I prove this by considering an act of formal and actual and explicit disobedience to and rebellion against the divine will. For if such an act can be conformed to right reason, then God must be disobeyed according to right reason. Therefore the will of God is not right, but an action opposed to it and deviating from it. So the following can be argued. There is some dictate concerning what is to be done or what is to be avoided which is necessarily true and cannot be false. Therefore, an action deviating from it is necessarily evil. Proof of the antecedent: This dicate is necessarily true, *One must not be disobedient to God nor rebellious against him but must live conformably to his will*, nor is this living and acting wrongly but rightly.

Confirmation: If such an act of formal disobedience and rebellion can fail to deviate from right reason and fail to be evil, then one is not disobedient to nor rebellious against the divine decree by an act of disobedience.

FIFTH, the act of contemning, blaspheming, and hating God or formally and actually placing a creature first and putting God after a creature cannot fail to be evil and vicious.

I prove this in the following ways.

First, if Socrates does not sin by such an act, then the command of God is not transgressed. Therefore, he is not disobedient. And therefore, he neither contemns nor blasphemes nor dishonors God nor places a creature before God.

Second, let *a* be an act by which the will formally and explicitly contemns God and puts him after a creature and wills to be disobedient and to transgress precepts and to deviate from the divine will. Then if the will in having *a* does not sin and licitly does this and conducts itself in this fashion, it is therefore licit and not irrational to forsake and contemn the precept of God on account of a creature. And therefore, the will of God and its decree is not supremely right nor the first rule of rectitude because something deviates from it and is at variance with it but is not unjust, and more than

irrationabile nec inordinatum est Deum non dominari nec praeponi sed creaturam praehonorari, et ultra; igitur licitem est frui creatura; igitur in creatura beatificari; igitur non irrationabile est creaturam esse finem ultimum et summum bonum.

Tertio, sequitur contradictio. Primo sequitur enim quod talis voluntas habens huiusmodi actum non deviat a prima regula rectitudinis nec a suo fine seu a debito ordine in finem ultimum nec inordinate se habet ad finem ultimum; et sequitur etiam contradictoriorum istorum. Prima pars patet: per te non peccat nec talis actus est vitiosus. Secunda pars probatur, quia voluntas per huiusmodi actum formaliter et expresse avertitur a Deo et abiicit Deum et reprobat et detestatur et recedit ab eo et adversatur illi.

Quarto, sequitur quod talis actus sit compossibilis beatitudini. Probo, quia non est ex se malus. Consequens est falsum, quia contraria essent simul et anima simul frueretur Deo et respueret illum et displiceret in eo.

Ex hiis arguitur falsum esse quod Deus possit se solo causare odium vel actum odii in voluntate et quod tunc anima odiret Deum non vitiose; quia, ut probatum est, sequitur contradictio, et quia voluntas per illum actum est mala per quem inordinate tendit et fertur in Deum. Sic est per *a* actum odii a quocumque causetur, quia per illum voluntas abiicit, contemnit, postponit Deum.

Non valet etiam dicere quod odium Dei et voluntatem odire Deum non est ex se et necessario vitiosum et iniustum, sed voluntatem creatam eligere sponte et libere odium Dei seu sponte et elicitive odire Deum. Si enim sic dicatur contra media posita quod odire Deum non potest esse non illicitum et iterum si voluntas tenetur non eligere *a* odium Dei, aut ideo eligere [v] *a* est illicitum quia talis actus est ex natura sua malus et vitiosus, et propositum; aut quia voluntati creatae est a Deo prohibitum eligere. Voluntas enim subdita et regulabilis non tenetur hoc eligere vel eligere et illud cavere et fugere nisi vel quia hoc est antecedenter ex natura sui bonum et illud malum vel quia hoc est praeceptum ei et illud prohibitum voluntate et lege superiori, aut igitur non potest a Deo esse non prohibitum et reprobatum. Et adhuc stat propositum, quia cum multi actus nunc a Deo prohibiti possint esse non prohibiti, si *a* non potest esse non prohibitum, hoc non erit nisi quia est ex se essentialiter malus et inordinatus; si potest esse a Deo non prohibitus creaturae rationali, igitur possibile est voluntatem libere eligere [w] illum licite et sponte.

Confirmatur: propter quod unumquodque tale est [x] illud magis [41]. Sed ideo malum est voluntatem elicere odium Dei quia malum est voluntatem odire Deum; et ideo prohibitum est voluntati elicere odium Dei quia prohibitum est odire Deum, sicut ideo bonum et debitum est elicere dilectionem Dei quia bonum et debitum est diligere Deum. Unde obiectum et notitia et Deus secundum generalem influentiam, licet eliciant effective huiusmodi actum, non peccant. Igitur aeque vel magis est ex se malum odire Deum sicut elicere odium Dei, et voluntas non minus inordinata est quatenus odiens formaliter Deum quam quatenus eliciens huiusmodi actum causaliter.

Item, inconvenientia videntur aeque sequi ex hoc quod est voluntatem odire Deum et voluntatem elicere odium Dei, et aeque declinantur inconvenientia.

Confirmatur: omnia ista, per articulum Parisiensem in posterioribus dicentem sic: *Quod tenentes intellectionem, volitionem, sensationem, esse qualitates existentes subiective in anima, habent dicere et concedere quod Deus potest facere se solo quod anima odiret Deum et proximum et non demeritorie--Error* [42].

that. Therefore, it is licit that a creature not be subject to the creator but be set above the creator. And therefore it is licit and neither irrational nor disordered that God not be lord and not be put first but that a creature be honored first, and more than that. Therefore it is licit to enjoy a creature and to find beatitude in a creature, and it is not irrational that a creature be the find end and the highest good.

Third, a contradiction follows. For first it follows that such a will performing such an act does not deviate from the first rule of rectitude or from its end or from the due ordering towards it final end nor does it behave in a disordered manner in relation to its final end; and the contradictory of these claims also follows. The first part is evident. According to you, the will does not sin and such an act is not vicious. The second part is proved because the will is formally and explicitly turned away from God and casts God aside and rejects and detests God and withdraws from him and stands opposed to him by such an act.

Fourth, it follows that such an act is compatible with beatitude. I prove this, because it is not evil of itself. The consequent is false because opposites would exist simultaneously and the soul would simultaneously enjoy God and reject him and be displeased with him.

By these arguments it is shown to be false that God by himself could cause hatred or the act of hatred in the will and that then the soul would hate God in a way that is not vicious. For, as has been proven, a contradiction follows. Further, the will is evil by that act by which it tends and is brought to God in a disordered manner. So it is by a, an act of hatred, by whomever it may be caused, because by that act the will casts God aside, contemns God, and puts God second.

It is also not valid to say that the hatred of God and the will hating God is not vicious and unjust of itself and necessarily, but rather, the created will choosing the hatred of God voluntarily and freely or hating God voluntarily and drawing it out of itself. For if it is thus said contrary to the means of proof set out that hating God cannot fail to be illicit, and again, if the will is obliged not to choose a, the hatred of God, then either it is the case that choosing [v] a is illicit because such an act is evil and vicious by its nature, and this is what is to be proven; or because choosing a has been prohibited to the created will by God. For a will which is subject to and regulated <by something else> is not obliged to choose this thing or to choose to guard against and flee that thing except for one of two reasons, either because this one is antecedently good of its nature and that one, evil; or because this one is commanded to it and that one prohibited by a superior will and law. Or therefore, it cannot fail to be prohibited and reprobated by God. And thus far, what is to be proven stands. For, since many acts which are now prohibited by God could fail to be prohibited, if a cannot fail to be prohibited, this will only occur because it is essentially evil and disordered of itself. If it can fail to be prohibited to a rational creature by God, then it is possible that the will freely choose [w] it licitly and voluntarily.

Confirmation: That because of which this is [x] such is itself greater than this [41]. But it is evil for the will to elicit the hatred of God because it is evil for the will to hate God, and therefore it is prohibited to the will to elicit the hatred of God because hating God is prohibited, just as it is good and dutiful to elicit the love of God because loving God is good and dutiful. So, although the object and knowledge and God effectively elicit such an act by a general influence, they do not sin. Therefore equally or more so is it evil of itself to hate God as to elicit the hatred of God, and the will is no less disordered in so far as it formally hates God than in so far as it causally elicits such an act.

SEXTO principaliter, ad confirmationem rationis praecedentis: si omnis actus voluntatis potest esse non malus, igitur potest esse bonus, virtuosus et meritorius et esse in homine iusto et grato et accepto Deo.

Consequentia probatur, quia actus ex se nec bonus nec malus potest permitti et concedi tanquam licitus, igitur postmodum potest praecipi non minus quam prohiberi; et quia actus qui ex se nullam habet malitiam non repugnat gratiae et acceptationi divinae cum etiam veniale stet cum gratia.

Falsitas consequentis probatur:

Primo, quia aliquis placeret Deo et ordinate et conformiter divinae voluntati se haberet in eo quod Deum contemneret et abiiceret, et esset amicus Dei in eo quod tempore inimicatur Deo.

Secundo, esset simul amicus et inimicus Dei.

Tertio, si mereretur et oboedit praecipienti, igitur diligit; igitur non odit.

Quarto, si meretur et iuste agit, igitur iustum est abiicere Deum et eius voluntatem; igitur ei deformari; igitur voluntas Dei non est summe recta.

Quinto, quia quanto magis contemneret et odiret Deum, tanto beatior esset quia iustior; et quanto magis recederet et averteretur a Deo [y] et quanto magis abiiceret et respueret Deum, tanto magis adhaereret Deo.

Sexto, quia simul frueretur Deo et uteretur, et simul praeponeret ipsum omnibus et postponeret ipsum alicui alteri.

Septimo, per articulum Parisiensem in posterioribus dicentem sic: *Quod Deus potest praecipere creaturae rationali quod habeat ipsum odio, et ipsa oboediens plus meretur quod si ipsum diligeret ex praecepto quoniam hoc faceret cum maiori conatu et magis contra propriam inclinationem--Reputo et assero falsum, erroneum et scandalosum* [43].

SEPTIMO principaliter, sicut falsitas ad primam et summam veritatem, sic malitia ad primam bonitatem; sed aliquid ita est ex se falsum quod non potest per primam veritatem esse non falsum; igitur...

OCTAVO, sequitur quod Lucifero damnato posset nunc bene vel non male esse culpabiliter et vituperabiliter sine mutatione reali.

Probo, quia Deus posset vel ab aeterno poterat instituere ut ea quae nunc Lucifero conveniunt forent ei non mala pro tempore praesenti sed bona.

Again, inconsistencies seem equally to follow from the fact that the will hates God and elicits the hatred of God, and to be avoided.

Confirmation: All of these are confirmed by the later articles of Paris stating, *That holding that understanding, volition, and sensation are qualities existing subjectively in the soul, they have to say and to concede that God could bring about by himself that the soul should hate God and neighbor and not demeritoriously--Error* [42].

SIXTH, in confirmation of the preceding reasoning: If every act of the will can fail to be evil, then it can be good, virtuous, and meritorious and be in a human being who is just and in a state of grace and accepted by God.

Proof of the inference: An act which of itself is neither good nor evil can be permitted and allowed as licit, then afterwards can be commanded no less than prohibited. Further, an act which of itself has no evilness is not incompatible with grace and with divine acceptance since even venial sin may remain with grace.

The falsity of the consequent is proved as follows.

First, someone would please God and conduct himself in an orderly manner and conformably to the divine will inasmuch as he would contemn God and cast God aside, and he would be the friend of God inasmuch as he is made the enemy of God for the moment.

Second, he would simultaneously be the friend and the enemy of God.

Third, if he would gain merit and if he gives obedience to God commanding, then he loves God; therefore, he does not hate him.

Fourth, if he gains merit and acts justly, then it is just to cast God and his will aside, and therefore, to deviate from it. And therefore, the will of God is not supremely right.

Fifth, how much the more he would contemn and hate God, so much the happier would he be in heaven because he would be more just. And how much the more he would withdraw and be turned away from God [y], and how much the more he would cast God aside and reject God, so much the more would he adhere to God.

Sixth, he would simultaneously enjoy God and use God, and simultaneously place God before all things and put God after something else.

Seventh, by the later article of Paris stating, *That God can command a rational creature to hold him in hatred, and that that creature in obeying would gain more merit than if he would love him according to a precept since he would do this with greater effort and more against his own inclination--I deem and assert to be false, erroneous, and scandalous* [43].

SEVENTH, just as falsity is related to the first and highest truth, so evilness is related to the first goodness. But something is false of itself in such a way that, through the first truth, it cannot fail to be false. Therefore...

EIGHTH, it follows that it could now be well or not bad for damned Lucifer, culpably and blamably, without an actual change.

I prove this as follows. God could establish or could have established from eternity that those things which are now found in Lucifer would not be evil for him for the present time, but good.

NONO, possibile esset *a* malum poenae esse aeque vel magis malum quam *b* malum culpae.

Probo: quod non ex se est malum sed mere contingenter ex ordinatione libera divinae voluntatis, sic quod potest esse minus et minus malum donec sit simpliciter non malum, posset fieri minus malum illo quo est nunc magis malum.

Probatur iterum consequentia, quia malum poenae sensus est ex se necessario malum essentialiter et per se, sed *b* tantum accidentaliter et contingenter est malum.

Falsitas consequentis probatur, tum quia creatura haberet plus fugere malum poenae quam peccatum, et haberet potius peccare quam incurrere poenam sensus; tum quia *a* poena [z] sensus esset poena condigna, immo ultra condigna culpae mortalis.

DECIMO, aliquis posset fieri impeccabilis sine dono beatitudinis talis gratiae confirmantis.

Probo, quia Deus poterit concedere Sorti facere et omittere quicquid voluerit ex quo nulla actio vel actionis privatio est necessario mala; et ita Sortes erit absolutus ab omni praecepto et obligatione.

UNDECIMO, sequitur quod Deus posset praecipere homini nolle beatitudinem et mentiri et peccare et volare et facere contradictoria simul.

Probatio consequentiae: quod est possibile homini et non est de se necessario malum, immo potest esse non malum et non male fieri ab homine, est possibile Deo; sed praecipere ista est possibile homini, et per te praecipere hoc non est ex se et necessario malum.

Igitur falsitas consequentis probatur, quia sequitur quod Sortes peccaret et non peccaret. Prima pars patet, quia deformaretur praecepto iusto et legi procedenti a voluntate Dei quia praecipitur sibi impossibile et ita non observat praeceptum, et quia mentiendo et peccando peccat. Secunda pars probatur, quia Sortes non obligatur ad contradictoria rationabiliter. Ratio enim recta non dictat hominem obligari ad volendum et faciendum contradictorium; alioquin bestiae et inanimata possent obligari praeceptis et peccare. Mentiendo etiam non peccaret quia impleret praeceptum et oboediret.

DUODECIMO, aliqua actio ex se et ex propria natura sui et obiecti est peior alia; igitur ex se et ex natura sua est mala.

Antecedens probatur, quia sumptis duabus actionibus vitiosis alterius generis vel speciei, ceteris paribus, una est peior quam alia; nec est differentia in circumstantia aliqua accidentali, nisi in propria natura actus et obiecti.

Ad ista, non asserendo conclusionem supra positum sed probabili collocutione sustinendo; illae enim rationes in oppositum aeque videntur concludere de actionibus furiosi vel somniantis.

NINTH, it would be possible that an evil of penalty, *a*, be just as evil as or a greater evil than an evil of fault, *b*.

I prove this as follows. That which is not evil of itself but merely contingently from the free decree of the divine will, and thus what can become evil to a lesser and lesser degree until it is simply not evil, can become a lesser evil than that which is now a greater evil.

Again the inference is proved as follows. An evil of penalty for the senses is of itself necessarily evil, essentially and through itself; but *b* is evil only accidentally and contingently.

Proof of the falsity of the consequent: First, a creature would be in the position of fleeing an evil of penalty more than sin and of sinning rather than incurring a penalty for the senses. Second, a penalty [z] for the senses, *a*, would be a deserved punishment, indeed beyond that of a mortal fault.

TENTH, someone could become impeccable without the gift of beatitude confirming such grace.

I prove this as follows. God will be able to allow Socrates to do and to omit whatever he shall have willed inasmuch as no action or privation of action is necessarily evil. And so Socrates will be released form every precept and obligation.

ELEVENTH, it follows that God could command a human being that beatitude be unwilled and that he lie and sin and fly and do contradictory things at the same time.

Proof of the inference: What is possible for a human being and is not necessarily evil from itself, indeed what can fail to be evil and wrongly done by a human being, is possible for God. But to command those things is possible for a human being and, according to you, to command this is not of itself and necessarily evil.

Proof of the falsity of the consequent: It follows that Socrates would sin and would not sin. The first part is evident. First, he would be deviating from a just precept and a law proceeding from the will of God since the impossible is commanded to him and so he does not observe the precept. Second, he sins by lying and by committing a sin. The second part is proved because Socrates is not reasonably obligated to contradictories. For right reason does not dictate that a human being be obligated to willing and doing what is contradictory; otherwise, beasts and inanimate beings could be obligated by precepts and could sin. Also, he would not sin by lying because he would fulfill and obey a precept.

TWELFTH, some action is worse than another of itself and by its own nature and the nature of the object. Therefore, it is evil of itself and by its nature.

Proof of the antecedent: Taking two vicious actions of different genus or species, one is worse than another, other things being equal. And the difference does not lie in some accidental circumstance, only in the particular nature of the act and the object.

I reply to these objections not by asserting the conclusion stated above but by maintaining it with a probable discussion. For those reasons in opposition seem equally probative with regard to the actions of a madman or a dreamer.

AD PRIMUM negatur minor sumendo actionem vel actionis privationem secundum illud quod sunt in se formaliter et quidditative, non sub nomine significante actionem vel actionis privationem cum circumstantia indebita quam etiam possibile est non convenire illi actioni vel privationi.

Ad probationem minoris dicendum quod huiusmodi nomina non sunt imposita ad significandum talem actionem vel privationem actionis talis, sed sub circumstantia indebita. Licet autem secundum leges positas et secundum ordinem iuris naturalis a Deo instituti huiusmodi circumstantiae concomitantur inseparabiliter huiusmodi actiones libere elicitas, tamen per potentiam Dei absolutam possunt eis non convenire. Quod autem sic intellegat Aristoteles patet, quia dicit, *quaedam nominata statim sunt convoluta* [a*] *cum malitia,* ita quod conceptus correspondentes sunt per se inferiores ad peccatum. Patet etiam quia exemplificat de actione furti quam contingit esse et non esse furtum, ut patet.

AD SECUNDUM negatur minor quoad hoc, quod non possit excusari loquendo de potentia absoluta.

Ad probationem: Augustinus loquitur secundum leges Dei ordinatas, non solum temporaliter a Deo humanae naturae promulgatas sed etiam aeternas et in mente divina aeternaliter determinatas. Nam et tibi enumerat ebrietatem [44]; contingit tamen inebriari sine culpa, saltem de potentia absoluta. Ponit etiam exemplum de furto [45], et tamen actio furti potest in sensu divisionis esse non furtiva.

AD TERTIUM negatur consequentia, tum quia quaedam sunt quae secundum legem naturae et legem Dei scriptam non possunt libere fieri nisi male; tum quia ex quo tale est prohibitum sive lege naturali aeterna sive lege Dei scripta sive lege humana, si verisimiliter et probabiliter praesumitur quod scienter et libere fecit, immo nisi probabiliter aliunde notum sit ipsum excusari, condemnandus est. Unde idem argumentum potest reduci de his quae lege scripta et positiva sunt instituta.

AD QUARTUM: conceditur maior si necessario sit deformis rectae rationi praeceptivae et dictanti hominem debere non habere illam. Et sic negatur minor; patet si habetur a furioso inculpabiliter.

Ad probationem dicendum quod haec nomina in obiectiva, *rebellio, contemptus, transgressio,* et *blasphemia,* possunt notare circumstantiam et condicionem actionis sive voluntatis agentis, vel possunt notare obiectum actus voluntatis. Primo modo conceditur in sensu compositionis quod actus inoboedientiae et rebellionis etc., necessario est deformis rectae rationi et est vitiosus necessario; sed ex hoc non sequitur quod aliqua realis actio vel privatio actionis sit necessario peccatum, quia quaecumque actio vel privatio actionis est inoboedentia, ipsa poterat esse non inoboedientia. Ideo non sequitur, *Transgressio praecepti est necessario peccatum, igitur aliqua actio vel actionis privatio non potest esse non mala,* sicut non [b*] sequitur, *Respicere b inordinate non potest esse non peccatum, igitur aliqua visio non potest esse non peccatum.* Sumendo secundo modo, puta quod voluntas habeat actum quo formaliter vult esse inoboediens vel transgredi praeceptum Dei et

REPLY TO THE FIRST OBJECTION: The minor is denied by taking the action or the privation of action according to that which they are in themselves formally and with reference to quiddity, not under a name signifying the action or the privation of action with an undue circumstance, a circumstance which it is also possible not to find in that action or privation.

Reply to the proof of the minor: Such names are not imposed for signifying such an action or the privation of such an action, but for signifying them under the form of having an undue circumstance. Although it is the case that, according to the laws which have been set down and according to the order of natural law established by God, such circumstances inseparably accompany such actions elicited freely, nevertheless, such circumstances can fail to be found in them through the absolute power of God. It is evident, however, that Aristotle understands it in this way, because he says that *certain ones named immediately are involved* [a*] *with evilness*, so that the corresponding concepts are per se subsequent to sin. This is likewise evident because he brings forward as an example the action of theft which happens to be or not to be theft, as is evident.

REPLY TO THE SECOND OBJECTION: The minor is denied with respect to the claim that it could not be excused, speaking with regard to absolute power.

Reply to the proof: Augustine is speaking according to the ordained laws of God, not only those temporally promulgated by God to human nature but also those which are eternal and eternally determined in the divine mind. For he enumerates drunkenness for you [44]; it happens, however, that one can be inebriated without fault, at least with respect to absolute power. He also offers the example of theft [45], and yet the action of theft can, in the sense of division, fail to be thievery.

REPLY TO THE THIRD OBJECTION: The inference is denied. First, there are certain things which, according to the law of nature and the written law of God, cannot freely be done except wrongly. Second, since such is prohibited either by the eternal natural law or by the written law of God or by human law, if it is presumed with likelihood and probability that someone has done it knowingly and freely, indeed unless it be otherwise known with probability that he is excused, he must be condemned. So the same argument can be repeated with respect to those things which have been established by written and positive law.

REPLY TO THE FOURTH OBJECTION: The major is conceded if the action necessarily deviates from right reason which is preceptive and which prescribes that a human being ought not to perform it. And so the minor is denied; this is evident if the action is performed inculpably by a madman.

Reply to the proof: These names in the ojects of thought, *rebellion, contempt, transgression,* and *blasphemy,* can signify a circumstance and condition of the action or of the will of the agent, or they can signify the object of the act of the will. In the first way it is conceded that, in the sense of composition, an act of disobedience and rebellion etc., necessarily deviates from right reason and is necessarily vicious. But it does not follow from this that any real action or privation of action is necessarily a sin, because whatsoever action or privation of action is an instance of disobedience could itself have failed to be disobedience. Therefore it does not follow, *Transgression of a precept is necessarily a sin, therefore some action or privation of action cannot fail to be evil,* just as it does not [b*] follow, *To look at b in a disordered manner cannot fail to be a sin, accordingly some vision*

vivere et agere in contemptum et blasphemiam Dei, sic diceretur quod talis, secundum illud quod est realiter et physice, non necessario est sic deformis rationi praeceptivae dictanti vere quod sic habens vel eliciens illum debet et obligatur sic carere illo ex Dei praecepto. Patet, quia potest haberi a furioso inculpabiliter; et tunc talis actus non est formaliter inoboedentia nec secundum illum est formaliter voluntas inoboediens. Sicut actus quo Sortes vellet esse peior Lucifero vel melior beato Petro nec faceret ipsum peiorem Lucifero nec meliorem beato Petro. Sicut etiam secundum Anselmum, *De Casu Diaboli* cap. 14, *Si voluntas acciperet aliquod velle a Deo totaliter, licet vellet inconvenientia et iniusta, non tamen vellet iniuste et inconvenienter; sicut igitur contingit aliquem velle iusta et non iuste, ita contingit velle iniusta non iniuste* [46].

Ad confirmationem patet ex dictus.

AD QUINTUM patet per idem. Si enim actus contemnendi, blasphemandi, inhonorandi, postponendi Deum et utendi eo sumantur pro actibus quibus formaliter voluntas vult ese contemnens etc., sic negatur assumptum ut scilicet illa notant condicionem obiective volitam. Nec sequitur, *Sortes non iniuste nec illicite nec irrationabiliter vult esse inoboediens, igitur licitum et rationabile est Deo esse inoboedientem*; nec igitur ratio recta est quae dictat Deo esse inoboediendum . Si vero illa sumantur ut notant condicionem actus, sic potest distingui, quia vel improprie ut notant proprietatem actus naturalem et physicam, vel proprie et stricte ut notant circumstantiam actus moralem et ethicam. Si secundo modo, conceditur assumptum, nec est contra propositum. Si primo modo, negatur assumptum, ut si demens habeat formaliter actum contemtivum Dei, vel verbo vocali et mentali dicat blasphemias Dei vel habeat actum quo formaliter fruatur creatura et utatur Deo in respectu ad creaturam et postponat formaliter Deum vel odiat; non enim agit libere, sed magis agitur ut brutum. Iste igitur utitur Deo et ipsum postponit et contemnit naturaliter et physice, non autem moraliter et ethice nisi in quadam similitudine. Diceretur igitur quod large iste contemnit Deum, sed non contemtibiliter; blasphemat, sed non blasphemarie; detestatur, sed non detestabiliter; et irreveretur, sed non irreverenter; et sic de aliis, licet desint interdum nomina. Non enim committit vel omittit contra praeceptum Dei vitiose. Iuxta hunc modum loquendi dicit Gregorius in homilia quod interdum iusti *dedignantur, non dedignantes; desperant, sed non desperantes*, etc. [47].

De actu autem odiendi Deum dicetur infra in speciali.

Ad primam probationem: conceditur consequentia [c*] accipiendo illa ut notent circumstantiam moralem actus.

Ad secundum negatur prima consequentia, nisi consequens sumatur ut illi termini notent condicionem obiective volitam et non condicionem moralem actionis vel agentis, et tunc negatur secunda consequentia.

Ad tertiam: voluntatem per aliquem actum deviare et averti a Deo et fine ultimo potest intellegi quod non velle et non approbare Deum nec complacere in illo, sed nolle ipsum et displicere in ipso; et sic non necessario est vitiosum et iniustum et culpabile. Alio modo est voluntatem se habere erga Deum indebite et inordinate et inconvenienter et contra dictamen rectae rationis praeceptivae et legis Dei; et sic conceditur pars negativa.

cannot fail to be a sin. Taking it in the second way, namely, that the will performs an act by which it formally wills to be disobedient or to transgress the precept of God and to live and act in contempt and blasphemy of God, it would be said that such an act, according to that which it is really and physically, does not necessarily deviate from preceptive reason truly prescribing that someone thus performing or eliciting that act ought and is obliged to abstain from it by the precept of God. This is evident because it can be performed inculpably by a madman; and then such an act is not formally disobedience nor is the will formally disobedient in accordance with it. Just as it is the case that the act by which Socrates should will to be worse than Lucifer or better than blessed Peter would make him neither worse than Lucifer nor better than blessed Peter. Likewise, just as, according to Anselm in *The Fall of the Devil*, chap. 14, *If the will should receive some volition totally from God, although it would will unsuitable and unjust things, it would not, however, will unjustly and unsuitably. Therefore, just as it happens that someone wills just things but not justly, so it happens that someone wills injustices but not unjustly* [46].

Reply to the confirmation: This is evident from what has been said.

REPLY TO THE FIFTH OBJECTION: The reply is evident through the same considerations. For if the acts of contemning, blaspheming, dishonoring, and putting God second and of using him are taken for acts by which the will formally wills to be contemning, etc., what is accepted <as a basis for the conclusion> is denied as these signify a condition objectively willed. Neither does it follow, *Socrates neither unjustly nor illicitly nor unreasonably wills to be disobedient, therefore it is licit and reasonable to be disobedient to God*; nor therefore is it right reason which prescribes disobedience to God. If in fact these are taken as they signify a condition of the act, distinctions can be made, because they signify either improperly as they signify a natural and physical property of the act, or properly and strictly as they signify a moral and ethical circumstance of the act. If they are taken in the second way, then what is accepted <as a basis for the conclusion> is conceded, and this does not go against what we propose to prove. If they are taken in the first way, what is accepted <as a basis for the conclusion> is denied, as, for example, if a madman formally performs an act contemptuous of God, either in uttering blasphemies of God with vocal and mental language or in performing an act in which he formally enjoys a creature and uses God with respect to a creature and formally puts God second or hates him; for he does not act freely, but more is impelled as is an animal. Therefore he uses God and puts him second and contemns him naturally and physically, but not morally and ethically, except with a certain similarity. Therefore it would be said that, in a broad sense, he contemns God, but not contemptuously; that he blasphemes, but not blasphemously; that he detests, but not detestably; and that he shows irreverence, but not irreverantly; and so with respect to the others, although they sometimes lack names. For he does not viciously commit or omit something contrary to the precept of God. According to this mode of speaking, Gregory states in a sermon that sometimes the just *are scorned but are not scorning; that they despair but are not despairing,* etc. [47].

The act of hating God in particular is discussed below.

Reply to the first proof: The inference [c*] is conceded in taking those as they signify a moral circumstance of the act.

Reply to the second proof: The first inference is denied, unless the consequent is taken as those terms signify a condition objectively willed and not a moral condition of the action or the agent,

Ad quartum negatur consequentia. Contrariatur enim perfectae beatitudini quae est incompossibilis talibus defectibus naturalibus.

De actu autem odiendi, an talis possit esse non malus, procedendo non asssertive sed collative et disputative.

Dicunt quidam quod actus huiusmodi odii potest esse in creatura et a creatura rationali sine peccato.

Patet de somniante vel furioso, ex quo ultra arguitur quod etiam in homine sano; quia non est ex se essentialiter et necessario vitiosus et iniustus cum in furioso sit non iniustus, igitur in quolibet potest esse et non esse culpabilis de potentia absoluta.

Item, huiusmodi actus non magis per se et necessario est malus quam actus diligendi Deum super omnia sit bonus et iustus et virtuosus; sed talis est contingenter huiusmodi.

Patet, si sit in somniante vel furioso, vel in infideli, vel si contra conscientiam obligatur pro tempore et loco.

Item, potest a solo Deo causari in voluntate; igitur voluntas non erit iniusta secundum illum.

Consequentia probatur per Anselmum, *De Casu Diaboli* cap. 14 et 15 [d*]: quia voluntas se haberet pure passive, non active libere, igitur sibi non esset imputandum [e*] ad peccatum [48].

Antecedens probatur per articulum Parisiensem, *omne enim effectum et omnem formam quam Deus potest causare mediante causa secunda, potest se ipso immediate* [49]; et quia omnem rem quam Deus potest annihilare, potest iterum producere.

Dices, potest eam creare extra subiectum, non autem in voluntate. Contra: omnem effectum causae secundae potest Deus se solo producere; sed compositum ex anima et illo actu est effectus producibilis a causa secunda. Immo magis per se terminat productionem quam forma secundum Aristotelem, 7 et 8 *Metaphysicae* [50]. Etiam in motu alterationis.

Item, omnem formam natam informare subiectum potest Deus ponere in illo subiecto; si enim virtus finita potest illam causare in subiecto, igitur et infinita virtus.

Confirmatur, quia Deum producere illam se solo extra subiectum continet; secundo, supernaturalia et miracula causare aut illum totaliter in subiecto non continet, nisi unum illorum.

Si vero aliter dicatur quod *b* actus odii, si causetur totaliter a Deo in voluntate, non erit tunc formaliter odium Dei, nec voluntas per illum formaliter erit odiens Deum, sed erit quaedam qualitas absolute informans animam, sicut albedo parietem.

Probatur, quia si voluntas formaliter odit Deum, igitur formaliter operatur; igitur agit; igitur se habet effective. Dicitur igitur quod sicut ille actus non est meritorius nec demeritorius, ita non [f*] esset formaliter odium Dei.

Contra:

Volitio et dilectio, non ex hoc quod totaliter causaretur [h*] in anima, non foret non volitio et dilectio [g*]; igitur pari ratione de actu odii et nolitionis.

Consequentia probatur pari ratione, quia sicut quidam actus diligendi sunt boni et quidam mali, ita de actibus nolendi et odiendi; et quia ille actus non minus naturaliter et essentialiter est odium et nolitio quam ille sit volitio et dilectio, quia non minus est sibi naturale tendere in obiectum et terminari ad obiectum.

Antecedens probatur, tum quia si Deus causet fruitionem sui in beato, beatus fruetur Deo; tum quia Deus non posset infundere animae amorem Dei super omnia, immo nec aliquod bonum velle,

in which case the second inference is denied.

Reply to the third proof: That the will deviate and be turned away from God and its final end by some act can be understood in this way, that it does not will and approve God and is not pleased with God, but rather, that God is unwilled by him and that he is displeased with God. And in this way, it is not necesssarily vicious and unjust and culpable. In another way, it is for the will to behave towards God in a manner that is undue and disordered and unsuitable and contrary to the dictate of preceptive right reason and the law of God. And in this way, the negative part is conceded.

Reply to the fourth proof: The inference is denied. For it is opposed to perfect beatitude, which is incompatible with such natural defects.

With regard to the act of hating God and whether it can fail to be evil, I will proceed not in the manner of making an assertion but in the manner of discussion and disputation.

Certain persons say that such an act of hatred can be in and from a rational creature without sin.

This is evident with regard to a dreamer or a madman, from which it is further argued that the same holds true in the case of a sane person. For that act is not essentially and necessarily vicious and unjust of itself since it is not unjust in a madman. Therefore, with respect to <God's> absolute power, it can be in anyone whomever and not be culpable.

Again, such an act is no more evil through itself and necessarily than is the act of loving God above all things good and just and virtuous; but such an act is contingently of this type.

This is evident if it is in a dreamer or a madman, or in an infidel, or if, contrary to conscience, it is obligatory for a time and place.

Again, the act of hating God can be caused in the will by God alone; therefore the will will not be unjust in accordance with it.

The inference is proved by Anselm in *The Fall of the Devil*, chaps. 14 and 15 [d*]. Since the will would be functioning purely passively, not actively and freely, the act would not be imputed [e*] to it as a sin [48].

The antecedent is proved by the article of Paris, *for every effect and every form which God can cause through the medium of a secondary cause, God can cause by himself immediately* [49]. And further, everything which God can annihilate, he can produce again.

But you will say that God can create the form outside the subject, but not in the will. In opposition to this the following may be said. God can produce by himself alone every effect of a secondary cause. But the compound out of the soul and that act is an effect producible by a secondary cause. Indeed, taken in itself it completes production more than does a form according to Aristotle in the *Metaphysics* 7 and 8 [50]. Likewise, in a motion of alteration.

Again, every form designed to give form to a subject can be put by God into that subject. For if a finite power can cause it in a subject, then likewise an infinite power can.

Confirmation: It involves God producing the form by himself outside the subject. Second, it does not involve causing supernatural events and miracles or causing that totally in the subject, but only one of these.

Or again, suppose it is said that an act of hatred, *b*, if caused in the will totally by God, will not then be formally the hatred of God nor will the will be formally in a state of hating God by that act, but it will be a certain quality absolutely informing the soul, just as whiteness informs a wall.

quia eo ipso non esset velle nec dilectio cum secundum Anselmum, *De Casu Diaboli* 14, si voluntas acciperet velle a Deo, adhuc voluntas vellet licet secundum illud non esset iusta nec iniusta [51].

Praeterea, Deum movere voluntatem ad actum speciali et supernaturali auxilio et influentia non tollit nec diminuit in illa rationem volitionis nec nolitionis; igitur, si supernaturaliter se solo moveat ad illam...

Praeterea, sicut actus potentiae visivae ad videre et actus intelligendi ad intellectum [i*], ita actus volendi ad velle et actus nolendi ad nolle; sed actus videndi vel intelligendi sic est essentialiter visio vel intellectio quod etiam si a solo Deo causetur, visus erit videns et intellectus intelligens, alioquin Deus nihil posset se solo revelare intellectui angelico vel humano infundendo notitiam prophetalem; igitur...

Patet maior, quia actus voluntatis non minus naturaliter seruntur in aliquid obiective quam actus potentiae cognitivae.

Praeterea, sicut habitus voluntatis ad volendum vel nolendum habitualiter, sic actus voluntatis ad volendum vel nolendum actualiter; sed habitus voluntatis, etiam si a solo Deo causetur, dabit voluntati esse volentem vel nolentem habitualiter.

Patet, quia habitus caritatis est a solo Deo, et tamen voluntas secundum illum diligit habitualiter. Patet etiam de fide infusa et de donis Spiritus Sancti infusis a solo Deo, sive voluntati sive intellectui.

Praeterea, Deus potest causare [j*] totaliter in Sorte actum quo odiatur aliud a Deo; igitur *b* actus odii Dei cessabit esse odium ex hoc quod sit a solo Deo.

Antecedens probatur, quia aliter Deus non posset mihi infundere actum odiendi peccatum et actum paenitentiae et contritionis quo detestarer priorem vitam peccati vel actum peccati si in tentatione proponeret quod est inconveniens, cum talis actus sit bonus et secundum aliquod non possit haberi nisi a Deo per specialem motionem adiuvante.

Consequentia principalis probatur, quia actus odii respectu alterius obiecti non magis essentialiter et naturaliter est odium quam actus respectu Dei.

Praeterea, si *b* actus a solo Deo causaretur, non esset odium Dei obiective secundum te; igitur nec fiet odium Dei si causetur a voluntate creata.

Probatio consequentiae: quia in potestate voluntatis non est quod talis actus terminetur ad hoc obiectum vel illud; alioquin per unicum actum posset [k*] velle quodlibet. Et quia si per hoc quod noviter sit a voluntate accipit [l*] terminari et tendere ad aliquod obiectum, maxime accipiet terminari ad voluntatem et esse odium voluntatis, non Dei; actio enim et causalitas voluntatis dabit illi actui referri ad ipsam magis quam ad aliud, saltem non ad Deum magis quam ad obiectum, nisi ratione notitiae concurrentis. Pone igitur quod Deus, supplendo praecise causalitatem voluntatis, coagat notitiae ad causandum illum actum; igitur erit actus odii Dei, et stat propositum.

Praeterea, quod convenit *b* actui non ex eo quod causatur effective a voluntate sed ex eo quod recipitur subiective in voluntate, non minus convenit actui *b* a quocunque causetur in voluntate; sed dare voluntati formaliter esse volentem vel nolentem convenit *b* actui ex eo quod recipitur in voluntate, non ex eo quod efficitur ab illa.

Probo, tum quia potentia sensitiva vel intellectiva non est formaliter sentiens vel intelligens ex eo quod elicit, sed ex eo quod recipit actum sentiendi vel intelligendi; *sentire enim et intelligere est pati*, secundum Aristotelem [52]. Et quia licet obiectum et Deus efficiant partialiter, tamen non dicuntur velle vel nolle secundum illum actum.

Proof: If the will formally hates God, then it formally operates; therefore, it acts; and therefore, it is in an effective condition. Therefore it is said that, just as that act is neither meritorious nor demeritorious, so it would not [f*] be formally the hatred of God.

In opposition to this the following may be said.

Volition and love would not cease to be volition and love [g*] from the fact that they were totally caused [h*] in the soul; therefore, in like manner in the case of an act of hatred and unwillingness.

The inference is proved in like manner, for just as certain acts of loving are good and certain ones are evil, so it is with respect to the acts of unwillingness and hating. Further, this act is no less naturally and essentially hatred and unwillingness than that one is volition and love, for it is no less natural to it to tend towards and be determined to its object.

Proof of the antecedent: First, if God causes the enjoyment of himself in someone happy in heaven, he will enjoy God. Second, God could not infuse the love of God above all things into the soul, nor indeed, willing any good, because by that very fact it would be neither willing nor love. This is so since, according to Anselm in *The Fall of the Devil* 14, if the will should receive a volition from God, the will would still will although it would be neither just nor unjust in accordance with that [51].

Moreover, that God move the will to an act by special and supernatural help and influence neither takes away from nor diminishes in the will the quality of volition or unwillingness. Therefore, if he by himself alone supernaturally moves to that...

Moreover, just as an act of the visual faculty is related to seeing and an act of understanding is related to the intellect [i*], so is an act of willing related to the will and an act of unwillingness to unwillingness. But an act of seeing or understanding is in such a way essentially sight or understanding that even if it is caused by God alone, the sight will be seeing and the intellect understanding. For otherwise, God could reveal nothing by himself to the angelic intellect or to the human intellect in infusing prophetic knowledge. Therefore...

The major is evident because an act of the will is no less naturally joined to something objectively than an act of the cognitive faculty.

Moreover, just as a habit of the will is related to willing or to be unwilling habitually, so an act of the will is related to willing or to be unwilling actually. But a habit of the will, even if it is caused by God alone, will give to the will the state of willing or being unwilling habitually.

This is evident because the habit of charity comes from God alone and yet the will loves habitually in accordance with it. This is likewise evident with respect to infused faith and with respect to the gifts of the Holy Spirit infused by God alone, whether to the will or to the intellect.

Moreover, God can totally cause [j*] in Socrates the act by which something other than God is hated. Therefore, the act of hating God, *b*, will cease to be hatred from the fact that it comes from God alone.

Proof of the antecedent: Otherwise, God could not infuse into me the act of hating sin and the act of repentance and contrition by which I should detest my former life of sin or a sinful act if he should propose something unsuitable in a temptation, since such an act is good and, according to some, cannot be performed except by God assisting with a special impulse.

Proof of the principal inference: An act of hatred with regard to another object is no more essentially and naturally hatred than that act with regard to God.

Moreover, if act *b* were caused by God alone, it would not, according to you, be the hatred

Praeterea, quod *b* actus tendat et feratur in tale obiectum et terminetur ad illud, aut hoc habet ex sua natura, et propositum; aut ex hoc quod causatur ab obiecto vel eius notitia. Et hoc non, quia cum causatur a voluntate et Deo, ferretur obiective super ista; et quia Deus non posset supplere causalitatem obiecti vel notitiae et quod actus terminaretur ad tale obiectum.

Confirmatur: aut *b* actus est amor vel odium talis obiecti se ipso per suam essentiam, aut per formam absolutam vel respectivam sibi additam. Si primam, igitur non tollitur esse huiusmodi per hoc quod a solo Deo causatur. Si secundum, contra: tum quia illam rem dico odium, et de illa stat principale argumentum; tum quia non erit relatio realis quia obiectum interdum nihil est.

Praeterea, erit transitus contradictionis sine mutatione, puta si Deus prius non supplens causalitatem voluntatis postea suppleat, vel econtra.

Si vero dicitur quod tolletur vel ponetur respectiva forma quae est actus, contra: quia illa, cum sit formaliter res causati quod agitur ad causam, non agit vel econtra, sequitur quod actus voluntatis dabit illi tendere in voluntatem magis quam in aliud obiective.

Praeterea, si convenienter dicitur quod idem actus *b* est odium cum est a voluntate creata et non est odium cum est a solo Deo, aeque vel magis convenienter poterat dici quod cum a voluntate vel cum est prohibitus est vitiosus et culpabilis, non autem cum est a solo Deo.

Cum igitur arguitur supra quod si voluntas secundum illum actus odiret, igitur operaretur, igitur ageret, diceretur quod *operatio* potest sumi pro usu vitali et actuali potentiae vitali et pro eius secundaria et accidentali perfectione actuali, non habituali, ut actualis usus distinguitur contra otium vel quietem; et sic conceditur prima consequentia et negatur secunda. Alio modo, pro actione et causatione immanente et actuali exercitio causalitatis effectivae secundum formam immanentem et causatam in effectivo; et sic negatur prima consequentia sustinendo igitur quod talis voluntas a solo Deo recipiens huiusmodi actum odiret Deum non vitiose, sicut etiam furiosus.

Ad articulum Parisiensem dicitur quod si *odium* [m*] sumatur large et generaliter pro actu naturaliter contrario dilectioni, sic ille actus diceretur *odium Dei*; sed sumendo *odium Dei* proprie et stricte secundum acceptionem in qua solet accipi, sic, sive ex impositione sive ex usu, implicat circumstantiam inordinatam et deviationem a rectitudine rationis et debito ordine in finem et quamdam perversionem convenientis ordinis in finem. Licet enim terminus *odii* absolute et per se sumpti non importet hoc quia convenit non inordinate odire peccatum, tamen ut determinatur per terminum significantem summum bonum et ut specificatur ferri in finem ultimum implicat circumstantiam inordinationis, sicut et isti termini eodem modo determinati obiective, *blaphemia Dei*, *contemptus Dei, inoboedientia, rebellio*, etc.. Per se enim sumpta non important deformitatem et obliquitatem a recta ratione quia possunt non inordinate haberi respectu obiecti alicuius, tamen cum determinantur [n*] obiective per summum bonum et finem ultimum important deformitatem et inordinationem et circumstantiam deviationis a ratione. Et sic negatur quod a solo Deo possit causari in voluntat

of God objectively. Therefore, neither will it become the hatred of God if it is caused by a created will.

Proof of the inference: First, it is not within the power of the will that such an act be determined to this object or to that one; otherwise, it could [k*] will anything whatever by a single act. Second, if from the fact that an act newly receives [l*] from the will a determination and tendency towards some object, most of all it receives a determination towards the will and towards being the hatred of the will, not of God. For action and causality of the will will give that act reference back to itself more than to another, at least not to God more than to an object, except by reason of concurrent knowledge. Suppose, therefore, that God, supplying precisely the causality of the will, acts together with knowledge for causing that act. Then it will be an act of the hatred of God, and what we propose to prove stands.

Moreover, what is found in an act, *b*, not because it is caused effectively by the will but because it is received subjectively in the will, is no less found in act *b* on account of whatever way it may be caused in the will. But giving the will willing or unwillingness formally is found in an act *b* because it is received in the will, not because it is effected by the will.

I prove this as follows. First, the sensitive or intellectual faculty does not formally perceive or understand because it elicits but because it receives the act of perceiving or of understanding. For, according to Aristotle, *to perceive and to understand is to undergo something* [52]. Second, although the object and God effect it partially, nevertheless they are not said to will or to be unwilling in accordance with that act.

Moreover, given that an act, *b*, tends toward and is brought to bear upon such an object and is determined to it, it either does this by its nature, and this is what we propose to prove; or because it is caused by the object or by the knowledge of it. But the latter is not the case. First, since it is caused by the will and by God, it would be brought to bear objectively upon them. Second, God could not supply the causality of the object or its knowledge while the act would be determined to such an object.

Confirmation: Either an act, *b*, is the love or hatred of such an object by itself through its essence, or through an absolute or relative form added to it. If the first is the case, then its being an act of that type is not taken away by the fact that it is caused by God alone. If the second alternative is chosen, the following may be said in opposition to it. First, I call that thing hatred, and with respect to that the principal proof stands. Second, it will not be a real relation because the object sometimes is nothing.

Moreover, a contradiction will pass away without a change, namely, if God at first does not supply the causality of the will and afterwards supplies it, or the contrary.

If in fact it is said that the relative form which belongs to the act will be taken away or put in, the following may be said in opposition to it. That form, since it is formally the matter of the effect which is brought to the cause, does not act, or rather the contrary, it follows that the act of the will will give that act a tendency to the will more than to something else objectively.

Moreover, if it is suitably said that the same act, *b*, is hatred when it comes from a created will but is not hatred when it comes from God alone, then equally or more suitably it could have been said that this act is vicious and culpable when it comes from a <created> will or when it is prohibited, but not when it comes from God alone.

Therefore when it is proved above that if the will would hate in accordance with that act, then

AD SEXTUM principale negatur consequentia quoad illam partem, quod talis actus sit virtuosus et meritorius. Talis enim actus non est virtuosus nisi eliciatur libere ab habente et conformiter rationi inexistenti et dictanti et quod fiat propter Deum ut finem ultimum summe dilectum ordinate, quod non convenit somnianti vel furioso. Talis etiam actus habet deformitatem aliquam naturalem et malitiam moralem ex genere quae, quamvis necessario non inferat ipsum esse universaliter et simpliciter peccatum et demeritorium, repugnat tamen virtuoso et meritorio laudabili. Quaedam igitur sufficiunt ad ipsum non esse vitiosum, quae non sufficiunt ad ipsum esse virtuosum.

Ad probationem consequentiae dicendum quod non potest praecipi accipiendo proprie *praeceptum*, quia importat obligationem ex parte eius cui praecipitur et executionem conformem esse iustam et laudabilem. Consequens autem principale conceditur quoad istam partem, scilicet quod in

it would operate, and therefore it would act, it would be said that *operation* can be taken in two ways. First, it can be taken for the vital and actual use of vital power and for its secondary and accidental perfection, actual not habitual, as actual use is distinguished from inactivity or rest. And, in this way, the first inference is conceded and the second is denied. In another way, *operation* can be taken for immanent action and causation and the actual exercise of effective causality according to a form which is immanent and caused in the effecting. And in this way, the first inference is denied in maintaining then that such a will, receiving such an act from God alone, would hate God in a way that is not vicious, just as a madman also does.

Reply to the article of Paris: If *hatred* [m*] is taken in a broad sense and generally for the act which is naturally contrary to love, that act would be called *hatred of God*. But in taking *hatred of God* properly and strictly according to the meaning in which it is accustomed to be taken, then, whether from imposition or from use, it implies a disordered circumstance and divergence from right reason and the due order towards its end and a certain perversion of the suitable order towards its end. For although the term *hatred* taken absolutely and in itself does not signify this because it is suitable to hate sin in a way that is not disordered, nevertheless, as *hatred* is determined by a term signifying the highest good and as it is specified to be brought to bear upon the final end, it implies a circumstance of disorder, just as do those terms *blasphemy of God, contempt of God, disobedience, rebellion*, etc., determined objectively in the same way. For taken in themselves they do not signify deviation and divergence from right reason because they can be performed in a way that is not disordered with respect to some object. Nevertheless, when they are determined [n*] objectively by the highest good and the final end they signify deviation and disorder and a circumstance of divergence from <right> reason. And in this sense, it is denied that the hatred of God can be caused in the will by God alone, nor do they have to assert this in saying that understanding and volition are qualities of the soul. Otherwise it might be said that the article speaks not with respect to the bare and absolute power of God, but with respect to the ordained power of God and what is possible according to the established laws of God, not only according to those delivered to human beings by a special Scripture but also according to the eternal laws as it were naturally imprinted on the created mind, which are called immutable natural law. Or it is to be said that the article condemns the opinion stating that, in asserting understanding and volition to be qualities of the soul, they would be necessitated to concede the consequent as if they probably could not say or respond otherwise. For this is false, since they can probably say otherwise in many ways, although these ways are not apparent.

REPLY TO THE SIXTH OBJECTION: The inference is denied with respect to this part, that such an act is virtuous and meritorious. For such an act is not virtuous unless it is elicited freely by the one performing it and conformably to reason existing in him and prescribing to him and that he does it for the sake of God as the final end supremely loved in an orderly manner, which is not found in a dreamer or a madman. For such an act has some natural deviation and generic moral evilness which, although it will not necessarily cause that act to be universally and simply sinful and demeritorious, is inconsistent with laudable virtuousness and meritoriousness. Therefore certain things suffice for that act not to be vicious, which do not suffice for it to be virtuous.

Reply to the proof of the inference: It cannot be commanded in taking *precept* properly because this implies an obligation on the part of him to whom the precept is given and that execution

habente gratiam potest esse huiusmodi actus; patet de furioso qui post baptismum ante annos discretionis sive sine culpa incidit in furiam.

AD SEPTIMUM: non est simile quoad contingentiam [o*] vel necessitatem et quoad perfectionem [p*] et actualitatem, sicut dictum est quaestione praecedenti [53], quia verum et falsum sumuntur ex respectu signi ad significatum obiective, sed bonitas et malitia ex respectu ad divinam ordinationem.

AD OCTAVUM negatur consequentia. Semper enim sibi est pessime et misere quoad malum poenae sensus, et scienter et libere [q*] contemnit et odit Deum quod non potest sine aliqua deformitate aut saltem sine mutatione in eo. Cui non sufficit hoc, concedat consequens.

AD NONUM negatur consequentia.
Ad probationem negatur de bonis alterius generis improportionabilibus, cuius modi sunt malum poenae tantum et malum culpae. Quicquid enim intrat malitiam culpae eo ipso fugibilius est quolibet malo poenae tantum, quia oppositum esset postponere Deum creaturae.

AD DECIMUM: consequens non videtur absolute impossibile, quia homo a pueritia potest fieri demens; loquendo tamen de homine habente usum liberi arbitrii, negatur consequentia. Talis enim non potest absolvi quin teneatur subici Deo et eius praeceptis; Deus autem potest illi aliquid praecipere, et ille potest non oboedire nec habet in se unde sit invertibilis ad malum; igitur non est impeccabilis.

AD UNDECIMUM negatur consequentia, quia praecipere proprie implicat obligationem ex parte illius cui est praeceptum, et ex parte praecipientis implicat obligare aut velle obligare et debitorem facere, non tamen orationem imperativi modi formare. Repugnantia autem est Deum velle obligare Sortem et non posse obligare Sortem, aut obligare ad actiones repugnantes humanae naturae est impossibile sicut nec lapis potest obligari ad intellegere.
Ad probationem: figura dictionis est. Conceditur enim quod Deus potest causare huiusmodi orationes imperativi modi et actum volendi praecipere in Sorte vel furioso, sed non potest praecipere; non quia hominem alteri principantem proferre huiusmodi orationes imperativas cum voluntate et intentione obligandi sit impossibile, nec quia talis actus in homine sit universaliter et necessario peccatum, sed quia Deum hominem ad hoc obligare est impossibile, et Deum velle hoc est Deum velle facere quod non est factibile et ita irrationabiliter et frustrabiliter velle vel impotentem esse.

AD DUODECIMUM: licet antecedens sit verum secundum leges Dei temporaliter datas et

conformed to it is just and laudable. The principal consequent is conceded, however, with respect to this part, namely, that such an act can be in someone in a state of grace. This is evident in the case of a madman who falls into madness after baptism but before the age of discretion or without fault.

REPLY TO THE SEVENTH OBJECTION: It is not similar with respect to contingency [o*] or necessity and with respect to perfection [p*] and actuality, as has been stated in the preceding question [53]. For truth and falsity are taken from the respect of the sign in relation to the thing signified objectively, but goodness and evilness are taken with respect to the divine decree.

REPLY TO THE EIGHTH OBJECTION: The inference is denied. For it always goes very badly and miserably for him with respect to evil of penalty for the senses. And he knowingly and freely [q*] contemns and hates God, which he cannot do without some deviation or at least without a change in him. For whom this reply does not suffice, let him concede the consequent.

REPLY TO THE NINTH OBJECTION: The inference is denied.
Reply to the proof: It is denied with respect to goods of a different genus which are disproportionate; the mere evil of penalty and the evil of fault are of this mode. For whatever enters into an evil of fault is by that very fact to be avoided more than any mere evil of penalty because the opposite would be to put God after a creature.

REPLY TO THE TENTH OBJECTION: The consequent does not seem absolutely impossible because a human being can be rendered insane from the time of childhood. Speaking, however, of a human being having the use of free will, the inference is denied. For such a human being cannot be released so that he is not bound to be subject to God and his precepts. God, however, can command something to him and he can fail to obey and not have in himself the power to be impervious to evil. Therefore, he is not impeccable.

REPLY TO THE ELEVENTH OBJECTION: The inference is denied because *to command* implies, properly speaking, an obligation on the part of him who is commanded, and implies, on the part of the one commanding, obligating or willing to obligate and making a debtor; nevertheless, it does not imply forming a sentence of the imperative mode. The inconsistency, however, is that God will to obligate Socrates but not be able to obligate Socrates, or rather, it is impossible to obligate to actions which are inconsistent with human nature, just as a stone cannot be obligated to understand.
Reply to the proof: It is a figure of speech. For it is conceded that God can cause such sentences of the imperative mode and command an act of willing in Socrates or in a madman, but he cannot command <the acts in question>. This is so not because it is impossible that a human being ruling over another produce such imperative sentences with the will and intention of obligating, nor because such an act is universally and necessarily a sin in a human being, but because it is impossible that God obligate a human being to this. For God to will this is for God to will to do what is not doable and thus for God to will irrationally and in a way subject to frustration, or to be powerless.

REPLY TO THE TWELFTH OBJECTION: Although the antecedent is true according to

aeternaliter veras secundum ordinem a Deo institutum, tamen loquendo de potentia [r*] Dei absoluta negatur antecedens. Concesso autem antecedente secundum ordinem institutum quod *a* ex natura actus et obiecti est peior quam *b*, ceteris paribus, cum hoc stat quod tam ille quam iste potest esse simpliciter non malus, et quod *a* potest esse in casu simpliciter minus malus secundum varietatem circumstantiarum; immo contingit *a* non esse malum in Sorte et esse malum in Platone.

Dices, cum *a*, ceteris paribus, sit peior quam *b*, quaeritur unde iste est excessus malitiae. Si ex propria natura specifica talis actus, habetur propositum quod talis malitia consequitur essentialiter quidditatem specificam talis actus vel actionis. Si quia deputatur ad poenam maiorem vel prohibetur sub poena maiori, contra: quia malitia culpae est prior quam malum poenae quo est dignum, ideo non est dignum maiori poena quia est maior et gravior malitia; et quia si ad nullum poenam determinatam deputaretur actualiter sed relinquerentur punienda arbitrio iudicis, adhuc haec actio, ceteris paribus, esset gravior illa prima. Huius causa et ratio est lex divinae voluntatis quae statuit hoc, si fieret, esse maius malum. Alia etiam ratio est ex parte actus et obiecti, sed haec ratio reducitur in alias leges universales divinae voluntatis priores. Cum enim Deus ordinavit actionem talem secundum speciem vel genus esse malam et prohibitam et deformem suis ordinationibus, ex hoc sequitur quod illa, ceteris paribus, quae pluribus modis deformatur vel magis nocet et corrumpit creaturam rationalem et quae magis directe obviat amori Dei est peior.

Ad argumentum in principio quaestionis patet supra.

the laws of God which are given temporally and are true eternally according to the order established by God, nevertheless, speaking with respect to the absolute power [r*] of God, the antecedent is denied. However, with the antecedent conceded according to the established order that *a* is worse than *b* by the nature of the act and the object, it still holds true, other things being equal, that as much the latter as the former can simply fail to be evil and that *a* can, in a special case, be simply a lesser evil in accordance with a difference of circumstances. Indeed, it happens that *a* fails to be evil in Socrates but is evil in Plato.

But you will say that when *a* is worse than *b*, other things being equal, it is asked from what source the former has an excess of evilness. If it is from such an act's own specific nature, we have what is to be proven, viz., that such evilness follows essentially the specific quiddity of such an act or action. If it is because it is assigned to a greater punishment or prohibited under the condition of a greater punishment, the following may be said in opposition to this. First, an evil of fault is prior to an evil of penalty, which it deserves, but <on the supposition> it is not deserving of a greater punishment because it is a greater and more grievous evil. Second, if it were actually assigned to no determined punishment but the infliction of punishments would be left to the free judgment of a judge, thus far this action would be more grievous than that first one, other things being equal. The cause and reason of this is the law of the divine will which established that this be a greater evil if it should be done. Also, another reason is on the part of the act and the object, but this reason is reduced to other universal laws of the divine will which are prior. For since God decreed such an action, according to its species or genus, to be evil and prohibited and deviant from his decrees, it follows from this that, other things being equal, an action which deviates in more ways or which harms and destroys a rational creature more and which more directly opposes the love of God is worse.

The reply to the proof in the beginning of the question is evident from what has been said above.

TEXTUAL NOTES

DISTINCTION 48, QUESTION 1

a. *Bonum delectabile*, also translated as *delightful good*.
b. *Bonum honestum*.
c. *Bonum commodi*, also translatable as *beneficial good*.
d. conformabiles: conformales.
e. de circumstantiis eligibilis et fugibilis: de circumstantiis et fugibilis.
f. in lumine naturali rationis naturalis: in lumine naturali rationum naturalium.
g. seu dicitur integritas: seu differentia integritas.
h. moralis: naturalis.
i. se ipsum: reipu.
j. Bonitas supernaturalis seu theologica et caritativa: Bonitas supernaturalis seu theologica vel caritativa.
k. secundum legem et ius naturae - redundant phraseology eliminated in translation.
l. in se et absolute: in se absolute.
m. in se et absolute: in se absolute.
n. bonum alicui alteri: bonum alicui.
o. sit: sit ei.
p. *et* omitted.
q. et: est.
r. quia: vel quia.
s. ut eligeret: et eligere.
t. bonitatem: beatitudinem.
u. concomitantur: concomitatur.
v. igitur: etiam.
w. veritatem: virtutem.
x. naturalis: naturale.
y. *et* omitted.
z. rationi: tationi.
a*. voluntatem: voluutatem.
b*. probationem: improbationem.
c*. verbi gratia: verbi gatia.
d*. postmodum: post modum.
e*. demonstratrum: demonstrato.
f*. bonitatis: bonitas.
g*. *gratiae* omitted.
h*. huiusmodi: huius.
i*. actualiter: actu.
j*. consequentem: consequente.
k*. Bernardum: B.
l*. spes: species.
m*. malle debuimus in vitiorum conflictationis molestia: male debuimus in vitiorum conflictationis malitia.
n*. dominationem: damnationem.
o*. meritorium gratiae: meritorim bonitatis.
p*. prima: primo.
q*. recta: rectam.
r*. voluntas: voluntatis.

s*. convenientissime: inconvenientissime.

t*. aliquid: aliquis.

u*. profecto: perfecto.

v*. The translation of *ex puris naturalibus* given by Heiko A. Oberman in *a Nominalistic Glossary*, in *The Harvest of Medieval Theology* (Durham, NC: Labyrinth Press, 1983), p. 468.

w*. deformitate: deformiter.

x*. reprobatum: reprobum.

y* confirmationem: probationem.

z*. praesentia: privatione.

a**. determinantem: determinantam.

b**. *Figura dictionis* is "the logical fallacy of mistaking one term for another and thus of equivocating in an argument; the designation is explained as coming from the fact that one object can be mistaken for another because of similarity in shape or figure (*figura*)..." R.J. Hennessey, O.P., explanatory note to St. Thomas Aquinas, *Summa Theologiae* IIIa, q. 3, a. 7 (Blackfriars in conjunction with Eyre & Spottiswoode, London, and Mc-Graw-Hill, New York, 1976), vol. 48, p. 105.

c**. antecedenter: antedenter.

d**. acta: actu.

e**. *probatio* omitted.

f**. Being of feminine gender and singular number, the Latin pronoun *haec* has no antecedent in the preceding sentence. Given the use of *verum*, perhaps *veritas* is to be understood.

g**. *non* omitted.

h**. propter quid: secundum quid.

i**. primo: primae.

j**. primo: prima.

k**. ad extra: ab extra.

l**. istum: iustum.

m**. *Intellectual reason* (or *universal* or *higher* or *properly so-called reason*) contrasts with *the particular* or *individual reason* or *reason in the improper sense of the term*. See Roy J. Deferrari, *A Latin-English Dictionary of St. Thomas Aquinas* (Boston: Daughters of St. Paul, 1960), s.v. *ratio*, p. 889.

n**. *elec*ti, literally, *the chosen*, often translated as *the elect*.

o**. Quarto: quartus. The text may contain a mistake in numbering objections, with this objection in fact being the second. The replies to the objections follow the apparent error.

p**. rationale: rationabiliter.

q**. *Dominus* omitted.

r**. Number 1 omitted.

s**. veritati: voluntati.

t**. praeter ea: praeterea.

u**. comitatur: comicatur.

v**. aliquos: aliquorum.

w**. eius benignitati. Libertas: eius benignitati et benignitati libertas.

x**. *Proslogii*: prosa.

y**. es: est.

z**. es: est.

a***. esses: esset.

b***. *De* omittted.

c***. constituti: costituti.

d***. ad hoc: ad huc.

e***. *bonum* omitted.

f***. *et* omitted.

g***. *Deo* omitted.

h***. *non* omitted.

i***. *non* omitted.

j***. talem: taem.

k***. aliquo: aliqua.

l***. *et* omitted.

m***. ad quod: ad quem.

n***. causabilis multipliciter: causabilis multipliciter scibilis; *scibilis* is superfluous.

o***. ordinavisset: ordinasset.

p***. salvandorum: salvandarum.

q***. congruens correspondentia: congruentia correspondentia.

r***. oboedientiae: obiective.

s***. oboedientiam: obiectivam.

t***. contemnendo: contemnerando.

u***. mortalis: moralis.

v***. si: sic.

w***. praeponeret: proponeret.

x***. 26: ro.

y***. illas: illa.

z***. Bernardum: Bedam.

a****. *Canone*: casu.

b****. quia: quae.

c****. realiter est: realiter nec est.

d****. *non* omitted.

e****. oboedientiae: obiective.

f****. sed: se.

g****. dationem: dilectionem.

h****. iustus: verus.

i****. actus: auctus.

j****. ad honorem: ad ad honorem.

k****. habitualiter nec implicite et interpretative: habitualiter et implicite nec interpretative.

l****. Cf. Oberman's translation of *facere quod in se est* in *a Nominalistic Glossary*, in *The Harvest of Medieval Theology*, p. 468.

m****. approbat: appobat.

n****. Bernardum: Bedam.

o****. Lacuna in printing of the text.

p****. Bernardus: Beda.

q****. monte: mente.

DISTINCTION 48, QUESTION 2

a. *Malum poenae. Poena* can mean either *punishment* or *penalty.* Andrew's discussion makes better sense if the idiom *malum poenae* is translated as *evil of penalty.* Cf. Thomas Gilby (trans.), St. Thomas Aquinas, *Summa Theologiae*, vol. 18 (Blackfriars in conjunction with Eyre & Spottiswoode, London, and McGraw-Hill, New York, 1965), Appendix 19 and glossary.

b. esse: est se.

c. poeta: posita.

d. demeriti: demerit.

e. iniusta: iusta.

f. vetatur: vitatur.

g. iniustum: iustum.

h. citra: circa.

i. consenserit: consenserint.

j. si: sic.

k. Latin text reads *...boni vel mali per se et principaliter et ultimate...*; inclusion of *per se* seems inappropriate in terms of contextual meaning, and may represent a textual error. It has been omitted in the translation.

l. praecipit vel prohibet: prohibet vel praecipit. Textual word order is reversed to accord with the order of the remainder of the sentence.

m. nolitum a Deo: nolitum fieri a Deo.

n. *non* omitted.

o. Dei: rei.

p. ordinat: ordinet.

q. eam: eum, referring to *prohibition.*

r. probationem: improbationem.

s. iniustum: iustum.

t. *Dispensatione*: Dispensative.

u. divortiis. Gaudemus: divortiis cap. Gaudemus.

v. ideo eligere: ideo tenetur non eligere *a* odium Dei, et ideo eligere (prior stretch of text   repeated).

w. eligere: elicere.

x. est: et.

y. averteretur a Deo: converteretur ad Deum.

z. poena: poenam.

a*. convoluta: involuta.

b*. non: enim.

c*. consequentia: conclusio.

d*. cap. 14 et 15: cap. 14 et 5.

e*. imputandum: putandum.

f*. *non* omitted.

g*. volitio et dilectio: dilectio.

h* causaretur: crearetur.

i*. intellectum: intelligere.

j*. causare: creare.

k*. A printing error occurs after fol. 261rb by way of repetition; fol. 261v repeats the text of 260v; 261r is then reprinted. The subsequent 261v resumes the text and pagination correctly.

l*. accipit: accipir.

m*. si odium: odium si.

n*. determinantur: determinatur.
o*. quoad contingentiam: quod contahentiam.
p*. quoad perfectionem: quod perfeitatem.
q*. libere: liberum.
r *. potentia: impotentia.

REFERENCE NOTES

ABBREVIATIONS

A   Anselm, *Opera Omnia*, edited by Franciscus Salesius Schmitt. Edinburgh: Thomas Nelson & Sons, 1946.

AC   *Anselm of Canterbury*, edited & translated by Jasper Hopkins & Herbert Richardson. Toronto & New York: Edwin Mellen Press, 1976.

B   Bernard of Clairvaux, *Opera*, edited by J. Leclercq & H.M. Rochais. Rome: Editiones Cistercienses, 1963.

BWA Richard McKeon (ed.), *The Basic Works of Aristotle*. New York: Random House, 1941. CC *Corpus Christianorum*, series Latina. Turnholt: Brepols, 1954--.

CIC   *Corpus Iuris Canonici*, edited by A.L. Richteri. Leipzig: Bernhard Tauchnitz, n.d.

CSEL   *Corpus Scriptorum Ecclesiasticorum Latinorum*. Vienna, 1866--.

PL   *Patrologiae Cursus Completus*, series Latina, edited by J.P. Migne. Paris, 1844-65; ed. Alt. 1866 seqq.

DISTINCTION 48, QUESTION 1

1. Augustine, *De Libero Arbitrio* I, 3, 6 (CC 29:214; CSEL 74:7). "Since your question has to do with the cause of our doing evil, we must first have a discussion on the nature of evil. State your opinion on this matter. If you cannot express it fully, all at once and in a few words, let me at least know what you think by mentioning, in particular, some evil deeds themselves. Ev<odius> Adultery, murder, and sacrilege, to say nothing of others which time and my memory do not allow me to mention. Can anyone think that these are not evil? Aug<ustine> Tell me first, then, why you think it is wrong to commit adultery. It is because the law forbids it? Ev. It is not wrong just because the law forbids it; rather, the law forbids it because it is wrong." Translated by Robert P. Russell, , O.S.A., in *The Fathers of the Church*, vol. 59 (Washington, D.C.: Catholic University of America Press, 1968), p. 76.

2. Aristotle, *Nicomachean Ethics* I, 6; 1096b (BWA 940). See also *Nicomachean Ethics* VII, 9; 1151b (BWA 1050).

3. Aristotle, *Nicomachean Ethics* I, 6; 1096a (BWA 939).

4. Augustine, *De Vera Religione* XI, 21 (CC 32:201; CSEL 77-2:17*)*; *De Genesi ad Litteram* XI, 13 (CSEL 28-1:345). Texts paraphrased in citation.

5. *Mark* 10:18.

6. Aristotle, *Nicomachean Ethics* I, 7; 1097b (BWA 941-2).

7. Augustine, *De Diversis Quaestionibus Octaginta Tribus*, q. 30 (CC 44A:38-40).

8. Anselm, *De Veritate* 12 (A 1:192-3).

9. Anselm, *De Casu Diaboli* 14 (A 1:258). "T<eacher> So let us consider the will-for-justice. If this will were given to this same angel to will only what was fitting for him to will, would he be able to will anything other <than what was fitting>? Or would he be able by himself to keep from willing what he had received to will? S<tudent> What we saw in the case of the will-for-happiness must in every respect hold true in the case of this will too. T. Then, <Satan> would have neither a just or an unjust will. For even as *there* <in the case of the will-for-happiness> the will would not be unjust if it willed unfitting things, since it would not be able to keep from willing them, so *here* <in the case of the will-for-justice> if the will willed fitting things, it would not thereby be just, since it would have received this capability in such way that it would not have been

able to will otherwise." (AC 2:157-8).

10. Augustine, *De Libero Arbitrio* II, 18, 50 (CC 29:270-1; CSEL 74:84-5). Text paraphrased in citation.

11. *Ibid.*, II, 18, 49-50 (CC 29:270-1; CSEL 74:84-5). Text paraphrased in citation.

12. Bernard of Clairvaux, *De Diligendo Deo* VII, 17 (B 3:133).

13. Augustine, *De Civitate Dei* XXI, 15 (CC 48:781; CSEL 40-2:546).

14. Peter Lombard, *Sententiae in IV Libros Distinctae*, 3rd ed., II, d. 24, cap. 1 (Grottaferrata (Rome): Collegium S. Bonaventurae Ad Claras Aquas, 1971-81).

15. *Ibid.*

16. *Ibid.*, d. 5, cap. 5.

17. Aristotle, *Metaphysics* II, 1; 993b (BWA 712-13). Cf. Thomas Aquinas, *Summa Theologiae* Ia, q. 2, a. 3, c., Quarta Via (London: Blackfriars, in conjunction with Eyre & Spottiswoode and New York: McGraw Hill, 1964) and *In XII Libros Metaphysicorum* II, Lect. II in *Opera Omnia* 20 (New York: Musurgia Publishers, 1949).

18. Anselm, *Proslogium* 11 (A 1:109).

19. Anselm, *Cur Deus Homo* I, 8 (A 2:59).

20. Hugh of St. Victor, *De Sacramentis* I, IV, 1 (PL 176:233-5; Roy J. Deferrari (trans.), *Hugh of Saint Victor on the Sacraments of the Christian Faith* (Cambridge, MA: Mediaeval Academy of America, 1951), p. 61, a translation based on an unpublished critical edition prepared by Brother Charles Henry).

21. The identification of authorship is incorrect; the work in question is to be attributed to the *Pseudo-Cyprian*.

22. Pseudo-Cyprian, *De Singularitate Clericorum* 16 (CSEL 3-3:190). Compare Andrew's list of authorities with that given by Francisco Suarez in *De Legibus ac Deo Legislatore* II, VI, 4, edicion critica bilingue, edited by Luciano Perena et al. (Madrid: Consejo Superior de Investigaciones Cientificas, Instituto Francisco de Vitoria, 1971). "These authorities also add that the whole basis of good and evil in matters pertaining to the law of nature is in God's will, and not in a judgment of reason, even on the part of God Himself, nor in the very things which are prescribed or forbidden by that law. Their opinion would assuredly seem to be founded upon the fact that actions are not good or evil, save as they are ordered or prohibited by God; since God Himself does not will to command or forbid a given action to any created being, on the ground that such an action is good or evil, but rather on the ground that it is just or unjust <simply> because He has willed that it shall or shall not be done as Anselm (*Proslogion*, Chap. xi), indicates, saying, *That is just which Thou dost will; and that is not just which Thou dost not will.* Such is the view held also by Hugh of St. Victor (*De Sacramentis*, Bk. I, pt. iv, chap. 1); and by Cyprian, in a work *(De Singularitate Clericorum)* attributed to him." Translation from James Brown Scott (ed.), *Selections from Three Works of Francisco Suarez, S.J.*, vol. 2, translated by Gwladys L. Williams, Ammi Brown, & John Waldron (Oxford: Clarendon Press, 1944). Note that Suarez gives the same list of authoritative sources, and in the same order, as does Andrew. This leads to the speculation that Suarez borrows from Andrew's text.

23. Anselm, *De Casu Diaboli* 14 (A 1:258). See n. 9.

24. Anselm, *Cur Deus Homo* I, 12 (A 2:70).

25. "...therefore that the divine intellect knows that *a* will be because the divine will determines and wills that *a* will be...". Andrew of Neufchateau, *Primum Scriptum Sententiarum*, d. 38-39, q. 5, a. 2; fol. 176rb (Paris: Granjon, 1514). Translations of stretches of text from *Primum Scriptum Sententiarum* are those of the present author.

26. Andrew of Neufchateau, *Primum Scriptum Sententiarum*, d. 48, q. 1, a. 2, concl. 2.

27. *Matthew* 11:26. Compare Thomas Bradwardine, *De Causa Dei* I, 21, section answering the question *Does reason move and direct the divine will?*, arguments for a negative answer: "So in the Gospel the Lord, when he spoke of the cause of this kind of thing, says, *I acknowledge you, Father, Lord of heaven and earth,*

who hid these things from the wise and the prudent and revealed them to children; yes, Father. And he immediately, as if adding some reason for the concealment and the revelation, says: *Because so it was pleasing before you.* (London: Ioannis Billius, 1618; reprint Frankfurt am Main: Minerva GMBH, 1964). Translations of Bradwardine are those of the present author.

28. *Matthew* 20:1-16.

29. *Matthew* 20:15. Compare Thomas Bradwardine, *De Causa Dei* I, 21, section answering the question *Does reason move and direct the divine will?*, arguments for a negative answer: "And that landowner of the Gospel acted in this way, as recounted in *Matthew* 20, in giving as generously to those working in his vineyard one hour as to others working the whole day, saying to whomever was grumbling: *I want to give to this last just as I give to you. Am I not allowed to do what I want?* ...So also in the case of paying wages to those working in the vineyard, when he made equal in recompense certain laborers unequal in work and the one who had put in more work sought more in wages, he says: *Did we not agree on one denarius? But I want to give also to this last just as I give to you. Am I not allowed to do what I want?*"

30. "SECOND CONCLUSION: Every real being actually other than God, in so far as it is a real being, exists because God wills it to exist, especially in the case of real beings which are not evil and are not unsuitably and badly made...". Andrew of Neufchateau, *Primum Scriptum Sententiarum*, d. 38-39, q. 1; fol. 164ra.

31. Compare Thomas Bradwardine, *De Causa Dei* I, 21, section answering the question *Does reason move and direct the divine will?*, arguments for a negative answer: "If reason moves the divine will, that reason is not caused in God by any creature...but it is intrinsic and essential to him; therefore it is necessary. And therefore the will of God necessarily agrees with it; for otherwise there could be an opposition of will and reason in God, and also sin done knowingly contrary to a rationally informed conscience. And so it would be the case that God necessarily acts with respect to things outside himself, whatever he does."

32. Compare Thomas Bradwardine, *De Causa Dei* I, 21, section answering the question *Does reason move and direct the divine will?*, arguments for a negative answer: "Again, if reason moved the divine will, a stronger reason would move it more. Since, therefore, God could make everything better than he does make it, and this would be to do it in a better and more rational way if he made it, consequently this moves his will more. Therefore he so wills and does."

33. *Romans* 9:20-1. Compare Thomas Bradwardine, *De Causa Dei* I, 21, section answering the question *Does reason move and direct the divine will?*, arguments for a negative answer: "The Apostle agrees with these speaking thus in *Romans* 9: *Who may oppose his will? O man, who are you, who answer back to God? Does a thing which has been produced say to the one who fashioned it, What did you make me in this way?* And he proves this by an argument from the indifference of reason for different deeds, just as I was arguing above. *Does not a potter of clay have the power,* he says, *to make from the same lump one particular vessel for honor and another for abuse?*"

34. Compare Thomas Bradwardine, *De Causa Dei* I, 21, section answering the question *Does reason move and direct the divine will?*, arguments for a negative answer: "This is confirmed by analogy with a human being. For if to a man able to save only one person from death comes two who are about to die unless he come to their assistance, and assuming they are equal in all respects, he acts rightly in saving whichever one of them and abadoning the other. And this is so without any reason prior to will, for there is no better reason for choosing this one than for choosing that one. And the same is true of preferring one of two who are equally deserving for some high office, and of generously giving a gift to one of many who are equally worthy, or even, among those not equally deserving, to someone less deserving."

35. *Wisdom* 8:1. Compare Thomas Bradwardine, *De Causa Dei* I, 21, section answering the question *Does reason move and direct the divine will?*, arguments for an affirmative answer: "And his wisdom proves this, which reaches from one end of the earth to the other with strength, and arranges all things delightfully.

36. *Ephesians* 1:11.

37. *Glossa Ordinaria*, Ad Ephesios. In *Bibliorum Sacrorum cum Glossa Ordinaria* (Lyon: 1589), 529-30.

38. Aristotle, *Nicomachean Ethics* III, 2; 1112a (BWA 969); see also n. 39. Compare the entire paragraph with Thomas Bradwardine, *De Causa Dei* I, 21, section answering the question *Does reason move and direct the divine will?*, arguments for an affirmative answer: "Again, the Apostle speaks thus of God in *Ephesians* 1, *who administers all things according to the counsel of his will,* where a gloss explains the verse thus, *that is, according to your will which comes from reason.* As if he would say, we do not know why he chose us to a greater extent for the office of preaching or apostleship; but yet he did it with counsel, not thoughtlessly. And this can be confirmed since counsel is a certain discourse of reason, as can be ascertained from the *Ethics* III, 7 and the following discussion."

39. Aristotle, *Nicomachean Ethics* VI, 2; 1139a (BWA 1024). See also n. 38.

40. Compare Thomas Bradwardine, *De Causa Dei* I, 21, section answering the question *Does reason move and direct the divine will?*, arguments for an affirmative answer: "And otherwise that unseemly jest would be justified with respect to God: *So I will, so I order, let will serve as the reason.*" Compare Thomas Buckingham, *Quaestiones, On the Divine Causality*, article two, *Whether everything which is rational or just is rational or just because it is willed by God to be such,* arguments for a negative answer: "But if God willed to create the world naturally prior to knowing the creation of the world to be rational and expedient, the will and willing would precede being wise and wisdom. According to that it follows that in the works of God there would not be any explanation other than *So I will, so I order, let will serve as the reason.* Since in the case of a human being it would be unsuitable and condemnable to act or to will and not from previous reason, for much stronger reason this would seem unsuitable in the case of God." (MS. New College (Oxford) 134, fol. 354rb-va). Translations of Buckingham are those of the present author.

41. Anselm, *De Veritate* 12: "Even as every will wills something, so it also wills for the sake of something. And just as we must consider *what* it wills, so we must also notice *why* it wills. For a will ought to be upright in willing what it ought and, no less, in willing for the reason it ought. Therefore, every will has both a *what* and a *why*. Indeed, whatsoever we will, we will for a reason." (AC 2:96).

42. Compare Thomas Bradwardine, *De Causa Dei* I, 21, section answering the question *Does reason move and direct the divine will?*, arguments for an affirmative answer: "Again, if God would rightly will anything and would do it without reason making a judgment beforehand, for the same reason a human being could act in this manner... . This line of reasoning is confirmed, because a human being is made in the image of God with respect to his soul, namely, with respect to memory, intelligence, and will. If therefore will guides reason in God, so it ought to be likewise in a human being; for otherwise there would not be imitation, nor a complete similarity."

43. *Proverbs* 16:4. Compare Thomas Bradwardine, *De Causa Dei* I, 21, introduction: "Moreover, objection can also be made specifically against the statement, *For if things formerly willed are the cause of the divine volition, the divine will has some cause... .* Again, every rational agent acts for the sake of some end, as is evident in the second book of the *Physics* and elsewhere often enough; but the end moves the agent, as natural, metaphysical, and moral philosophy all frequently teach. ...In the case of the fourth argument it must be understood that the end is twofold, as is evident in the *Ethics* I, and in many other places, namely, the final end and the intermediate end. The final end on account of which God wills and effects anything whatever is himself... So *Proverbs* 16, *The Lord has made all things for himself... ".*

44. Compare Uthred of Boldon: " 'That, whatever the designated effect, it is necessary that there be some cause why God wills that effect, and to say finally, *because God wills it,* is the response of little old women.' I said this more often because God wills nothing except what comes from reason." (M.D. Knowles, "The Censured Opinions of Uthred of Boldon," *Proceedings of the British Academy* 37 (1951): 305-42 at 339, no. XXV.) The translation is that of the present author.

45. Peter Lombard, *Sententiae in IV Libros Distinctae* II, d. 1, cap. 4.

46. *Ibid.*, II, d. 18, cap. 1.

47. *Ibid.*, II, d. 18, cap. 1.

48. *Ibid.*, II, d. 18, cap. 2.

49. *Ibid.*, II, d. 18, cap. 3.

50. *Ibid.*, II, d. 21, cap. 7.

51. *Ibid.*, II, d. 23, cap. 1.

52. Compare the paragraph to Thomas Buckingham, *Quaestiones, On the Divine Causality,* article two, *Whether everything which is rational or just is rational or just because it is willed by God to be such,* arguments for a negative answer: "According to that, reason would not move the divine will, nor would there be any reason to be assigned in the works of God other than *because it is pleasing to the sovereign.* Further, holy people very frequently take pains to show the reason for divine action in Scripture, and from that reason they show God thus to have acted rationally." (MS. New College (Oxford) 134, fol. 354va)

53. Pseudo-Augustine, *Quaestiones Veteris et Novi Testamenti*, q. 97 (CSEL 50:172); cited in Peter Lombard, *Sententiae in IV Libros Distinctae* I, d. 42, cap. 1.

54. Pseudo-Augustine, *Quaestiones Veteris et Novi Testamenti*, q. 106 (CSEL 50:244); cited in Peter Lombard, *Sententiae in IV Libros Distinctae* I, d. 42, cap. 1. Compare Thomas Bradwardine, *De Causa Dei* I, 21, section answering the question *Does reason move and direct the divine will?*, arguments for an affirmative answer: "And the same comes from *Questions of the Old and New Law*: God was able to make the whole at the same time, but reason prohibited this."

55. Peter Lombard, *Sententiae in IV Libros Distinctae* I, d. 42, cap. 3, quoting Hugh of St. Victor's *De Sacramentis.*

56. Anselm, *Cur Deus Homo* I, 10 (A 2:67).

57. *Ibid.*, II, 10 (A 2:108).

58. *Ibid.*, I, 12 (A 2:69).

59. *Ibid.*, I, 12 (A 2:69-70).

60. Anselm, *Proslogium* 9 (A 1:107).

61. *Ibid.*

62. *Ibid.*, 9 (A 1:108).

63. *Ibid.*, 10 (A 1:108-9).

64. *Ibid.*, 11 (A 1:109).

65. Augustine, *De Trinitate* XIII, X, 13 (CC 50A:399-400). Text paraphrased in citation.

66. Anselm, *Cur Deus Homo* I, 16 (A 2:74-5).

67. The meaning of the reply is unclear. Possibly, it can be elucidaed by considering a parallel text in *Primum Scriptum Sententiarum*, and the intellectual background of Andrew's work.

In considering the topics of predestination and reprobation in distinction 40-41, Andrew argues for the negative thesis that God did not predestine some persons to receive the grace which justifies and makes one worthy of eternal life because he foresaw their future merits (d. 40-41, q. 1, concl. 1; fol. 179r). The second objection to this thesis which Andrew mentions closely parallels the objection presently under consideration (viz., d. 48, q. 1, a. 2, concl. 3, 1m):

> SECOND, God does not do or will anything concerning a creature unless rationally and wisely; therefore he wills nothing except from reason antecedently prescribing and seeing beforehand and as it were moving, and he has a rational *why*. For he could give a human being the reason for that which he wills to be done so and not otherwise.

> Confirmation: Augustine says in *To Orosius*, q. 7: *In God will cannot precede wisdom.* And in *Wisdom* 8 it is said that God's *wisdom reaches from one end of the earth to the other, and arranges all things.* (fol. 179v)

The structure of the reply to this objection is also similar to the reply presently under consideration, but with the difference that Andrew speaks in terms of *ratio concomitans (accompanying reason)*:

> REPLY TO THE SECOND OBJECTION: The inference is denied. It suffices that it be according to accompanying reason.

This statement can be read against the background of Thomas Bradwardine's *De Causa Dei* I, 21, section answering the question *Does reason move and direct the divine will?*:

> There is, however, as yet something more which must be considered as the second part of those rational things, namely, that the reason in question is of three kinds: obligating, preferential, and truly fitting and accompanying. Obligating reason is that which prescribes that anyone ought and is bound to do or to omit this or that. He who has this reason and does not follow it, sins. And such reason is not in God with respect to later objects of volition, but frequently is in us. Preferential reason, on the other hand, is that which prescribes that it would be better to do this than that, or that it would be better to do this than to omit it. And such reason does not move and neither is conclusive to the divine will nor determines it to action. For God could make better things than he does, and many good things which he does not make. Reason truly fitting and accompanying is that which prescribes that it is fitting and good to do or to omit this or that. And speaking of reason in this way, God wills rationally every posterior object of volition. And in this way a human being rationally wills to prefer, and does prefer one of two equals, or perhaps the less deserving among unequals in some cases of things premised. For if this be done, it is fitting and good. And such reason does not obligate and does not determine God or a human being, but only suffices for willing. For a human being, however, it is always prudent and holy to conform his will to preferential reason, and wherever he can have such reason. And perhaps the Apostle understood things in this way when he was saying, *May you do nothing without a preceding decision,* namely, where such a preferential, or even obligating, preceding judgment can be procured. Where in fact it cannot, as is the case in the preference of one of two equals, wills suffices as a reason, or at least a fitting and accompanying reason, as has been stated. And the authority cited could likewise be understood of such preceding judgment. God, however, cannot follow preferential reason in all matters unless he were to do everything possible, and anything infinite among these, which includes a contradiction as has been shown elsewhere. Therefore in such cases will suffices him as a reason, or at least the aforementioned fitting and accompanying reason suffices.

Also relevant to consider is Thomas Buckingham's *Quaestiones, On the Divine Causality,* a. 2, *Whether everything which is rational or just is rational or just because it is willed by God to be such,* reply to the arguments for a negative answer:

> In reply to the next reason I say that such a decree or volition of God is rational and just by *accompanying* reason and justice, not by previous or prior reason or justice. Just as is the case with respect to many human statutes and laws, which are rational and just because they are enacted as statutes and laws and are established before they are rational or just, so that decree is rational and just by accompanying reason. And if it be conceded that in that instant of nature they are not rational or just, this is not a cause for concern; it is sufficient that in the present they are rational and just.
>
> In reply to the other reason I say that holy people frequently take pains to show the reason accompanying the divine volition, not a previous or moving reason. (fol. 354vb)

68. The citation from *Ephesians* and accompanying gloss given in d. 48, q. 1, a. 2, concl. 3, 2m is also given by Andrew in the aforementioned d. 40-41, q. 1, concl. 1, 3m (fol. 179va). In his reply to that objection Andrew also distinguishes different senses of *counsel* (fol. 180ra), but again brings in the concept of *ratio concomitans (accompanying reason)*:

> ...In reply to the authority of the gloss it can be said that <God's will> comes from reason because <God wills> conformably to accompanying reason.... (fol. 180ra)

69. "Like all genuine thought, practical thinking involves generalities. Every human action is describable

in terms of a generalized rule... More, since actions consist of particulars, practical reasoning must also take them into account. The deliberation preceding a choice, therefore, includes at least one universal and one particular judgment.

All discursive reasoning, whether theoretical or practical, is done correctly only if our inferences have a valid logical form. Aristotle describes correct deliberation, therefore, in terms of a model which has come to be called the *practical syllogism*, in which a universal (a practical rule setting out the end to be attained by acting) is related to particulars (of an actual situation). He writes:

> ...the one premise or judgment is universal and the other deals with the particular (for the first tells us that such and such kind of man should do such and such kind of act, and the second that *this* is an act of the kind meant, and I a person of the type intended.)"

Roger J. Sullivan, *Morality and the Good Life* (Memphis, TN: Memphis State University Press, 1977), p. 66. The text cited is *De Anima* 3, 11; 434a16-19. For the connection of the practical syllogism with deliberation Sullivan also cites *Nicomachean Ethics* 6, 8; 1142a20-23 and 6, 9; 1142b22-25 and 5, 7; 1135a6-13 and 7, 3; 1146b36-1147a7 (p. 76).

70. Hugh of St. Victor, *De Sacramentis* I, II, 22 (PL 176:216; Deferrari, *Hugh of Saint Victor on the Sacraments of the Christian Faith*, p. 41).

71. Anselm, *De Casu Diaboli* 14 (A 1:258). See Reference Notes to Distinction 48, Question 1, n. 9.

72. Augustine, *De Genesi ad Litteram* VIII, 6 (CSEL 28-1:239-40).

73. Augustine, *Enchiridion de Fide, Spe et Caritate* 18, 69 (CC 46:87); see also 19, 70-71 (CC 46:87-8). These texts merely distinguish degrees of sin.

74. Augustine, *De Civitate Dei* XXI, 26 (CC 48:796-99; CSEL 40-2:568-73). This text connects the distinction between degrees of sin with the notion of setting a creature above God.

75. Bernard of Clairvaux, *De Praecepto et Dispensatione* II, 4; III, 6-8 (B 3:256-9).

76. Gratian, *Decretum, Concordia Discordantium Canonum* I, d. 13, I (CIC 1:31).

77. I *Corinthians* 4:4.

78. Augustine, *In Joannis Evangelium*, Tractatus 51, 10 (CC 36:443).

79. *John* 12:25.

80. *Psalm* 11:5 (Lat. 10:6).

81. *Tobit* 12:10.

82. *Proverbs* 1:18.

83. *Romans* 8:38-9.

84. Andrew of Neufchateau, *Primum Scriptum Sententiarum*, d. 14-16, q. 1 (fol. 65ra).

85. Bernard of Clairvaux, *De Praecepto et Dispensatione* III, 7 (B 3:258).

86. Andrew of Neufchateau, *Primum Scriptum Sententiarum*, d. 1, q. 3 (fol. 23va).

DISTINCTION 48, QUESTION 2

1. Andrew of Neufchateau, *Primum Scriptum Sententiarum*, d. 48, q. 1, a. 2, concl. 2.

2. Boethius, *Philosophiae Consolatio* I, Prosa 4, 44 (CC 94:11).

3. *Psalm* 142:7 (Lat. 141:8).

4. Augustine, *Enarrationes in Psalmos* CXLI, 17 (CC 40:2057).

5. Reference not located.

6. Andrew of Neufchateau, *Primum Scriptum Sententiarum*, d. 48, q. 1, a. 2, concl. 2.

7. Aristotle, *De Anima* I, 5; 411a (BWA 553). Cf. Thomas Aquinas, *Sentencia Libri De Anima* I, Lect. XII in *Opera Omnia* 45-1, Commissio Leonina, Rome (Paris: J. Vrin, 1984); *Summa Theologiae* IIaIIae, q. 9, a. 4, 1m.

8. Peter Lombard, *Sententiae in IV Libros Distinctae* II, d. 35, cap. 1: "Sin is, as Augustine says, every word or deed or desire which is contrary to the law of God. ...Ambrose likewise says in his book *Paradise*, What is sin, except transgression of the divine law and disobedience to divine precepts?" The translation is that of the present author.

Compare Gregory of Rimini, *Lectura Super Primum et Secundum Sententiarum* II, d. 34-37, q. 1, a. 2, corr. 2, *Many things are sins of themselves and not precisely because they are prohibited*: "Again, Ambrose states in his book *Paradise*, and this statement is reported by the Master in bk. 2, dist. 35, sect. 1: *What is sin, he says, except transgression of the divine law and disobedience to divine precepts? Thus there is sin in transgression , but there is not fault in commanding. For sin would not exist if there were not a prohibition.* Ambrose says these things. From these considerations it seems to follow without exception that all sin is prohibited by God, nor would anything be a sin on account of something else except because it is prohibited." Translated by the present author from A. Damasus Trapp, OSA & Venicio Marcolino (eds.), *Lectura Super Primum et Secundum Sententiarum* VI (New York: Walter de Gruyter, 1980).

9. *Psalm* 36:10 (Lat. 35:11).

10. Augustine, *Enarrationes in Psalmos* XXXV, 16 (CC 38:334).

11. Augustine, *De Peccatorum Meritis et Remissione et De Baptismo Parvulorum* II, 16, 23 (CSEL 60:95-6).

Compare Gregory of Rimini, *Lectura Super Primum et Secundum Sententiarum* II, d. 34-7, q. 1, a. 2, corr. 2, *Many things are sins of themselves and not precisely because they are prohibited*: "But Augustine seems to be in opposition to that correlary conclusion when he says in the second book of *The Baptism of Infants, To Marcellinus*: *For sin will also not exist, if something will be, if it is not divinely commanded that it not be.* Further, we subsequently find in the same text: *How, he says, is it not prohibited by the justice of God, if there is sin?*"

12. Gregory of Rimini draws the distinction between *indicative* and *imperative* precepts and laws in replying to the objections against the correlary *Many things are sins in themselves and not precisely because they are prohibited, Lectura Super Primum et Secundum Sententiarum* II, d. 34-7, q. 1, a. 2, corr. 2, ad ista respondeo... .

13. Augustine, *De Libero Arbitrio* I, 3, 6 (CC 29:214; CSEL 74:7). Text paraphrased in citation.

14. *Leviticus* 19:11.

15. Augustine, *Quaestionum in Heptateuchum* III, Quaestiones Levitici, q. LXVIII, lb. 19, 11 (CC 33:221; CSEL 28-2:296).

Compare this paragraph and the previous one with Gregory of Rimini, *Lectura Super Primum et Secundum Sententiarum* II, d. 34-7, q. 1, a. 2, corr. 2, *Many things are sins of themselves and not precisely because they are prohibited*: "The correlary is likewise evident from the authorities. For Augustine says in *The Free Choice of the Will* I, sect. 3: *Adultery is not evil because it is prohibited by the law, but it is prohibited by the law because it is evil.* The same thing is said in his gloss on the verse in *Leviticus* 19, *You shall not lie...*

And he responds saying, *But rather it is the case that because lying was unjust, therefore it is prohibited; it is not the case that because it is prohibited, it is therefore unjust.*"

16. Heinrich Denifle & Aemilio Chatelain, *Chartularium Universitatis Parisiensis* (Paris: Fratrum Delalain, 1889-97), II, 1147, no. 27. Article of John of Mirecourt condemned in 1347.

17. *Exodus* 20:13, 15.

18. Andrew of Neufchateau, *Primum Scriptum Sententiarum*, d. 48, q. 1, a. 2, concl. 4, 9m.

19. Peter Lombard, *Sententiae in IV Libros Distinctae* I, d. 46, cap. 3.

20. *Malachi* 1:2-3; *Romans* 9:13. For a discussion of uses of this text in the medieval literature, see H.A. Oberman, *Thomas Bradwardine* (Utrecht: Drukkerij En Uitgevers-Maatschappij v/h Kemink & Zoon N.V., 1957), p. 156.

21. Andrew of Neufchateau, *Primum Scriptum Sententiarum*, d. 48, q. 1, a. 2, concl. 4, ad 9m.

22. Andrew of Neufchateau, *Primum Scriptum Sententiarum*, d.22, q. 3, ad 1m: "Reply to the first objection against the two conclusions set out above: With respect to this kind <of complex signifiable> which is that Socrates sin, God does not have a will according to which he wills formally that Socrates sin, nor does he have unwillingness according to which he is simply and formally unwilling that Socrates sin, but he has an unwillingness which is prohibitory, just as, with respect to goods which he commands and yet are not done, he has an imperative will.... With respect to evilness he also has the unwillingness of reprobation and detestation as it were, contrary to acceptance and pleasure. Likewise with respect to an act, as it is a real thing, he has a will of general influence and a prohibitory unwillingness. Therefore it is more suitably said in common speech that, with respect to evil qua evil, he has simply neither a will nor unwillingness but permission, because we likewise say in ordinary conversation that we permit those things with respect to which we have a will mixed with involuntariness." (fol. 96va23-9, 33-40)

23. Anselm, *De Casu Diaboli* 14 (A 1:258). For Anselm's text, see Reference Notes to Distinction 48, Question 1, n. 9.

24. Denifle & Chatelain, *Chartularium Universitatis Parisiensis* I, 473, no. 63: "That God cannot produce the effect of a secondary cause without that secondary cause itself." This is one of the propositions condemned in 1277 by Stephen Tempier, bishop of Paris. Translations of sections of the *Chartularium Universitatis Parisiensis* are those of the present author.

25. Bernard of Clairvaux, *De Praecepto et Dispensatione* III, 6 (B 3:257-8).

26. *Ibid.*, III, 6 (B 3:258).

27. Augustine, *De Civitate Dei* I, 21 (CC 47:23; CSEL 40-1:40).

28. On the case of Abraham, see, for example, Augustine, *De Civitate Dei* I, 21 (CC 47:23; CSEL 40-1:39), I, 26 (CC 47:27; CSEL 40-1:46); *Contra Gaudentium* I, 31, 39 (CSEL 53:239).

29. See, for example, Augustine, *De Adulterinis Conjugiis* I, 18, 20 (CSEL 41:367), on the case of the Israelites being commanded, through the prophet Esdras, to divorce foreign wives they had taken.

30. On the case of Jacob's lying, see, for example, Augustine, *Contra Mendacium ad Consentium* X, 24 (CSEL 41:499-502).

31. On the case of the Israelists plundering the Egyptians as they left Egypt, see, for example, Augustine, *Quaestionum in Heptateuchum* II Quaestiones Exodi, q. 39, lb. 11, 2 (CC 33:84-5; CSEL 28-2: 112-3).

32. See Reference Notes to Distinction 48, Question 2, n. 26-7.

33. On polygamy in the Old Testament, see, for example, Augustine, *De Doctrina Christiana* III, XII, 20 (CC 32:90; CSEL 80:91-2); *De Bono Conjugali* XV, 17 (CSEL 41:209-10).

34. Aristotle, *Nicomachean Ethics* II, 6; 1107a (BWA 959).

35. *Matthew* 7:1.

36. Augustine, *De Sermone Domini in Monte* II, 18, 59 (CC 35:154-5). Text paraphrased in citation.

37. That one ought not to lie for the sake of a good end is a thesis of Augustine in *Contra Mendacium ad Consentium* (CSEL 41:466-528) in its entirety. Current editions do not divide this treatise into books.

38. Peter Lombard, *Sententiae in IV Libros Distinctae* II, d.40, cap. unicum. Lombard here reports the views of Augustine in *Contra Mendacium*.

39. Anselm, *Cur Deus Homo* I, 12 (A 2:70).

40. Anselm, *De Conceptu Virginali et De Originali Peccato* 4 (A 2:144). Text paraphrased in citation.

41. Aristotle, *Posterior Analytics* I, 2; 72a (BWA 113).

42. Denifle & Chatelain, *Chartularium Universitatis Parisiensis* II, 1147, no. 31: "That maintaining, as is commonly held, that understanding, volition, and sensation are qualities existing subjectively in the soul which God can create by himself and put where he wishes, they have to maintain or concede that God could bring about by himself that the soul should hate neighbor and God not demeritoriously." Proposition of John of Mirecourt condemned in 1347.

43. *Ibid.*, II, 1124: "That God can command a rational creature to hold him in hatred, and that that

creature in obeying would gain more merit than if he would love him according to a precept since he would do this with greater effort, and more against his own inclination--False, erroneous, and scandalous with respect to the antecedent and the consequent, but, with respect to the inference, it could be maintained." Proposition of Nicholas of Autrecourt condemned in 1346.

44. Augustine, *De Sermone Domini in Monte* II, 18, 59 (CC 35:154).

45. *Ibid.*

46. Anselm, *De Casu Diaboli* 14 (A 1:258). For Anselm's text, see Reference Notes to Distinction 48, Question 1, n. 9.

47. Gregory the Great, *XL Homiliarum in Evangelia* II, Homilia 34 (PL 76:1246-7). See also Dom David Hurst (trans.), *Gregory the Great Forty Gospel Homilies* (Kalamazoo, MI: Cistercian Publications, 1990), p. 281. Hurst notes: "There is no modern critical edition of his forty Gospel homilies, and for the foreseeable future one must rely on the Maurist text reprinted in volume seventy-six of Migne's Patrologia Latina. For this English translation, therefore, we have created an interim critical edition based primarily on three early manuscripts..." . *Ibid.*, p. 3.

48. Anselm, *De Casu Diaboli* 13 (A 1:257). "T<eacher> Therefore, he wills to be happy in proportion to his recognition that a greater happiness is possible. S<tudent> Without doubt, he so wills. T. Therefore, he wills to be like God. S. Nothing is clearer. T. What do you think:? Would his will be unjust if in this manner he willed to be like God? S. I do not wish to call it just, because he would be willing what was not fitting; nor do I wish to call it unjust, because he would will of necessity. T. But we posited that someone who wills only happiness wills only benefits. S. That's right. T. Therefore, if that <angel>, who willed only benefits, were not able to have greater and truer benefits, would he not will whatever lesser benefits he was able to use? S. By all means. In fact, he would not be able to keep from willing even the very lowest of benefits if he was not able <to have> greater ones. T. When he willed unclean and very base benefits in which irrational animals take pleasure, wouldn't this same will be unjust and blameworthy? S. How would it be unjust and blameworthy, for it would will what it had received not to be able to keep from willing? T. However, it is evident that this will is the work of God and the gift of God (even as is life or sensibility), whether when it wills the loftiest benefits or when it wills the basest ones. And it is evident that neither justice nor injustice are in this will. S. No doubt about it. T. Therefore, insofar as <this will> is a being, it is something good. But as far as justice or injustice is concerned, <this will> is neither good nor evil. S. Nothing is clearer." (AC 2:156-7) See also Reference Notes to Distinction 48, Question 1, n. 9.

49. See Reference Notes to Distinction 48, Question 2, n. 24.

50. Possibly Aristotle, *Metaphysics* I, 9; 991b (BWA 708). See also *Metaphysics* I, 7; 988b (BWA 702-3) and XIII, 5; 1080a (BWA 897).

51. Anselm, *De Casu Diaboli* 14 (A 1:258). For Anselm's text, see Reference Notes to Distinction 48, Question 1, n. 9.

52. Aristotle, *De Anima* I, 5; 410a (BWA 551).

53. Andrew of Neufchateau, *Primum Scriptum Sententiarum*, d. 48, q. 1, a. 2, concl. 4, ad 1m.

APPENDICES

APPENDIX A

THE DISPUTED BIOGRAPHY OF ANDREAS DE NOVO CASTRO

Some biographical information on Andreas de Novo Castro is provided in *Primum Scriptum Sententiarum*, an edition of his commentary on the first book of the *Sentences* printed in Paris in 1514 [1]:

Title: *Primum scriptum Sententiarum editum a fratre andrea de novo castro: ordinis fratrum Minorum doctore ingeniosissimo*

Incipit: *Incipit prologus super primum Scriptum Sententiarum editum a fratre Andrea de novo castro: ordinis Fratrum minorum doctore ingeniosissimo.*

Colophon: *Expliciunt quaestiones In primum sententiarum subtilissimi ac perdocti viri Fratris Andreae de novo castro doctoris ingeniosissimi ordinis fratrum minorum provinciae Franciae custodiae lothoringiae et conventus novi castri...*

From this it is learned that Andreas de Novo Castro was a Franciscan belonging to the province of France, custody [2] of Lorraine, and house of *Novum Castrum*, and that academically he was given the honorific title *most ingenious doctor*. This indeed constitutes a modest biography, and even some of these alleged facts have been a matter of dispute in standard biographical sources.

The geographical name *Novum Castrum* admits of various translations into vernacular. In *Repertorium Commentariorum in Sententias Petri Lombardi* Stegmuller lists, without indication of preference, two possibilities for the location and nationality of Andrew: he is to be placed either in Neufchateau in Lorraine in France, or in Newcastle (on-Tyne) in England [3]. Clearly, the former interpretation of *Novum Castrum* is indicated by the colophon of *Primum Scriptum Sententiarum* [4], and a good number of biographical sources identify the author of this text as being from Lorraine [5] or from Neufchateau specifically [6]. On the other hand, Tanner's *Bibliotheca Britannico-Hibernica* places Andrew in Northumberland, the region in which Newcastle-on-Tyne is located, and further describes him as a Dominican rather than a Franciscan [7]. Quetif-Echard, Hurter, and Sbaralea all make mention of the identification of Andrew as an English Dominican in a number of earlier sources [8]. There are also biographical sources which claim Andrew to be English but which, in agreement with the information presented in *Primum Scriptum Sententiarum*, regard him as a Franciscan rather than a Dominican [9]. The confusion which exists over the identity of Andrew is exemplified by the *Dictionnaire de Theologie Catholique*: the 1923 edition contains an entry for *Andre de Neufchateau* while the 1931 edition changes the title of the entry to *Andre de Newcastle*, the latter describing Andrew as coming originally from England but belonging to the French Franciscan community in Lorraine [10]. The biographical confusion is further complicated by Peter of Alva and Astorga who considers Andrew to be Italian, thus interpreting *Novum Castrum* as *Castronuovo* [11]. In addition, there are to be found in various biographical sources explicit denials of the claims that the Andrew in question was Italian [12] or English [13] or an English Dominican [14].

Hubert Elie has advanced the hypothesis that this biographical controversy may be due, at least in part, to a conflation of two different persons caused by linguistic ambiguity. Elie suggests that there existed *two* authors whose names correspond to the Latin *Andreas de Novo Castro*: one was an English Dominican, Andrew of Newcastle, and the other, a French Franciscan, Andrew of Neufchateau [15]. This postulated distinction of persons is found in two earlier biographical sources, viz., that of Fabricius [16] and that of Chevalier [17].

Quite apart from Elie's hypothesis, questions can be raised about the accuracy of claims competing with the biographical information contained in *Primum Scriptum Sententiarum*. Titus Szabo raises two considerations against the contention that Andrew was English [18]: Andrew is not mentioned in the *Catalogum scriptorum Anglorum ex Ordine Fratrum Minorum* of Angelus a S. Francisco [19]; and, in the *Scriptores Ordinis Praedicatorum* of Quetif-Echard, the entry on Andreas de Novocastro declares him to be "Franciscanus...nostrisque nomenclatoribus omnino ignotus" [20]. The former piece of evidence counts against the view that the Andrew in question was an English Franciscan, and the latter, against the view that he was an English Dominican [21]. Against the claim that Andrew was Italian, Szabo points out that the proponent of this view, Peter of Alva and Astorga, confuses two different persons, namely, Andreas de Novo Castro and Hugo de Novo Castro, and that such a confusion automatically casts doubt upon his ascription of nationality [22]. Thus, on balance, it seems reasonable to take the Andreas de Novo Castro of *Primum Scriptum Sententiarum* as the French Franciscan Andrew of Neufchateau.

One of the most significant pieces of information omitted from the biographical information contained in *Primum Scriptum Sententiarum* is any indication of the *date* of the life of Andrew or of the composition of his commentary on the *Sentences*. Two seventeenth century writers, Francisco Suarez and Ralph Cudworth, have provided a list of medieval proponents of the divine command ethical theory. In Suarez's enumeration of divine command moralists, Andrew is associated with philosophical theologians known to belong to the fourteenth and earlier fifteenth centuries: William Ockham, Peter of Ailly, and Jean Gerson [23]. Cudworth's list likewise mentions Andrew together with William Ockham and Peter of Ailly [24]. Among biographical sources, Quetif-Echard [25], Touissant [26], Stegmuller [27], and Chiettinni [28] locate Andrew in the fourteenth century generally. More precise attempts at dating are not lacking. Hurter places Andrew in the period 1276-1300 [29]. A number of biographical sources, including Bale [30], Le Mire [31], Moreri [32], Oudin [33], Wharton [34], Fabricius [35], Posada [36], and Chevalier [37], locate him around 1300, while Du Pin [38], Pauwels [39], and Teetaert [40] place him more broadly *at the beginning* of the fourteenth century. On the other hand, Courtenay locates Andrew in the period of Parisian theology from 1349-1364 [41]. Similarly, Ehrle postulates a date of c. 1350 for Andrew's commentary on the *Sentences* [42]. Andrew is placed in the second half of the fourteenth century by Fussenegger [43]. A much later date of c. 1500 is given by Calmet [44]; and Digot locates Andrew in the period 1508-1544 [45]. Fortunately, various pieces of evidence are available to help resolve this dispute among biographical sources.

Some chronological information is provided by the content of *Primum Scriptum Sententiarum*. In "Le Criticisme et le Scepticisme dans la Philosophie du XIVe Siecle,' Konstanty Michalski reports finding in *Primum Scriptum Sententiarum* a position of *more probabilism*: Andrew does not consider as certain or demonstrable propositions which had formerly been regarded as such, but only assigns to them a greater degree of probability [46]. Hubert Elie locates the articulation and

popularity of such an epistemological position around or after 1350 [47]. Less speculative is a consideration of references made in the text, which are informative at least as a means of determining a date after which the text must have been composed. Among the authors and works explicitly cited in *Primum Scriptum Sententiarum*, the latest references occurring in the text proper are to Gregory of Rimini's commentary on the *Sentences* [48] and to Thomas Bradwardine's *Summa*, that is, to his *De Causa Dei* [49]. While the exact date of Gregory's reading of the *Sentences* is a matter of dispute, the dispute centers on the years between 1342 and 1344 [50]. Bradwardine's *De Causa Dei* is commonly dated 1344 [51]. Further, *Primum Scriptum Sententiarum* contains a large number of citations of condemned articles, over half of which belong to the condemnations of Nicholas of Autrecourt and John of Mirecourt in 1346-47 and 1347 respectively [52]. Specifically, seven different propositions of Nicholas of Autrecourt are mentioned [53], while citation is made of twenty-two of the forty-one propositions of John of Mirecourt which were finally condemned [54]. In addition, at least one other of the condemned propositions cited may belong to Parisian articles compiled during the mid-fourteenth century [55]. Thus the internal textual evidence indicates that *Primum Scriptum Sententiarum* could not have been written prior to the second half of the fourteenth century.

Further, it has been noted by Elie that the editor of *Primum Scriptum Sententiarum* names John of Ripa in the marginalia [56]. There are four instances in which the marginal notes of the editor indicate that a position of John of Ripa is being discussed or refuted in the body of the text [57]. Katherine H. Tachau dates Ripa's lectures on the *Sentences* during the academic year 1352-53 [58], and concomitantly, suggests that Andrew's references to Ripa's lectures provide "the *terminus a quo* for dating his own" [59].

From the second half of the fourteenth century Titus Szabo has located in the *Chartularium Universitatis Parisiensis* two references to an *Andreas de Novo Castro* [60]. The first reference occurs in a roll of the Faculty of Arts dated 1362. Listed under the *Nomina magistrorum provincie Remensis* of the *Nacio Gallicana* is found:

> Magistro Andree Hugonis Denisoti de Novo Castro, clerico Tullensis dioc. (de can. eccl. S. Deodati in Vosago Tull. dioc.). [61]

In a similar roll of 1379 is again found:

> Andree Denisoti de Novocastro, presb., mag. in art. et bac. in theol. ante creationem fe. re. Gregorii XI -- de can. in eccl. Tullens. [62]

On the basis of the considerations of name, geographical location, time period, and professional training, Szabo has argued that the individual cited in these entries is to be identified as our Andrew of Neufchateau [63]. The alleged point of concordance which is least obvious is that of geographical location. In the administration of the Franciscan order, the custody of Lorraine in the province of France had four constituent subdivisions: Metis (Metz), Virdunum (Verdun), Tullum (Toul), and Novum Castrum (Neufchateau) [64]. Thus, the descriptions of the Andrew in question as "clerico Tullensis dioec(esis) " and "de can(onico) in eccl(esia) Tullens(is)" serve to place him in the same area as Neufchateau, and moreover, cohere with specifically Franciscan geography.

If the individual named in these entries of the *Chartularium Universitatis Parisiensis* for the years 1362 and 1379 is in fact the Andrew of *Primum Scriptum Sententiarum* [65], they provide evidence that Andrew's scholarly activity, and concomitantly, his adult life, is indeed to be located in the second half of the fourteenth century. These references, if correct, also serve to locate Andrew's academic activity at the University of Paris [66]. In fact, it seems that Andrew was among those commemorated in the stained glass windows adorning the library of the Sorbonne built in the late fifteenth century [67].

` In the second aforementioned reference in the *Chartularium Universitatis Parisiensis*, Andrew is listed as a bachelor in theology before the election to office of Pope Gregory XI [68], an event which took place in 1370 [69]. From the fact that 1370 is used as a reference point for Andrew's academic status, Szabo concludes that Andrew must have written his commentary on the *Sentences* in the years immediately preceding this date. Szabo postulates a date between the years 1365 and 1370 [70]. Concomitantly, on the basis of this and other considerations, he hypothesizes a life span of 1340 - 1400 [71].

Courtenay and Elie also place Andrew's commentary on the *Sentences* in the decade of the 1360's, but give it an earlier date than does Szabo. Tachau has argued for pushing back the date even further, to the late 1350's.

Elie claims that discussion of the issue of the *complexe significabile* by Bonsembiante includes a response to arguments put forward by Andrew [72]. On the assumption that Bonsembiante's work dates from c. 1363, Elie postulates a date of c. 1360 for Andrew's commentary on the *Sentences* [73]. Tachau likewise finds the figure of Bonsembiante significant in locating Andrew of Neufchateau:

> In all four of his *principia* Bonsembiante quotes his fellow *sententiarii* at length. Prominent among these is an unnamed Franciscan bachelor, whom Trapp supposed to be Ludovicus de Padua. In fact, however, Bonsembiante's Franciscan *socius* is Andreas de Novocastro, as a comparison of their texts shows... [74]

Tachau dates Bonsembiante's commentary on the *Sentences* during the academic year 1358-59 [75], which in turn pushes back the date of Andrew's commentary.

Courtenay has suggested that a "Brother Andrew" who is mentioned in *MS. Vatican Latin 986* is in fact Andrew of Neufchateau [76]. He believes the work in which Andrew is mentioned "can be dated around 1365 or shortly before" [77]. Tachau reports that further investigation of *MS. Vatican Latin 986* reveals that "Andreas is cited in *two* of the *Sentences* commentaries it contains" [78], specifically, in one by an anonymous Franciscan and in another by a certain Registre [79]. Tachau maintains that the latter belongs either to the academic year 1357-58 or 1358-59 [80]. On the basis of textual parallels between Bonsembiante and Registre, Tachau argues that the "Andreas" of Registre's commentary is the same Andrew who is discussed by Bonsembiante, i.e., Andrew of Neufchateau [81].

However, in constructing textual parallels between Andrew of Neufchateau and Registre and Bonsembiante Tachau recognizes that

> ...the extant text of Andreas' *Sentences* is not precisely the work to which

Bonsembiante refers: after all, he responds to Andreas' *principia*, but we find the latter's arguments in his prologue instead. Moreover, neither Registre's nor the anonymous Franciscan's resumes of Andreas' views can be matched *verbatim* against his surviving lectures, however accurately they appear to repeat his positions [82].

From this Tachau postulates the following *curriculum vitae* for Andrew of Neufchateau:

(1) Andreas lectured at a Franciscan *studium* (possibly Amiens) other than Paris between 1353 and 1358, where an anonymous confrere and Registre confronted his views;

(2) Andreas lectured as a bachelor on the *Sentences* at Paris, debating his *socii* (including Bonsembiante Badoer) in principial lectures in 1358-59;

(3) Andreas prepared an *ordinatio* of his lectures on the first book of the *Sentences*, incorporating pre-Parisian lectures and Parisian debates. [83]

And Tachau further speculates that the printed edition *Primum Scriptum Sententiarum* descends from Andrew's revised work [84].

NOTES

1. See Appendix B, n. 40 for the location of the extant copies of this text printed by John Granjon. We are indebted to the British Library for a microfilm of the copy from their collection.

2. A *custody* was a subdivision of a province in the administrative structure of the medieval Franciscans; see J.F. Niermeyer, *Mediae Latinitatis Lexicon Minus* (Leiden: Brill, 1976), s.v. custodia.

3. Friedrich Stegmuller, *Repertorium Commentariorum in Sententias Petri Lombardi* (Wurzburg: F. Schoningh, 1947), I, 36: "Natus Neufchateau (Lotharingia) vel Newcastle (Anglia)." Note that Stegmuller is postulating the *birthplace* of Andrew.

4. Note, however, that the colophon serves to identify Neufchateau as the local Franciscan community to which Andrew belonged, *not* as his birthplace as Stegmuller postulates.

5. Peter Rodulphe (Petrus Rodulphius/Radulphius), *Historiarum Seraphicae Religionis* (Venice, 1586), 307 cited in Titus Szabo, *Introduction to De Conceptione Virginis Gloriosae* by Andreas de Novo Castro in *Bibliotheca Franciscana Scholastica Medii Aevi,* XVI (Quaracchi: Collegium S. Bonaventurae, 1954), p. 105, n. 4; A. Possevin (Possevinus), *Apparatus Sacer* (Venice, 1606), I, 85 cited in Szabo, *Introduction*, p. 105, n. 5; Lucas Wadding, *Scriptores Ordinis Minorum* (Rome: Nardecchia, 1906), 16b; Quetif-Echard, *Scriptores Ordinis Praedicatorum* (Paris: 1719-23; reprint New York: Burt Franklin, 1959), I, 740; C. Oudin (Oudinus), *Commentarius de scriptoribus Ecclesiae antiquis* (Leipzig, 1722), III, c. 699 cited in Szabo, *Introduction*, p. 105, n. 8; John Albert Fabricius, *Bibliotheca Latina Mediae et Infimae Aetatis* (Padua: Joannem Manfre, 1754), I, 96; John de Soto, *Bibliotheca Universa Franciscana* (Madrid: Causa V. Matris de Agreda, 1732; reprint Gregg Press, 1966), I, 76; H. Hurter, *Nomenclator Literarius Theologiae Catholicae* (Innsbruck: 1906-26; reprint New York: Burt Franklin, 1962), II, 392.

6. D. Calmet, *Bibliotheque Lorraine* (Nancy, 1751), c. 46 cited in Szabo, *Introduction*, p. 105, n. 11; Digot, *Histoire de Lorraine* (Nancy, 1856), IV, 144 cited in Szabo, *Introduction*, p. 105, n. 12 and in Hubert Elie, *Le Complexe Significabile* (Paris: J. Vrin, 1936), p. 242; J.B. Glaire, *Dictionnaire des Sciences Ecclesiastiques* (1868), I, 101 cited in Elie, *Le Complexe Significabile*. p. 243; P. Pauwels, *I francescani e la Immacolata Concezione* (Rome, 1904), 93 cited in Szabo, *Introduction*, p. 105, n. 15; Louis Moreri, *Le Grand Dictionnaire Historique* (Basle: Jean Louis Brandmuller, 1940), I, 338 and I, p. 105, n. 10; R. Coulon, *Dictionnaire d'histoire et de geographie ecclesiastiques* (Paris, 1914) II, c. 1685; C. Toussaint, *Dictionnaire de Theologie Catholique* (1923), I, c. 1185; Emanuele Chiettini, *Enciclopedia Cattolica* (Vatican City: l'Enciclopedia Cattolica & il Libro Cattolico, 1948-54), I, c. 1200; G. Fussenegger, *Lexicon fur Theologie und Kirche* (Freiburg: Herder, 1957), c. 518; Elie, *Le Complexe Significabile*, pp. 225-54; Szabo, *Introduction*, pp. 104-7; William J. Courtenay, *Adam Wodeham* (Leiden: Brill, 1978), p. 139.

7. Thomas Tanner, *Bibliotheca Britannico-Hibernica* (London: 1748; reprint Tuscon, AR: Audax Press, 1963), p. 41.

8. "ANDREAS DE NOVOCASTRO sacrae theologiae magister, a Baleo, Simlero, Caveo, Dupinio & Oleario nostris accensetur scriptoribus, & Anglis asseritur, sed omnes delusi...," Quetif-Echard, *Scriptores Ordinis Praedicatorum* I, 740. "Demum Andreas a Novocastro O.Min. , Lotharingius, quem aliqui Anglum et Dominicanum fuisse opinati sunt," Hurter, *Nomenclator Literarius Theologiae Catholicae* II, c. 392. "ANDREAS DE NOVOCASTRO...Oudinus... qui et Henricum Warthonum in Append. Ad Hist liter. Gulielmi Cavi sub an. 1301, asserentem hunc *Andream* natione Anglum, et Ordinis Praedicatorum extitisse reprehendit; ante quem Baleus, et Simlerus, postea Dupinus, et Olearius errorem ebiberunt," John Hyacinth Sbaralea, *Supplementum et Castigatio ad Scriptores Trium Ordinum S. Francisci* (Rome: Nardecchia, 1908), I, 37-8. For the identification of Andrew as an English Dominican, see also A. de Posada, *Biographia ecclesiastica completa* (Madrid, 1948), I, p. 648 cited in Elie, *Le Complexe Significabile*, p. 243.

9. Le Mire (Miraeus), *Bibliotheca ecclesiastica* (Antwerp, 1639), p. 267 cited in Elie, *Le Complexe Significabile*, p. 240; Louis Moreri, *Le Grand Dictionnaire Historique* (Paris: Denis Thierry, 1691), I, p. 227, and citation from edition of 1702 in Elie, *Le Complexe Significabile*, p. 240.

10. The entry in the 1923 edition (I, c. 1185) was written by C. Toussaint, while that in the 1931 edition (XI, c. 326) is due to A. Teetaert.

11. Peter of Alva and Astorga, *Militia Immaculatae Conceptionis V. Mariae* (Louvain, 1661), c. 79 and *Monumenta antiqua Seraphica pro Immaculata Conceptione V. Mariae*, 10 cited in Szabo, *Introduction*, p. 106.

12. Chiettini, *Enciclopedia Cattolica* I, c. 1200.

13. *Ibid.*

14. Quetif-Echard, *Scriptores Ordinis Praedicatorum* I, 740; H. Wharton, *Appendix ad Historiam Litterariam Gulielmi Cave* (Basel: Joh. Rudoph Im-Hoff, 1744), p. 4, s.v. Andreas Novocastrensis, n. (d); Coulon, *Dictionnaire d'histoire et de geographie ecclesiastiques* II, c. 1685.

15. Elie, *Le Complexe Significabile*, pp. 239-40, 241.

16. "ANDREAS NOVOCASTRENSIS Anglus Ord. Praed. circa A.C. 1300, cujus *Commentarios in quatuor libros sententiarum & in Boethia de Consolatione Philosophiae* memorat J. Baleus Centur. X pag. 44. Ex Philippi Wolfi de vitis peritorum virorum..."; "ANDREAS DE NOVOCASTRO in Lotharingia ad Mosam, circa idem tempus Ordin. Minorum Provincialis, inter Scholasticos *Doctor ingeniosissimus* cujus *Commentarii in primum Sententiarum* prodiere Parisiis 1514, fol. ...". Fabricius, *Bibliotheca Latina Mediae et Infimae Aetatis* I, pp. 95-6. Elie bases his hypothesis on this text specifically; see *Le Complexe Significabile*, pp. 240-1.

17. "Andre de NEUFCHATEAU (Vosges), franc., v. 1300; Andre de NEWCASTLE-on-Tyne, domin., v. 1300," Ulysse Chevalier, *Repertoire des Sources Historiques du Moyen Age* (Paris: Picard & Fils, 1905), I, c. 225.

18. Szabo, *Introduction*, p. 107.

19. *Certamen seraphicum Provinciae Angliae*, ed. altera (Ad Claras Aquas, 1885), 231-300.

20. Quetif-Echard, *Scriptores Ordinis Praedicatorum* I, 740.

21. Szabo also contends that the latter piece of evidence counts against the aforementioned distinction of persons made by Fabricius: "Immo nec dominicanus ille, quem recitat Fabricius, videtur in rerum natura exstitisse, utpote, teste Quetif-Echard, nomenclatoribus Praedicatorum omnino ignotus." Szabo, *Introduction*, p. 107.

22. "Si iam valorem historicum opinionum praedictarum perpendamus, omnium debilior apparet sententia P. de Alva et Astorga, utpote qui circa ispam personam erravisse convincitur. Apud Alva enim Doctor noster appellatur *Andreas seu Hugo de Novo-Castro*; dum constat Andream et Hugonem duas exstitisse personas. Qui vero circa personam errat, vix patriam poterit indicare. Ceterum, Alva nullum affert asserti sui argumentum, solusque hanc sententiam proponit." Szabo, *Introduction*, p. 107. For the confusion of Andreas de Novo Castro with *Hugo de Novo Castro*, see Elie, *Le Complexe Significabile*, pp. 244-5; Leo Amoros, O.F.M., "Hugo von Novo Castro O.F.M. und sein Kommentar zum ersten Buch der Sentenzen," *Franziskanische Studien* 20 (1933): 177-222; Szabo, *Introduction*, pp. 106-7, 110. For the confusion of Andrew of Neufchateau with Antonius Andreas (Antoine Andre), see Elie, *Le Complexe Significabile*, pp. 242-3.

23. Francisco Suarez, *De Legibus*, edicion critica bilingue, edited by Luciano Perena et al. (Madrid: Consejo Superior de Investigaciones Cientificas, Instituto Francisco de Vitoria, 1971), II, VI, 4. William Ockham lived c. 1280-1349; Peter of Ailly, 1350-1420; and Jean Gerson, 1363-1429.

24. Ralph Cudworth, *Treatise Concerning Eternal and Immutable Morality* I, I, 5 in *The True Intellectual System of the Universe* (New York: Gould & Newman, 1838).

25. Quetif-Echard, *Scriptores Ordinis Praedicatorum* I, p. 740.

26. Toussaint, *Dictionnaire de Theologie Catholique* (1923), I, c. 1185.

27. Stegmuller, *Repertorium Commentariorum in Sententias Petri Lombardi* I, 36.

28. Chiettini, *Enciclopedia Cattolica* I, c. 1200.

29. Hurter, *Nomenclator Literarius Theologiae Catholicae* II, 392.

30. Bale (Baleus), *Scriptorum illustrium maioris Britanniae,* centuria decima (Gippeswia, 1548), p. 44 cited in Elie, *Le Complexe Significabile*, p. 239.

31. Le Mire, *Bibliotheca ecclesiastica* 267 cited in Szabo, *Introduction*, p. 108.

32. Moreri, *Le Grand Dictionnaire Historique*, 1691 ed., I, p. 227; 1740 ed., I, p. 338.

33. Oudin, *Commentarius de scriptoribus Ecclesiae antiquis* III, c. 699 cited in Szabo, *Introduction*, pp. 107-8.

34. Whaton, *Appendix ad Historiam Litterariam Gulielmi Cave*, p. 4: "...claruit anno 1301."

35. Fabricius, *Bibiotheca Latina Mediae et Infimae Aetatis*, pp. 95-6.

36. Posada, *Biographia ecclesiastica completa* I, 648 cited in Elie, *Le Complexe Significabile*, p. 243.

37. Chevalier, *Repertoire des Sources Historiques du Moyen Age* I, 225.

38. DuPin, *Novelle Bibliotheque des Auteurs Ecclesiastiques: Histoire des Controverses et des Matieres Ecclesiastiques Traitees dans le Quatorzieme Siecle* (Paris: Pralard, 1701), p. 186.

39. Pauwels, *I francescani e le Immacolata Concezione* 93-4 cited in Szabo, *Introduction*, p. 108, n. 8.

40. Teetaert, *Dictionnaire de Theologie Catholique* (1931) XI, c. 326.

41. Courtenay, *Adam Wodeham*, p. 139.

42. Card. Ehrle, "Der Sentenzenkommentar Peters von Kandia," *Franziskanische Studien* 9 (1925): 53ff at 270.

43. Fussenegger, *Lexicon fur Theologie und Kirche*, 518.

44. Calmet, *Bibliotheque Lorraine*, p. 46 cited in Elie, *Le Complexe Significabile*, pp. 241-2 and in Szabo, *Introduction*, p. 108, n. 10.

45. Digot, *Histoire de Lorraine* IV, 144 cited in Elie, *Le Complexe Significabile*, p. 242 and in Szabo, *Introduction*, p. 108, n. 10.

46. "D'apres les degres de certitude, il distingue quatre categories de connaissances. Le plus haut degre de certitude revient a la science mathematique, dont le contenu s'exprime par des judgments necessaires et evidents... Un degre inferieur de certitude est propre aux sciences naturelles, qui s'appuient si fortement sur l'experience, que l'on constate immediatement l'impossibilite d'emettre des jugements contraires. ...La troisieme place est reserve a l'ancienne philosophie de la nature, qui reposait generalement sur des preuves beaucoup plus convaincantes, que les theories opposees. ...Le quatrieme degre de certitude revient aux doctrines morales, dont les jugements sont non seulement d'accord avec l'experience, mais rovent encore un appui dans le fait que les theories contraires entrainent une serie de consequences funestes dans la vie. (Omitted are citations from *Sent.* I, d. 45, q. 3). ...Il resulte de ce qui precede que, dans les deux premieres categories du savoir, regne l'evidence, tandis que les deux autres sont le domaine d'une plus ou moins grande probabilite. Dans la suite, on s'apercoit de l'importance du fait, qu'une serie de theses concernant la metaphysique et la theodicee, a ete rangee dans les deux dernieres categories du savoir, parfois memes encore plus en bas. En consequence, toutes les preuves a leur appui pourront etre considerees seulement comme plus probables, mais dans aucun cas comme evidents, que celles sur lesquelles reposent les theses contraires. Il en sera generalement de meme pour les autres preuves, pas toujours cependant, car on s'apercevra parfois, qu'elles sont moins convaincantes; aussi verrons-nous le probabiliorisme d'Andre de Novo Castro tomber de temps en temps dans le probabilisme, voire meme dans le fideisme.

Le probabiliorisme de cet auteur s'etendait a une serie de verites, qui aux yeux de la scolastique classique de XIIIe siecle passaient pour absolument certaines et pour fondees sur des preuves exactes, equivalent a une *demonstratio*. L'existence d'un etre absolument parfait, son independence a l'egard d'une cause efficiente superieure, l'unite et l'immaterialite de Dieu, sa substance inetendue, la creation par lui des esprits qui meuvent les spheres, le libre arbitre de l'homme---toutes ces verites reposent sur des preuves plus probantes que les theses diametralement opposees, mail elles n'atteignent tout de meme pas le degre de certitude, que donne une demonstration exacte (In lumine naturali tamquam probabilius ponendum est aliquod ens esse perfectissimum. Sent. I Parisiis 1514 fol. 42v. In lumine naturali tamquam probabilius et rationabilius ponendum est unicum deum esse, non plures. Sent. I, D. II-VII q. 5, fol. 46r. Dico tamen, quod tamquam probabilius in lumine naturali tenendum est primum ens esse substantiam spiritualem, incorpoream et inextensam. Sent. I, D. VIII, q. 1, fol. 50r)." Konstanty Michalski, *La Philosophie au XIVe Siecle   Six Etudes* edited by Kurt Flasch (Frankfurt: Minerva, 1969), pp. 113-5 (alternately, pp. 45-7 of "Le Criticisme et Le Scepticisme dans la Philosophie de XIVe Siecle").

47. Elie, *Le Complexe Significabile*, p. 247.

48. *Primum Scriptum Sententiarum*, fol. 2ra, on the issue of the *complexe significabile*: "...per Gregorium li. 1 d. 28 q. 1."

49. The views of Bradwardine are explicitly discussed at some length in *Primum Scriptum Sententiarum*, d. 46, q. 2, *Utrum Deus habeat scientiam immutabilem de eventu futuri contingentis* (fol. 226ra, 227ra, 227rb, 230rb); in d. 47, q. 1, *Utrum divina praescientia et praeordinatio futurorum necessitet antecendenter voluntatem humanan ad agendum* (fol. 240vb-241ra, 241va-vb, 247va-vb, 248ra-rb, 248va); and in d. 47, q. 2, *Utrum omne quod est futurm eveniet de necessitate simpliciter absoluta* (fol. 249rb-vb, 250rb). The name is variously spelled *Thomae Bradoardum* (fol. 226ra), *Thomam Bradonardim* (fol. 230rb), *Thomas/Thomae Bradouardini* (fol. 240vb, 249rb). The references are to the third part (i.e., book) of Bradwardine's *Summa* (i.e., *De Causa Dei*). Specific citations include chapters 1 (fol. 240vb), 2 (fol. 226ra, 227ra, 240vb, 248ra), 3 (fol. 230rb, 248va), 4 (fol. 227ra, 227rb, 241ra, 247vb, 248va), 5 (fol. 227rb, 241ra, 248va), 8 (fol. 240vb, 241ra), 9 (fol. 227ra), 15 (fol. 241ra), 26 (fol. 226ra, 227rb), 27 (fol. 227rb, 241ra, 248va, 249rb), 28 (226ra, 249vb), 29 (fol. 241va, 241vb, 249rb), 30 (fol. 226ra), 39 (fol. 227rb).

In attempting to date Andrew's commentary on the first book of the *Sentences*, Hubert Elie notes that

"Andre nous parle egalement de la *Summa theologica* de Thomas Bradwardine" (*Le Complexe Significabile*, p. 247). However, Elie is cognizant of only one reference, namely, that occurring at fol. 249rb (*Le Complexe Significabile*, p. 247, n. 5). The extent of Andrew's explicit citation of Bradwardine is an important piece of evidence in attempting to determine possible sources for his discussion of the divine command theory, see *Introduction*, sect. IV of the present book.

50. Gordon Leff, *Gregory of Rimini* (Manchester: University of Manchester Press, 1961), pp. 7-8; Damasus Trapp, "Gregory of Rimini Manuscripts: Editions and Additions," *Augustiniana* 8 (1958): 425-43 at 425-28; William J. Courtenay, "John of Mirecourt and Gregory of Rimini on Whether God Can Undo the Past," *Recherches de Theologie Ancienne and Medievale* 40 (1973): 147-74 at 157.

51. Gordon Leff, *Bradwardine and the Pelagians* (Cambridge: Cambridge University Press, 1957), pp. 265-6. William Courtenay has claimed that "Andrew's work...is distinguished in part by the total absence of references to authorities later than the twelfth century" (*Adam Wodeham*, p. 139). Clearly, Courtenay is mistaken.

52. Andrew also cites articles from several sets of thirteenth century condemnations, viz., 1240 (fol. 241rb), 1270 (fol. 226rb), 1276 (fol. 226rb), and 1277 (fol. 1va, 51va, 53va, 53vb, 54ra, 85va, 89ra, 160rb, 226rb, 227ra, 227vb, 235va, 241ra, 245va, 248vb, 250va).

53. Following the listing of Denifle & Chatelain's *Chartularium Universitatis Parisiensis* (Paris: Fratrum Delalain, 1891-99), II, no. 1124, pp. 576-87, these are the articles cited:

PRIMA CEDULA

Dixi et scripsi quod hec propositio: homo est animal, non est necessaria secundum fidem, non attendens pro tunc connexionem necessariam predictorum terminorum--Falsam et revocandam. (fol. 13va-vb)

Item, dixi in quadam disputatione quod contradictoria ad invicem idem significant.--Falsam. (fol. 10rb, 155va)

Item, dixi in quadam disputatione quod Deus et creatura (non sunt ali)quid.--Falsam et scandalosam prout verba sonant. (fol. 3vb)

ALIA CEDULA

Ite(m quod propositiones): Deus est, Deus non est, penitus idem significant, licet (alio modo).--Falsum. (fol. 155va)

ARTICULI MISSI DE PARISIUS

Item, quod Deus et creatura non sunt aliquid.--Falsum et scandalosum prout jacet. (fol. 3vb)

Item, quod significabile complexe per istud complexum: Deus et creatura distinguntur, nichil est.--Falsum et scandalosum. (fol. 1va, 4ra)

Quod Deus potest praecipere rationali creature quod habeat ipsum odio, et ipsa obediens plus meretur, quam si ipsum diligeret ex precepto, quoniam hoc faceret cum majori conatu, et magis contra propriam inclinationem.--Falsum, erroneum et scandalosum quantum ad antecedens et consequens, quantum ad consequentiam posset tolerari. (fol. 260rb)

In attempting to date Andrew's commentary on the first book of the *Sentences*, Hubert Elie discusses at some length Andrew's citation of condemned articles of Nicholas of Autrecourt (*Le Complexe Significabile*, pp. 246-7). However, our list of the condemned articles cited by Andrew is more complete than Elie's.

54. Following the text of the Second Apology of John of Mirecourt (edited by F. Stegmuller, "Die zwei Apologien des Jean de Mirecourt," *Recherches de Theologie Ancienne et Medievale* 5 (1933): 40-78, 192-204), these are the articles cited by Andrew:

(1)   Quod satis erat possibile, quod per volitionem creatam Christus aliquid voluit et nunquam sic debuit evenire. (fol. 234rb)

(2)   Quod Christus potuit dicere falsum et etiam asservisse assertione creata tam vocali quam mentali. (fol. 234rb, 236rb)

(4)   Quod Deus facit quod aliquis peccet, et quod sit peccator, et quod vult voluntate beneplaciti, quod iste sit peccator. (fol. 89vb, 92va, 93rb, 265va)

(5)   Quod nullus peccat volendo aliqualiter aliter quam Deus vult eum velle. (fol. 92va)

(6)   Quod Deus aliquid reprobat, quod ipse vult voluntate beneplaciti. (fol. 89va, 91vb, 265va)

(7)   Quod quemcumque peccantem Deus vult peccare voluntate beneplaciti et facit eum peccare et quod iste peccet. (fol. 6vb, 92va)

(8)   Quod Deus facit malum esse et peccatum esse. (fol. 6vb, 93rb)

(10) Quod aliquis facit aliquid omnino ut Deus vult eum facere voluntate beneplaciti, et tamen talis peccat. (fol. 92va, 265va)

(11) Quod quicumque peccet, conformat voluntatem suam voluntati beneplaciti Dei, sic quod ille vult sicut Deus vult eum velle. (fol. 92va)

(12) Quod possible est, Christum secundum voluntatem creatam errasse, et forte secundum hominem mendacium protulisse. (fol. 234rb)

(25) Quod odium proximi non est demeritorium nisi quia est prohibitum a Deo. (fol. 258rb)

(29) Quod tenentes ut communiter tenetur, quod intellectio, volitio et sensatio sint qualitates subiectivae existentes in anima, quas Deus causare potest se solo et ponere ubi vult, habent ponere seu dicere, quod Deus potest se solo facere, quod anima odiret proximum et Deum, et non demeritorie. (fol. 260rb)

(30) Quod Deus est causa aliqualiter actus demeritorii ut demeritorius est. (fol. 93rb)

(31) Quod Deus est causa peccati ut peccatum est, et mali ut malum est. (fol. 93rb)

(32) Quod qualitercumque voluntas aliquid causat, taliter causat in virtute primae causae. (fol. 98rb)

(33) Quod Deus est causa maxima et immediata privationis iustitiae in actu. (fol. 98ra)

(34) Quod Deus est causa et actor peccati ut peccatum est. (fol. 93rb)

(35) Quod Deus est causa cuiuslibet modi actus et cuiuslibet circumstantiae productae. (fol. 98rb)

(36) Quod a Deo est, quod actus demeritorius est, inquantum demeritorius est. (fol. 93rb)

(39) Quod propter opera alicuius futura bona Deus praedestinavit aliquem ab aeterno. (fol. 181vb)

(40) Quod aliquis est praedestinatus ab aeterno propter bonum usum liberi arbitrii, quem Deus praescivit eum habiturum. (fol. 181vb)

(41) Quod non sic gratis et misericorditer Deus praedestinavit etc. quem praedestinavit, quin etiam pro operibus bonis futuris ipsius vel alterius. (fol. 181vb)

As evidence to be used in dating Andrew's commentary on the first book of the *Sentences*, Hubert Elie brings forward the fact that "Andre mentionne aussi...un article de Jean de Mirecourt condamne en 1347: celui dans lequel il est dit que Dieu est cause du peche" (*Le Complexe Significabile*, p. 247); the specific reference given is to (7) in the above list (*ibid.*, p. 106). Clearly, Andrew's familiarity with and use of the condemned articles of John of Mirecourt is much more extensive than Elie recognized.

Our study of condemned articles cited by Andrew can shed some light on a hypothesis put forward by William Courtenay. Courtenay conjectures that "the phrase *posteriores articuli*...was a phrase commonly used to distinguish the articles condemned in 1347 and shortly thereafter from those of 1277" ("John of Mirecourt and Gregory of Rimini on Whether God Can Undo the Past," p 172). In support of this conjecture, Courtenay directs the reader to the phraseology of Andrew of Neufchateau (*ibid.*, p. 172, n. 177). On a number of occasions, Andrew does use the sort of terminology in question when citing the 1347 condemnations of John of Mirecourt: "articulum/articuli in posterioribus" (fol. 91vb, 93rb); "articuli in posterioribus condemnati" (fol. 92va);

"articulus parisiensis in posterioribus" and grammatical variants thereof (fol. 181vb, 234rb, 260rb); "articulis parisiensibus posterioribus" (fol. 258rb); and "errores parisius condemnatis in articulis posterioribus" (fol. 265va). However, there are instances in which condemned propositions of Mirecourt are referred to simply as an "article of Paris" (fol. 6vb, 89va, 98ra, 236rb), the same terminology frequently used by Andrew to refer to the comdemnations of 1277 (fol. 1va, 53va, 85va, 89ra, 160rb, 226rb, 227ra, 227vb, 235va, 245va, 248vb, 250va). When Andrew makes reference to condemned propositions of Nicholas of Autrecourt of 1346-47, he sometimes indicates them as an "article of the lord cardinal": "articulus/articulum domini cardinalis" (fol. 1va, 10rb, 13vb); "articulos qui sunt domini cardinalis" (fol. 3vb). But Andrew also uses the "posteriores articuli" formula in the case of Autrecourt: "articulus 4 in posterioribus per cardinalem condemnatus" (fol. 155 va); "articulum parisiensem in posterioribus" (fol. 260rb). This addresses another point made by Courtenay: "After 1347, although there were many references to *new* or *subsequent* Parisian articles, I know of only two references to the condemned propositions of Autrecourt," viz., "Paris, Bibl. Nat. lat. 16409, fol. 132v; Pierre d'Ailly, *Conceptus et insolubilia* (Paris: s.a., fol. 15v)..." ("John of Mirecourt and Gregory of Rimini on Whether God Can Undo the Past," p. 171).

55. William Courtenay has pointed out that "Hugolino of Orvieto, at the time of the founding of the theological faculty at the University of Bologna, in 1364, was familiar with three lists of prohibited articles contained in the acts of the Parisian faculty of theology" ("John of Mirecourt and Gregory of Rimini on Whether God Can Undo the Past," p. 170). Courtenay argues that the first list was probably constituted by the articles of 1277 (*ibid.*, pp. 170-1). He indicates that the second list, containing condemned articles of John of Mirecourt, was reproduced in its entirety by Hugolino in the Bolognese statutes (*ibid.*, p. 171). On the other hand, Courtenay speculates that "we probably know only a portion of the articles contained in the third Parisian list, drawn up some time between 1348 and 1364" (*ibid.*, p. 171). He further speculates that the following condemned article cited by Andrew at 216ra was probably contained in the third Parisian list: "Item, in posterioribus articulis Parisiensibus sic dicitur: Quod Deus potest facere omnem rem praeteritam non fuisse et quod potest facere Magdalenam non peccasse--Error." (*ibid.*, p. 171). Cf. Courtenay, *Adam Wodeham*, p. 139, where he again makes reference to the article cited by Andrew at 216ra but places it in the period 1347-13<u>54</u>.

56. Elie, *Le Complexe Significabile*, p. 247.

57. *Primum Scriptum Sententiarum*, fol. 51vb, 52rb, 73vb, 152vb.

58. Katherine H. Tachau, "The *Quaestiones in Primum Librum Sententiarum* of Andreas de Novocastro, O.F.M.," *Archives d'Histoire Doctrinale et Litteraire du Moyen Age* 67 (1992): 289-318 at 300-1. Tachau also notes the marginal references to John of Ripa; *ibid.*, pp. 294, 301.

59. *Ibid.*, p. 302.

60. Szabo, *Introduction*, pp. 109-111.

61. Denifle & Chatelain, *Chartularium Universitatis Parisiensis* III, n. 1265, p. 84.

62. *Ibid.*, no. 1433, p. 254.

63. "Hunc Andream alium non esse nisi nostrum Doctorem, suadet concordia nominis, loci, temporis et operositatis. Concordat namque nomen Andreae de Novo Castro, quod *Chartularium*, utpote documentorum officialium collectio, completum exhibet, vocans Andream *Hugonis Denisoti* (vel *Dynisoti*). ...Concordat locus; nam civitas Tullensis, cuius clericus, presbyter et canonicus vocatur Andreas *Chartularii*, ad eamdem Custodiam Lotharingiae pertinebat, cui etiam Novum Castrum (*Neufchateau*) annumeratum est cuiusque alumnus noster Andreas exstitit. --Concordat tempus; supra enim ostendimus nostri Andreae vitae cursum c. 1340-1400 esse reponendum. Si eius nativitatem posueris c. 1340, recte anno 1362 clericus, anno 1379 presbyter appellatur (ordinatus, ut innuitur, ante creationem Gregorii XI, ergo ante 1370). --Indicia tandem duplicis tituli, quo Andreas Denisoti pollet, haud obscure deteguntur in operibus nostri Doctoris. Ille siquidem magister in artibus et baccalareus in theologiae vocatur. Iam vero Comment. I Sent. nostri Doctoris est opus ex una parte baccalarei; ex alia vero in artibus, maxime in logica, versatissimi, ut data opera ostendit Elie. *Tractatus* eius de Conceptione pariter non solum eximii theologi, sed et clarissimi philosophi notam praetendit." Szabo, *Introduction*, p. 110.

On Szabo's postulation of Andrew life span, see below.

64. Szabo, *Introduction*, p. 109, n. 1.

65. Szabo's identification is disputed by Tachau, "The *Quaestiones in Primum Librum Sententiarum* of Andreas de Novocastro, O.F.M.*" p. 302, n. 32: "We can ignore the even later dating proposed by Titus Szabo, "Andreas de Novo Castro, O.F.M., De conceptione virginis gloriosae," in *Tractatus quatuor de Immaculata Conceptione b. Mariae Virginis* (*Bibliotheca Franciscana Scholastica Medii Aevi* 16), Quaracchi, 1954, pp. 109-13, 117, since Szabo quite mistakenly accepts references in CUP to a canon named Andreas de Novocastro earning his B.A. and M.A. in the 1370s-80s as alluding to our author."

66. Tachau does not dispute locating Andrew of Neufchateau at the *University of Paris*; "The *Quaestiones in Primum Librum Sententiarum* of Andreas de Novocastro, O.F.M.," pp. 291, 307.

67. Leopold Delisle, *Le Cabinet des Manuscrits de la Bibliotheque Imperiale*, vol. II, *Le Cabinet des Manuscrits de la Bibliotheque Nationale* (Paris: Imprimerie Nationale, 1874), pp. 200-1; see also Szabo, *Introduction*, pp. 110-11.

68. See n. 62 above.

69. Szabo, *Introduction*, p. 117.

70. *Ibid.*

71. *Ibid.*, p. 108.

72. Elie, *Le Complexe Significabile*, p. 247, which makes reference back to the following comments:

Si le signifiable par complexe est ainsi en dehors du temps considere par rapport a nous, on doit ajouter, dit Bonsembiante, que "Dieu etre" en tant que signifiable par complexe, et a supposer que le "etre" soit pris comme verbe et non comme substantif, n'est pas une entite, comme le serait un incomplexe, ni, par consequent, susceptible d'aucune perfection finie ou infinie. Contre cette assertion, de nombreux arguments peuvent cependant etre invoques, et Bonsembiante ne manque pas de les examiner en detail, apres les avoir fait exposer par le bachelier des Freres Mineurs.

Tout d'abord, dit-on, "Dieu etre" n'est pas moins quelque chose que "Dieu etre distinct de la creature." Or l'article de M. le Cardinal, declare qu'il est faux et scandaleux de dire que l('intelligible) signifiable par le complexe "Dieu et la creature se distinguent' n'est rien. Donc, conclut-on, "Dieu etre" est aussi une entite. Cet argument a donne naissance a differentes interpretations du mot "rien." Ou bien celui-ci s'oppose a "quelque chose," et par consequent le signifiable par complexe est une entite ou des entites, et Gregoire a demonstre qu'il ne pouvait etre plusieurs entites. Ou bien le mot "rien" s'oppose a "signifiable par un complexe vrai," mais cette hypothese ne saurait etre prise en consideration, car en ce cas l'article de M. le Cardinal serait sans utilite, puisque personne n'a jamais soutenu qu'il soit faux de dire que Dieu se distingue de la creature. L'article est donc bien dirige, dit Bonsembiante, contre ceux qui pretendent que le signifiable par complexe n'est ni une ni plusieurs entites signifiables par incomplexes, soit par identite, soit par illation... (*Le Complexe Significable*, p. 141)

Compare the following passage from *Primum Scriptum Sententiarum*:

Praeterea, articulus domini cardinalis vicesimus tertius est iste, *quod significabile complexe per istud complexum, Deus et creatura distinguuntur, nihil est, revoco tanquam falsum et scandalosum.* Quaero qualiter ly nihil accipitur in isto articulo. Si prout opponitur huic quod dico, *Aliquid pro aliqua entitate per se una vel non per se una vel pro collecto ex pluribus entitatibus aliquam habentibus unitatem,* habetur propositum. Si prout opponitur huic quod dico, *Aliquid pro significabili complexe per complexum verum,* contra: quia tunc vane conditus foret articulus quia per ipsum tunc non obviaretur opinioni erroneae alicuius, quia nullus dicit quod hoc complexum sit falsum, *Deus et creatura distinguuntur,* et tamen iste articulus est conditus ut excludatur opinio falsa cuiusdem.

Confirmatur: si falsum et scandalosum est dicere quod *Deum distingui a creatura* nihil est, ut dicit articulus, igitur falsum et scandalosum est dicere quod *Deum esse* vel *Deum esse bonum infinitum* nihil est... (fol. 1va)

73. Elie, *Le Complexe Significabile*, p. 247.

74. Tachau, "The *Quaestiones in Primum Librum Sententiarum* of Andreas de Novocastro, O.F.M.," p. 303. See also pp. 303-5; 306, n. 41.

75. *Ibid.*, p. 303.

76. In making the claim that "He also seems to be the Andrew referred to in a work that can be dated around 1365 or shortly before, " Courtenay simply gives the reference "Vat. lat. 986, fols. 15r, 94v, 97v" (*Adam Wodeham*, p. 139). He is apparently doing no more than repeating Augustus Pelzer's description of the MS. in *Codices Vaticani Latini* (*Bibliotheca Vaticana*, 1931), II, pt. 1: "Nominatur in marginibus, qui etiam notabilia et divisiones habent, aut in textu cum alii (ut Patres Ecclesiae) tum...andreas (ff. 94v, 97r; f. 15r ad rationem fratris andree)...".

77. Courtenay, *Adam Wodeham*, p. 139.

78. Tachau, "The *Quaestiones in Primum Librum Sententiarum* of Andreas de Novocastro, O.F.M.," p. 302.

79. *Ibid.*

80. *Ibid.*, pp. 302-3.

81. *Ibid.*, pp. 305-6.

82. *Ibid.*, p. 306.

83. *Ibid.*, p. 307.

84. *Ibid.*, p. 307.

APPENDIX B

THE PRESERVATION OF THE TEXT

In view of the significance of Andrew of Neufchateau's discussion of divine command ethics, the state of preservation of the text is regrettable, and on two counts. First, no manuscript copies are known to be extant of that part of his commentary on the first book of the *Sentences* which contains his treatment of the divine command theory. Thus reliance must be placed on the single printed edition of 1514. Second, even within this edition, the substantive editorial work is less complete for the questions on divine command ethics than for other parts of the text.

In general, medievalists have had difficulty locating manuscript copies of the first book of Andrew's commentary. Two twentieth century medievalists, Hubert Elie and Titus Szabo, explored five possible locations without success [1]. In *Scriptores ordinis minorum* Wadding reports that Peter Rodulphe attests to having seen a manuscript of the text in the Library of the Holy Savior in Bologna [2]. The same report on Rodulphe is given by Quetif-Echard [3]., Oudin [4], and de Soto [5], with the report of Oudin in turn recorded in a corrective note to the text of Wharton [6]. Both Elie and Szabo have correctly pointed out, however, that the actual statement of Peter Rodulphe in his *Historarium Seraphicae Religionis* does not make clear whether he saw a manuscript copy or a printed edition of the text of Andrew in the Library of the Holy Savior: "Vidi expositionem super primum Bononiae, in Bibliotheca S. Salvatoris" [7]. And Rodulphe's history, published in 1586, is sufficiently late to allow either interpretation of his statement. Szabo's consultation of a catalogue of the library compiled c. 1533 yielded the discovery of an entry *Andreae de Castro quaestiones super primum Sententiarum* [8], which could refer to Andrew of Neufchateau [9]. But again, the catalogue does not explicitly indicate whether a manuscript or a printed edition is being described. In fact, the editor of the catalogue notes the difficulty of attempting to distinguish the two [10]. Thus we are left without solid evidence that a manuscript copy of the text in question ever existed in the Library of the Holy Savior in Bologna; and even if it did, it may well have subsequently been lost. A catalogue of that library from 1695 does not contain any entry for Andrew of Neufchateau [11], as Elie has pointed out [12]. And Elie's continuing search did not succeed in locating an appropriate entry in a catalogue of the University of Bologna, where books from the Library of the Holy Savior were eventually transported [13].

According to Quetif-Echard and to Sbaralea, a manuscript of the first book of Andrew's commentary was once housed in the library of the College of Navarre in Paris [14]. In the more recent *Dictionnaire d'histoire et de geographie ecclesiastique* Coulon has speculated that *MS. Bibliotheque Nationale lat. 16584* might be the manuscript of the College of Navarre. Coulon's conjecture is based on Delisle's description in *Le Cabinet des Manuscrits de la Bibliotheque Nationale* of *MS. Lat. 16584* as being from Andreas de Novo Castro [15]. In the 1931 edition of the *Dictionnaire de Theologie Catholique* Teetaert unqualifiedly asserts that a manuscript of the text in question exists in the Bibliotheque Nationale in Paris [16].

Examination of *MS. Bibliotheque Nationale lat. 16584* indicates, however, that it contains several treatises of Aristotle [17], and it is so described by Delisle in the *Inventaire des manuscrits latins* [18]. In fact, Coulon appears to have misinterpreted Delisle's comments in *Le Cabinet des Manuscrits*. In the section in which Andreas de Novo Castro is mentioned, Delisle is not dealing with

the issue of *authorship* of texts; rather, he is offering brief notes on various *libraries* from which the Bibliotheque Nationale had acquired a small number of manuscripts [19]. The sources of acquisition are presented in an alphabetical list which, according to Delisle, includes "the names of religious establishments and of civil establishments, those of princes, or great lords, of prelates, of amateurs and of scholars" [20]. So we find:

> NOVO CASTRO (Andreas DE). --Ms. latin 16584, suivant une note du XIVe siecle [21].

Thus this entry is to be interpreted as meaning that, according to a note found in the codex and believed to date from the fourteenth century, *MS. Latin 16584* formerly belong to Andreas de Novo Castro. And Delisle's entry is based on a note in the codex which indicates that this book of Aristotelian treatises was *purchased* by a certain Andreas de Novo Castro [22]. Thus even if this is the same person as our Andrew of Neufchateau [23], the codex does not contain the desired text.

Elie raised the possibility of the desired manuscripts being found in the Library of St. Germain in Paris and in the Library of the Holy Cross in Florence [24]. He claims to find reference made to the former location by Sbaralea [25] and, with qualification, by Oudin, admitting that it is unclear whether Oudin's comments refer to a manuscript or to a printed edition [26]. For the latter location, he cites Sbaralea, although again admitting that his reference may be to a printed edition [27]. In both instances, Elie's search for a manuscript proved fruitless [28]. Indeed, his search of these two libraries appears misguided in the first place, for Szabo has pointed out that all three of the aforementioned references in Sbaralea and Oudin are unambiguously and unmistakably references to printed editions of Andrew's commentary [29].

Another possibility, raised and discussed by Szabo [30], is *MS. Colmar Stadbibliothek 232*, the binding of which bears the inscription: *De Novo Castro Super primum Sententiarum* [31]. Nevertheless, the codex presently lacks the indicated commentary on the first book of the *Sentences* and contains only a commentary on the second book [32]. So even if this codex does contain a manuscript copy of a text of Andrew of Neufchateau [33], it is not what is needed for study of his divine command ethics.

In an article published in 1992 Katherine H. Tachau reports "the discovery of two codices (both formerly part of the Sorbonne library) containing Andreas' questions," viz., *Paris, Bibliotheque Nationale, Latin 15908* and *Latin 15909* [34]. The attribution of these anonymous lectures to Andrew of Neufchateau was made on the basis of a comparison of the incipit of these manuscripts to the 1514 printed edition of Andrew's commentary on the first book of the *Sentences* [35]. Unfortunately, neither manuscript includes distinction forty-eight, questions one and two, the questions constituting Andrew's discussion of an ethics of divine commands [36]. However, these questions are listed in the *tabula quaestionum* of *MS. Bibliotheque Nationale, Latin 15908*, providing evidence for their authenticity [37].

Thus scholars must rely exclusively on *Primum Scriptum Sententiarum*, edited by Peter Honston [38] and printed in Paris in 1514 by John Granjon [39] for study of Andrew of Neufchateau's divine command ethics. At present, only five copies of this printed edition are known to be extant [40]. Tachau argues that neither of the aforementioned manuscripts in the Bibliotheque Nationale served as the basis for preparing this printed edition, and postulates that there was once

another manuscript from which, directly or indirectly, all remaining witnesses of Andrew's lectures descend [41].

Honston's edition represents an early attempt at a critical edition, with textual variants printed as marginalia. Tachau suggests that "Honston had before his eyes a codex...which he treated as his base text" and that "he also made use of a second manuscript" [42]. Tachau argues that neither manuscript in the Bibliotheque Nationale could have served as the source of these textual variants, and postulates the existence of yet another manuscript which served Honston as a second copy of Andrew's questions [43].

Honston's practice of noting textual variants extends only through distinction forty-five, question four, fol. 217rb. Regrettably, no variants whatever are noted for the discussion of divine command ethics in distinction forty-eight, questions one and two [44].

Primum Scriptum Sententiarum is a printed edition which still bears a strong resemblance to a manuscript in terms of type of script, layout, use of abbreviations, and the absence of a modern system of punctuation and of sentence and paragraph structure. Consequently, not only are there painfully few copies of Andrew's commentary still in existence, but it is preserved in a format which many find forbidding and inaccessible. In order to make Andrew's discussion of divine command ethics available to the community of philosophers and theologians interested in this ethical position, the present modernized Latin edition and English translation of distinction forty-eight, questions one and two has been prepared.

NOTES

1. Hubert Elie, *Le Complexe Significabile* (Paris: J. Vrin, 1936), pp. 233-8; Titus Szabo, *Introduction* to *De Conceptione Virginis Gloriosae* by Andreas de Novo Castro in *Bibliotheca Franciscana Scholastica Medii Aevi*, XVI (Quaracchi: Collegium S. Bonaventurae, 1954), pp. 113-9.

2. Lucas Wadding, *Scriptores Ordinis Minorum* (Rome: Nardecchia, 1906), p. 16. Elie points out that D. Calmet (*Bibliotheque Lorraine* (Nancy, 1751), p. 46) is mistaken in his report that Wadding claims to have himself seen the manuscript at Bologna (*Le Complexe Significabile*, p. 234).

3. Quetif-Echard, *Scriptores Ordinis Praedicatorum* (Paris, 1719-23; reprint New York; Burt Franklin, 1959), I, 740. Elie claims that R. Coulon wrongly states that it was Echard who saw the manuscript in Bologna (*Le Complexe Significabile*, p. 234). However, Elie may have misinterpreted Coulon: "Echard avait vu ce ms. faisant partie de la bibliotheque du college de Navarre; un autre ms. du meme ouvrage se trouvait dans la bibliotheque de Saint-Saveur de Bologne" (R. Coulon, *Dictionnaire d'histoire et de geographie ecclesiastiques* (Paris, 1914), II, c. 1685).

4. C. Oudin (Oudinus), *Commentarius de scriptoribus Ecclesiae antiquis* (Leipzig, 1722), III, 699 cited in Szabo, *Introduction*, p. 114, n. 6.

5. John de Soto, *Bibliotheca Universa Franciscana* (Madrid: Causa V. Matris de Agreda, 1732; reprint Gregg Press, 1966), I, 67.

6. H. Wharton, *Appendix ad Historiam Litterariam Gulielmi Cave* (Basel: Joh. Rudolph Im-Hoff, 1744), p. 4, s.v. Andreas Novocastrensis, n. (d).

7. Peter Rudolph (Petrus Rodulphius/Radulphius), *Historiarum Seraphicae Religionis* (Venice, 1586), 307 cited in Szabo, *Introduction*, p. 114. For the point of interpretation, see Elie, *Le Complexe Significabile*,

p. 234 and Szabo, *Introduction*, p. 114.

8. M.-H. Laurent, *Fabio Vigili et les Bibliotheques de Bologna* (Vatican City: Biblioteca Apostolica Vaticana, 1943), *Catalogue de la Bibliotheque de San Salvatore*, p. 309, n. 201; also Szabo, *Introduction*, p. 114.

9. Laurent so identifies the entry, but does not indicate on what basis the identification is made.

10. "L'etude de notre catalogue souleve d'autre part un probleme, car l'on est en droit de se demander si le plus grand nombre des ouvrages, qui y figurent, etaient des manuscrits. A premiere vue, on serait fort tente de la croire vu que la mention *ex impressione* est fort rare, mais l'identification que, pur un grand nombre de volumes, j'ai pu mener a bonne fin, m'a dicte une conclusion differente. Manuscrits et imprimes ont ete classes pele-mele et les livres edites sont de beaucoup les plus nombreux. Comment les distinguer les uns des autres? C'est un des problemes les plus difficiles que j'ai du affronter au cours de ce travail." Laurent, *Fabio Vigili et les Bibliotheques de Bologna*, p. XXXVI.

11. Catalogue of Blasius Albertinus, reprinted as "Katalog der Handschr. In der regulierten Chorherren z. San Salvator in Bologna," *Serapeum* 27 (1866), n. 14-16 cited in Elie, *Le Complexe Significabile*, p. 234.

12. Elie, *Le Complexe Significabile*, p. 234.

13. *Ibid.*, pp. 234-5.

14. Quetif-Echard, *Scriptores Ordinis Praedicatorum* I, 740; John Hyacinth Sbaralea, *Supplementum et Castigatio ad Scriptores Trium Ordinum S. Francisci* (Rome: Nardecchia, 1908), I, 38.

15. Coulon, *Dictionnaire d'histoire et de geographie ecclesiastiques* II, 1685; Leopold Delisle, *Le Cabinet des Manuscrits de la Bibliotheque Imperiale*, vol. II *Le Cabinet des Manuscrits de la Bibliotheque Nationale* (Paris: Imprimerie Nationale, 1874), p. 388.

16. Teetaert, *Dictionnaire de Theologie Catholique* (1931), XI, 326.

17. "Examinons en effet le ms latin 16.584... Nous sommes bien obliges de constater--et M. Coulon l'aurait fait avec nous s'il l'avait examine--qu'il ne contient nullement le *Sententiare* d'Andre, mais les *Ethiques* (p. 68 r *Explicit liber ethicorum de gratias*), les *Morales* (p. 95 v: *Explicit liber magnorum ethicorum aristotelis stragerice* (sic)) et les *Metaphysiques* d'Aristote (in fine; *explicit metaphisica*)." Elie, *Le Complexe Significabile*, pp. 236-7.

18. "16584   Aristote, Ethiques et metaphysique."

19. "CHAPITRE XVI. NOTES SUR DIVERSES BIBLIOTHEQUES DONT QUELQUES DEBRIS SONT ARRIVES AU DEPARTEMENT DES MANUSCRITS. Les collections du departement des manuscrits renferment beaucoup de volumes ayant fait partie de bibliotheques dont je n'ai pas eu l'occasion de parler dans les chapitres precedents. Je vais en enumerer quelques-unes et indiquer plusieurs de nos manuscrits qui en proviennent." Delisle, *Le Cabinet des Manuscrits de la Bibliotheque Nationale*, p. 335.

20. *Ibid.* Translation that of the present author.

21. *Ibid.*, p. 388.

22. "Apres l'*explicit metaphisica* se trouve l'annotation manuscrite suivante, qui avait ete remarquee par L. Delisle, et dont l'ecriture parait etre du XIVe siecle: *Iste liber in quo continentur ethicorum magnorum moralium et metaphisice Aristotelis est Andree de Novocastro quem emit pro...scutis 28 solidis 70 denariis pro initio scuri (studii)? philosophi;* (les mots du milieu sont presque effaces)." Elie, *Le Complexe Significabile*, p. 237. A somewhat different transcription is given in G. Lacombe et al., *Aristoteles Latinus* (Bruges & Paris: Desclee de Brouwer, 1957), Pars Prior, no. 694, p. 575: *Iste liber in quo continentur Ethicorum, Magnorum Moralium et Metaphysice Aristotelis est Andree de Novo Castro quem emit pro (verba erasa) 28 s...pro medio scuti Philippi.*

23. "Celui-ci se nommait assurement en latin Andreas de Novocastro, mais rien ne nous autorise a dire qu'il fut frere mineur ni *a fortiori* a l'identifier avec Andre de Neufchateau, bien que la date de l'ecriture de la note manuscrite precitee et la similitude de nom ne rendent pas cette hypothese improbable." Elie, *Le Complexe Significabile*, p. 237.

24. *Ibid.*, p. 233.

25. *Ibid.*, p. 233.

26. *Ibid.*, p. 234.

27. *Ibid.*, p. 233.

28. *Ibid.*, pp. 234-6.

29. "*Commentarius in 1. librum Senten.* ...item ibidem in Biblioth. S. Germani impressus Paris. an. 1514. in fol. apud Jo: Grantion; ...Extat et Florentiae in Biblioth. S. Crucis tantum *in librum primum Sentent.* editum Paris. in fol. Per Jo: Gration...," Sbaralea, *Supplementum et Castigatio ad Scriptores Trium Ordinum S. Francisci*, p. 38. "Scripsit prolixum Commentarium...quem ego vidi in Bibliotheca Sancti Germani Parisiensis, impressum Parisiis in folio anno 1514 in claustro Brunelli apud Ioannem Graudjon," Oudin, *Commentarius de scriptoribus Ecclesiae antiquis* III, 699, cited in Szabo, *Introduction*, pp. 116, n. 1. For the point of interpretation, see Szabo, *Introduction*, pp. 115-6.

30. Szabo, *Introduction*, pp. 116, 118.

31. *Ibid.*, p. 118.

32. "Continebat I et II Sent., ut insinuat inscriptio legaturae: *De Novo Castro, Super primum (librum) Sententiarum.* Reapse, liber II incipit mutilus, verba introductoria simul cum libro I desiderantur. ...Ex benigna communicatione D.P. Schmitt, Dir. Bibl. Civit. Colmar." Szabo, *Introduction*, p. 118, n. 2.

33. Friedrich Stegmuller attributes this manuscript to *Hugh of Novo Castro*; see *Repertorium Commentariorum in Sententias Petri Lombardi* (Wurzburg: F. Schoningh, 1947), I, 172. Szabo, on the other hand, has argued for the authorship of *Andrew* on grounds of stylistic similarities between *MS. Colmar 232* and the printed edition of Andrew's commentary on the first book of the *Sentences*, and stylistic dissimilarities between these two and the commentary on the *Sentences* belonging to Hugh; *Introduction*, p. 118. Szabo's conclusion is, at least tentatively, accepted by William Courtenay in *Adam Wodeham* (Leiden: Brill, 1978), p. 139, n. 62. *MS. Colmar 232* is also attributed to Andrew of Neufchateau by G. Fusseneger (*Lexicon fur Theologie und Kirche* (Freiburg: Herder, 1957), 518).

The *number* of books of the *Sentences* on which Andrew commented has been a matter of dispute. Some biographical sources attribute to him commentary on all four books. See Bale (Baleus), *Illustrium maioris Britanniae scriptorum* (Gippeswia, 1548), p. 44 cited in Elie, *Le Complexe Significabile*, p. 239; A. Possevin (Possevinus), *Apparatus Sacer* (Venice, 1606), I, 85 cited in Szabo, *Introduction*, p. 117, n. 8; Wadding, *Scriptores Ordinis Minorum*, p. 16; de Soto, *Bibliotheca Universa Franciscana* I, 67. Other sources explicitly take issue with this claim, maintaining that Andrew commented only on the first book; see Oudin, *Commentarius de scriptoribus Ecclesiae antiquis* III, 699 cited in Szabo, *Introduction*, p. 117, n. 11; Quetif-Echard, *Scriptores Ordinis Praedicatorum* I, 740; H. Hurter, *Nomenclator Literarius Theologiae Catholicae* (Innsbruck: 1906-26; reprint New York: Burt Franklin, 1962), II, c. 392; Coulon, *Dictionnaire d'histoire et de geographie ecclesiastique* II, c. 1685; Teetaert, *Dictionnaire de Theologie Catholique* (1931), XI, c. 326. A number of other sources make mention only of a commentary on the first book. See Louis Moreri, *Le Grand Dictionnaire Historique* (Paris: Denis Thierry, 1691), I, 227; I, 338 (1740 ed.); Wharton, *Appendix ad Historiam Litterariam Gulielmi Cave*, p. 4; John Albert Fabricius, *Bibliotheca Latina Mediae et Infimae Aetatis* (Padua: Joannem Manfre, 1754), I, 96; Du Pin, *Novelle Bibliotheque des Auteurs Ecclesiastiques: Histoire des Controverses et des Matieres Ecclesiastiques traitees dan le Quatorzieme Siecle* (Paris: Pralard, 1701), p. 186; Thomas Tanner, *Bibliotheca Britannico-Hibernica* (London, 1748; reprint Tuscon, AR: Audax Press, 1963), p. 41; C. Toussaint, *Dictionnaire de Theologie Catholique* (1923), I, 1185; Emanuele Chiettini, *Enciclopedia Cattolica* (Vatican City: l'Enciclopedia Catttolica & il Libro Cattolico, 1948-54), I, c. 1200.

34. Katherine M. Tachau, "The *Quaestiones in Primum Librum Sententiarum* of Andreas de Novocastro, O.F.M.," *Archives d'Histoire Doctrinale et Litteraire du Moyen Age* 67 (1992): 289-318 at 291-2.

35. *Ibid.*, p. 292.

36. *Ibid.*, pp. 296, 318.

37. *Ibid.*, p. 296.

38. See Dedicatory Epistle for *Primum Scriptum Sententiarum*, not paginated.

39. The correct spelling of the surname of the publisher has been something of a matter of dispute. Within the printed text itself, one finds three versions: Jehan *Granjon* (the insignia of the publisher on the title page), Johannis *Grantion* (the naming of the publisher on the title page), Jehan *Grantion* (the parliamentary permission to print the text), and Johannis *Granion* (colophon). Quetif-Echard has called attention to the appearance of variants in biographical sources: "Hoc idem scriptum in sententiarum primum typis prodiit Parisiis, Joannis Granjon 1514 fol. Ex his Possevinum & Wadingum emendabis...tum cum typographum corrupte Gratium vel Grantium..*Granjon* vocant." (*Scriptores Ordinis Praedicatorum* I, 740). In addition, the variant *Grantion* is used by Sbaralea (*Supplementum et Castigatio ad Scriptores Trium Ordinum S. Francisci*, p. 38). Elie follows Quetif-Echard in preferring *Granjon* (*Le Complexe Significabile*, p. 239, n. 1), and the legitimacy of this choice is supported by research initiated by Szabo (*Introduction*, p. 116, n. 3).

40. Vatican Barb. F. II. 3; Bibl. Nat. Victor Emmanuel (Rome) 14, 30, P. 10; British Library 472 b. 8 (1); Cambridge University G 10, 25; Bibl. Antoniana Patavina AB. V. 10. For this list of locations, see Elie, *Le Complexe Significabile*, p. 229 and Szabo, *Introduction*, p. 116.

41. Tachau, "The *Quaestiones in Primum Librum Sententiarum* of Andreas de Novocastro, O.F.M.," pp. 295-6.

42. *Ibid.*, p. 296.

43. *Ibid.*, pp. 296-9.

44. Variants are given at fol. 1ra, 1vb, 2ra, 2va, 3vb, 4rb, 5va, 6ra, 10rb, 10va, 12rb, 12va, 14rb, 15rb, 16ra, 17va, 18ra, 18va, 19rb, 20ra, 21vb, 22vb, 23vb, 26ra, 26rb, 30ra, 30rb, 30vb, 32vb, 33rb, 33va, 34rb, 35va, 36ra, 36va, 38rb, 38vb, 39ra, 39rb, 40ra, 40rb, 41vb, 42ra, 42rb, 43rb, 43va, 43vb, 44rb, 46rb, 46va, 48va, 51va, 51vb, 53va, 53vb, 54rb, 54vb, 55ra, 55rb, 55vb, 56ra, 58ra, 59ra, 61rb, 64ra, 64vb, 73vb, 75vb, 78rb, 79vb, 81ra, 81rb, 83ra, 91ra, 97ra, 98ra, 101va, 104vb, 107rb, 108va, 121vb, 132ra, 133ra, 133rb, 144ra, 148ra, 149vb, 150ra, 217rb. Text continues through fol. 270vb, with distinction 48, questions 1 and 2 found on fol. 251rb - 262ra. The indication of variants shows a distinct pattern: the notation of variants is initially quite regular, but becomes increasingly sporadic. Such a pattern may well be indicative of incomplete editorial work.